Praise for *The Other "F" Word*

"We are all in the innovation industry now. To adapt, most organizations must rise to a new level of risk-taking, experimentation, and tolerance for failure. In fact the winners continually reinvest in failure because they know it's a source of break-throughs. No one knows this better than Danner and Coopersmith, who have delivered a brilliant and engaging handbook in *The Other 'F' Word*. Let them help you find new levels of success by creating a culture of 'constructive failure' in your organization."

—**Randy Komisar, General Partner,**
Kleiner Perkins Caufield & Byers

"This excellent book is so needed. Failure is a gift. As a senior relationship manager (think sales), I make the Hall of Fame if I win 3 out of 10 pitches. That means I encounter the other F word 70 percent of the time. And that is a good day. So why not view 'no' as an invitation to 'yes,' and failure as the gateway to success? Learn, laugh, move forward differently—keep at it. Danner and Coopersmith's book shows you and your team how to do that, and win."

—**Barbara Byrne, Vice-Chair, Investment**
Banking, Barclays Capital

"Danner and Coopersmith present a very valuable perspective into the most important ingredient for entrepreneurial success: failure. This is an excellent guide to what gives Silicon Valley its unique global advantage—the acceptance and embrace of failure. Entrepreneurship is all about experimentation; learning from failure is the key to success. This tells you 'everything you wanted to know but were afraid to ask' about failure—and success."

—**Vivek Wadhwa, Distinguished Fellow of Policy & Research,**
Singularity University; faculty, Stanford and Duke University;
***TIME* magazine "Top 40 Minds in Tech"**

"I tell entrepreneurs around the world that the best way to avoid failure is to listen to the right people in the first place. If you want to learn about the power and potential of the other F word and what you can do to leverage it in your organization, the right people to listen to are John Danner and Mark Coopersmith. Hats off to them for creating this indispensable user's manual to becoming a more failure-savvy leader, avoiding it when you can and harnessing it when you can't."

—**Jeff Hoffman, co-founder, Priceline.com;**
Partner and co-founder, ColorJar

"Failure IS an option. By leaning into failure, entrepreneurial leaders can inspire new levels of creative capacity building and employee engagement. Simultaneously, organizations can develop, build, and grow talent-rich pipelines of 'failure resilient leaders' who can experiment, iterate more, and lead better. Danner and Coopersmith make it clear that 'failure' is not the buzz word du jour, but a strategic competitive advantage of high potential, adaptive leaders and failure-savvy organizations. It is my sincere hope this book encourages leaders to dream bigger and bolder and to shutter their incremental strategic plans in favor of institutionalizing a failure-smart culture that leverages and integrates organizational learning, growth, and innovation. Lean in and enjoy the ride!"

—**Karl R. LaPan, Chairman and Interim CEO,**
National Business Incubation Association (NBIA)

"Danner and Coopersmith have unlocked the way to make failing not just a 'lesson learned' in your company but a cultural transformation that accelerates growth and engagement. They provide the know-how for creating a culture that rewards risk-taking and inspires creative thinking."

—**Nancy Schlichting, CEO,**
Henry Ford Health System

"No one ever sets out to fail. But being afraid to fail means you'll be afraid to try. Playing it safe gets you nowhere. That's why the Lean Startup discipline embraces failure as a key resource for strategic insight. Whether you're an entrepreneur or an executive in a large company, this essential book shows you how to harness failure to get the results you want."

—**Steve Blank, father of the Lean Startup movement and**
author of *The Startup Owner's Manual*

"It is very rare to find a book such as *The Other 'F' Word* that is so fun, profound, and practical, all at the same time. The book needs to come with a warning that it is very hard to put down."

—**Derek Lidow, Princeton professor, entrepreneur,**
and author of *Startup Leadership*

"Whether you're a hardened CEO or a rising star, if you're looking for opportunity, don't overlook failure. It might be market failure that points the way to your next high-impact venture; or an internal failure that highlights where you ought to pivot. Either way, this novel, clear-thinking book can be your guide. Danner and Coopersmith have translated their decades of experience with startups, mid-size and global businesses into a practical and creative executive's guide to the other F word."

—Linda Rottenberg, co-founder and CEO, Endeavor;
author of *Crazy Is a Compliment*

"I've seen thousands of businesses over my career, from ambitious startups and growing small businesses to thriving multinationals and dying enterprises living in their past. As much as they all crave success, what can really separate the winners from the losers is how effectively they deal with the central topic of this must-read book: failure and the fear of it that stifles innovation and limits real employee commitment. Danner and Coopersmith offer a winning and refreshingly practical framework that can improve your company's odds of success."

—Pete Hart, retired Chairman and CEO, Silicon Valley Bank;
former CEO, MasterCard International

"Great innovators don't fear failure. They learn from it. They build on it. In this pragmatic guide, John Danner and Mark Coopersmith tell you how to think about failure in a positive way—and use it to create value."

—Walter Isaacson, President and CEO, Aspen Institute;
former Chairman/CEO, CNN; bestselling biographer of Steve Jobs,
Benjamin Franklin, Albert Einstein, and Henry Kissinger

"*The Other 'F' Word* profiles how to transform your organization from one which fears failure, assigns blame, and discourages breakthrough thinking into one which maximizes learning and embraces a way of working to establish a competitive edge and a pathway to winning performance. An important read!"

—Jim Goldman, former CEO, Godiva

"Leadership is a rare blend of confidence and humility, and nowhere is this more evident than in the way that leaders handle the inevitable failures that come their way. Danner and Coopersmith write about how to manage failure to your advantage, from moving through your fear to creating the failure-savvy organization that can thrive amid all sorts of disruptions. Whether you're in the C-suite or a leader on the front lines, I recommend that you make the bold move of putting failure to work. *The Other 'F' Word* will show you how."

—Charlene Li, Founder and CEO, Altimeter Group, speaker, and bestselling author of *Groundswell* and *Open Leadership*

"Danner and Coopersmith show you how to change your relationship with failure. Start putting this book to work before you make another move—if you want to succeed."

—Guy Kawasaki, Chief Evangelist, Canva; author of *The Art of Social Media*

"A great reminder why the world's best coaches and athletes spend endless hours watching game films just to embrace the power of *The Other 'F' Word*. This book's an All-Star playbook in any league."

—Leo Kiely, Director, Altria Group Inc.; retired CEO, MillerCoors

"While failure can be a great teacher, one has to be a willing student. But learning's only valuable when it's put into practice. That's where *The Other 'F' Word* makes such a powerful impact, showing how we can translate the lessons from failure into results that count. And that's why this book deserves its place on the desks of every executive trying to spark innovation and entrepreneurial spirit in their teams and organizations."

—Chris Kuenne, Founder and CEO, Rosemark Smart Capital

"Danner and Coopersmith deliver key insights that could not be more timely for healthcare and so many other fields where the urgent need for transformation is driving high-risk strategies, and where failures litter the landscape. Their Failure Value Cycle should be required reading for every hospital, health plan, or medical group executive."

—Molly Joel Coye, MD, MPH, Chief Innovation Officer, UCLA Health

"In this book, Danner and Coopersmith have framed failure as 'today's lesson for tomorrow.' I think that is exactly right. But more importantly the authors have gone beyond quotable sayings and feel-good framings and provided an actual field guide to harvesting this renewable resource. Read this. Share it and try their methods on for a while."

—**Mickey McManus, Visiting Research Fellow, Autodesk;**
Chairman and Principal, MAYA Design;
co-author of *Trillions*

"In our increasingly complex yet connected world, the organizations that are most likely to sustainably succeed are those where people are willing to discuss their failures and thus adapt faster, and feel closer. Discover exactly how in this spellbinding new book *The Other 'F' Word.*"

—**Kare Anderson, author of** *Mutuality Matters*;
TED talk on Opportunity Makers

"A lifetime in high-risk environments has taught me that failure can be an extra-ordinarily rich source of success. So take Danner and Coopersmith's spot-on advice: Don't just fail, learn. Don't just learn, grow. *The Other 'F' Word* shows you how, with a great deal to offer even the most canny executives."

—**Scott Delman, Tony Award–winning producer,**
The Book of Mormon; **private equity fund manager**

"Intelligent organizations become that way by being confident enough to set out in powerfully distinctive strategic directions yet humble enough to acknowledge and learn from their failures along the way. Whether facing the challenge of engaging an increasingly diverse workforce or building an organization for sustainable innovation, executives today need the no-nonsense, practical insights *The Other 'F' Word* delivers. The authors show how you can leverage failure to inform and even inspire your organization. And since failure knows no boundaries, their book promises to be a vital resource for intelligent leaders everywhere."

—**Tammy Erickson, Executive Fellow, Organizational**
Behavior, London Business School;
speaker; McKinsey Award-winning author, *Thinkers50*

"We all forget that enterprise is about experimentation, and most experiments don't work. *The Other 'F' Word* teaches us how to mine gold out of that giant steaming pile of failure! Whether you're an intrapreneur or entrepreneur, you'll gain fresh inspiration and advice about using failure as a valuable tool for reaching your goals."

—Jim Fruchterman, social entrepreneur;
Founder and CEO, Benetech

"Danner and Coopersmith are right: Failure is the most under-recognized, under-valued, and under-leveraged resource in business today. Leaders who can take advantage of its opportunities can achieve the impossible. Organizations that can harness failure can gain the top-tier advantages of greater employee engagement and resilience. The bottom line is, if you want to win you must master the art and science of failure. I recommend *The Other 'F' Word* to you and your team."

—William Hasler, Dean Emeritus at University of
California's Haas School of Business; former Vice Chair,
KPMG Peat Marwick; former Chairman, Solectron

"A leader's job is to deliver great results today—while simultaneously developing culture, new initiatives, and bold change for tomorrow. This demands enormous amounts of energy, courage, and willingness to take risks. Danner and Coopersmith provide invaluable hands-on advice for both taking risk and mastering the art of failure. *The Other 'F' Word* is a critical read for all innovators and leaders of breakthrough change."

—Dave Pottruck, Chairman, HighTower; former CEO, Charles Schwab;
author of *Stacking the Deck: How to Lead Breakthrough*
Change Against Any Odds

The *Other*

"F" Word

How **Smart Leaders, Teams,** and **Entrepreneurs** Put Failure to Work

John Danner • Mark Coopersmith

WILEY

To Peach and Lori

Contents

Foreword

By Jeffrey Bewkes
Chairman and CEO, Time Warner

I'm in the business of storytelling. Time Warner is one of the world's largest, most innovative entertainment enterprises. We search for powerful stories that our audiences care about, and develop the best platforms on which to share them, including news, movies, and TV programming delivered wherever and however our viewers, listeners, and readers want them.

Fortunately, our company has its share of huge successes, from *Game of Thrones, Girls, The Sopranos,* and *Sex & the City,* to *Batman, Superman, Harry Potter,* and *Lord of the Rings.* We know about blockbusters, what it takes to create them, and how wonderful it is to celebrate them.

We also know about box-office bombs, and have had our share of those as well. We made what I've called "the biggest mistake in corporate history" by merging with AOL, a move that almost destroyed our company. We've produced TV programs, feature films, magazines, and comic books that flopped—and I've personally green-lighted several of those during my career. Given the visibility of our business, those failures tend to become very public very quickly.

So I know a bit about the other F word, too—how failure happens, how it can test an organization's spirit, and, more importantly, how its lessons can be leveraged to drive innovation and future success. It may be the hardest resource to harness, but it is often the most valuable, precisely because it teaches you what you don't yet know and need to learn.

That's why I was delighted when the authors of this important book asked me to write its foreword. This is a powerful story for leaders, teams, and entrepreneurs to read and apply. John Danner and Mark Coopersmith show how failure has delivered often unexpected value to successful companies at every phase in their life cycle. Illustrated with fresh, honest insights from a fascinating array of executives in many spheres, the book is anchored by the authors' own pragmatic original framework for what to do with and about the other F word at every stage of failure itself.

You will find your time in these pages well spent. As organizational leaders trying to serve fast-changing, complex markets, we need every resource we can muster. We need experimentation, creativity, and innovation as well as disciplined execution and performance excellence. This book can help you unlock the power of failure as a resource on both fronts. It shows how you can take the other F word out of the realm of the unmentionable and apply its potential to more candidly engage your employees and embrace the risk that innovation, growth, and operational superiority require.

Failure doesn't need to be feared or revered—but it does need to be respected and understood if it is to be put to work effectively. As their title suggests, Danner and Coopersmith strike just the right balance here: failure happens, get over it, and get on *with* it.

The Other F Word can help you create a more "failure-savvy" culture, one that is better equipped to get on with the real business of success—whether you're in the business of telling and selling stories, as we are, or generating value in other ways for the customers at your box office.

—Jeffrey Bewkes

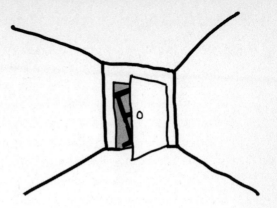

Preface: A Book About a Topic Nobody Wants to Talk About

Everybody wants to talk about success. But nobody wants to talk about failure. Whether you're an executive, an entrepreneur, or a member of a team in your organization, you'd probably like to improve your odds for success—and are willing to take steps to do that. Plus, you don't want to fail.

In your quest, you can become a more charismatic, inspiring, and effective leader. You can concentrate on creating disruptive innovations that transform your organization or industry. You can develop your skills as a thinker, a listener, a communicator, or a practitioner of your particular job skills.

These are each valuable paths to success. But you are likely sitting on top of a largely untapped and misunderstood strategic resource that can help you get there faster. That resource is failure.

Failure is one resource you and your organization create virtually every day. It's the result of the mistakes you and your colleagues make, the unfortunate results of good faith efforts by hard-working teams, the superiority of your competition or adversaries, or even the bad luck events that upset your organizations' best-laid plans.

Whatever its causes, failure is today's lesson for tomorrow. It contains the secrets that can show you what you still need to know, how you need to change your strategy and, handled wisely, can help you build and maintain an organizational culture that pursues excellence while accommodating fallibility.

Failure isn't just an unfortunate event. It's an everyday reality leaders and teams must address. Managed correctly, it can be a vital resource for resiliency in your career and company. But fear of failure limits most organizations' willingness to take risks, innovate, expand creativity, and fully engage their workforce—thus compromising their chances for success.

We've seen this issue from many different angles. As executives, consultants, speakers, board members, and teachers, both of us have spent decades helping businesses, nonprofits, and government organizations develop strategies, drive innovation, accelerate growth, and strengthen culture. We advise senior management teams at major global enterprises and startup ventures around the world. And we anchor executive education programs, leadership seminars, and keynote conferences on five continents.

We're also fortunate enough to teach leadership, innovation, and entrepreneurship at two of the finest universities in the world, the University of California Berkeley and Princeton. In fact, this book's title comes from a pioneering course called "The Other F Word," which we created at Berkeley's Haas School of Business to help MBA students figure out how to use failure to their advantage.

Why Did We Write This Book?

First, because our audiences, clients, and students asked us to. When we give talks on this topic the most frequent questions we receive are "How can we address this in my company, where failure is not an accepted topic of discussion?" and "What advice can you give me to help get started?" We suspect that, like so many others, you and your organization share this interest. You want ideas and suggestions to improve your odds of success. We will show you how to address failure in a more meaningful, productive way, so you can liberate it from the confines of whispered conversations. Failure benefits no one when it is the unmentioned elephant in the conference room.

Failure is a huge topic that impacts every aspect of business. As executives and advisors, we encounter failure in virtually every major organizational function and level—from the C-suite to the factory floor and from frontline sales teams to back-office support managers. In our work as consultants, we've tackled it firsthand at organizations in different phases in the business life cycle, from early-stage startups to well-established global enterprises. In all these settings, despite their many differences and shared commitment to success, the other F word looms large as a leadership and operational challenge.

We see the other F word in our classrooms, too. In our executive education programs, managers from across the organizational landscape and around the world offer candid examples of their struggles in pursuing their enterprises' innovation imperative while accommodating the fear of failure in their organizational culture.

Finally, we have not seen another book that offers truly practical suggestions for how savvy leaders can turn failure from a regrettable reality into a resource for resiliency. Numerous books and articles exist about failure, from the "I struggled, I persevered, I succeeded" personal memoirs to the "fail fast, fail often" cheerleading of Silicon Valley, and even spiritual and psychological self-help manuals. This book is not one of those. We will offer you specific ideas on what you can do *with* failure to improve your odds of success.

After all, that's really what we're each looking for, isn't it?

Our Failure Bona Fides

Everybody's an expert at failing. We all do it all the time. So, what credentials do we bring to writing a book about the other F word?

Fortunately, in addition to our university and teaching roles, we each start from the perspective of several successes we've enjoyed thus far. John has advised CEOs and senior management teams since his college years. He co-founded a widely read national newspaper for health-care executives, was a key staffer for then-governor Bill Clinton, helped launch the U.S. Department of Education, and practiced law at a prestigious international firm. Mark co-founded and built a substantial new business unit for Sony, has held leadership roles in startups and global enterprises alike, and led online-payments company WebOrder from its early stages through growth and acquisition (now part of Google).

But aside from the fact that we've thought, researched, and taught about the other F word, perhaps our most important qualification is that we, like you, have experienced failure directly.

A sampling? John here: I almost got kicked out of Harvard. I advised one of my first clients, CBS, not to buy a then-fledgling company called MCI (which later went on to reshape the modern telecom industry). I didn't make partner at that law firm (a blessing in disguise), launched a business that never made money, and sold my 100 shares of Walmart stock in 1981 for $40/share to help pay for a cross-country road trip with my wife (those shares would be worth close to $1M today—but that trip was great).

Mark's turn: I sold my company WebOrder as the stock market hit all-time highs (good for my investors) and then learned more than I wanted about restricted stock as the market plunged (not so good for me). While at Sony I led several new business initiatives that never made it to market. A number of the startups I advised have failed, and as an angel investor I own more than a few worthless stock certificates.

So we know the other F word firsthand. We also both come by this topic honestly through the work of our fathers. Mark's dad, Stanley, was a prominent psychologist, an early pioneer studying the importance of self-esteem in shaping classroom behavior and expectations. In fact, 40 years ago he noted just how strong the link between self-esteem and fear of failure can be. John's father dealt with failure through a different lens, but in a no less human way. He was a minister, and helped his congregations understand human fallibility, even while striving to live better lives.

But ours is not a book about self-esteem or sin; the first is too difficult to get a handle on, and the second too judgmental to help much. In fact, we think most people's fear of failure is already far too closely linked with their fear of shame, blame, and guilt. And none of that is very helpful to our task at hand—helping you address and leverage the power of failure to drive innovation, engagement, and success in your organization.

We wrote this book with the humility and authenticity our experiences have offered us, and encourage you to read it through the lens of some of your own. Welcome to the conversation.* Now, let's put failure to work.

John Danner   **Mark Coopersmith**

1

What's in It for Me?

Your Personal Guided Book Tour

This book will make you a better leader by helping you tap into a phenomenal resource all around you. You may not always be aware of it, and chances are you're not utilizing it very well right now. But the good news is you've already paid for it, and you and your organization continue to add to it every day in many ways. It's failure, the *other F word*. Although no one likes to fail, truly successful leaders know how to turn a bad experience from a regret into a resource. They put failure to work, driving innovation, strengthening genuine collaboration, and accelerating growth in their organizations.

We teach about innovation, leadership, strategy, and entrepreneurship. Our executive, graduate, and undergraduate students at University of California Berkeley and Princeton come from backgrounds ranging from business to engineering and healthcare to energy. In all our classes, we stress that entrepreneurs, innovators, product designers, and leaders of change initiatives need to answer the one key question on the minds of their potential customers, users, and colleagues: WIIFM? That's short for: *What's In It For Me?* Translate what you are trying to do into terms your audience can understand and benefits they can appreciate.

We're holding ourselves to that same standard. So to begin, we've created a personal crib sheet for you on the key points we'd like you to think about . . .

1. Failure matters. Why? Because we spend much, if not most, of our lives creating it, dealing with it, and trying to learn from it.
2. Failure's like gravity. It's everywhere—a fact of life for every organization at every organizational phase, from startup to growing business and established enterprise.
3. Failure is too often a taboo topic. That's why we call it the *other F word*. If you can't talk about it, you can't manage it, or learn from it. Take it out of the shadows.
4. You've already paid for it, so use it. As a leader or team member, you can convert failure from a repeated regret to a strategic resource that can help you drive innovation, better engage your colleagues' real capabilities, and accelerate growth.
5. Fear of failure is failure's force multiplier. It distorts the likelihood of failure and exaggerates its consequences. It is one of your most important challenges in getting your organization to go where you want it to go.
6. While we suggest a more open and practical direct relationship with failure, that doesn't mean tolerating it as an excuse for incompetence, negligence, or indifference.
7. How you deal with failures of your team members is the acid test of whether you trust them, and vice versa. And trust is essential to address the biggest failure in most organizations: Employees are not meaningfully engaged in their work or mission.
8. If you're serious about innovation or entrepreneurship, be prepared for the failure that often comes with the experiments and risks associated with those objectives. Use it to understand what you don't know or haven't yet delivered.
9. Our seven-stage Failure Value Cycle framework can help your organization to better understand and harness failure as a value-add resource:
   1. **Respect** the power and likelihood of failure
   2. **Rehearse** for your most significant failure scenarios to develop better, faster reflexes
   3. **Recognize** its signs sooner

4. **React** to failure situations more appropriately in the moment
5. **Reflect** deeply and honestly on their underlying causes so you can craft better strategies going forward
6. **Rebound** confidently, based on the lessons learned
7. **Remember** the insights you gained, to strengthen your culture's ability to leverage future failures
10. *Failure is today's lesson for tomorrow.* Put it to work to help you accelerate innovation, intensify employee engagement, and drive growth. You and your organization are fallible. Admitting that reality and leveraging the failures you create builds the trust you need to create those results.

Now that you know where we're headed, let's tell you four places we won't take you. First, we won't waste your time exploring the usual clichés about the other F word, like *to err is human* and *learn from your mistakes*. While we know how difficult it can be to put that understanding into action, ours is not a personal psychology book or self-help manual.

Second, we're not going to take out our pom-poms to join the *fail fast, fail often* cheerleading chorus from Silicon Valley. We think you've already heard that enough, too.

Third, this is not another one of those "I struggled, I persevered, I succeeded" heroic personal memoirs. Great, inspiring stuff, but we'll leave that genre to others.

Fourth, although we are teachers, this is not an academic book per se. We hope it will be used in classrooms worldwide, but it is not written as a textbook. Our tone is informal and straightforward. We want to engage in a conversation, not a lecture. We invite you to share your experience and perspectives with us on our book website: www.theotherfwordbook.com.

FIND YOURSELF HERE

We've written this book with a practical agenda in mind: to challenge you to think about failure differently, manage it more effectively, and leverage it more creatively in your organization. We'll offer you specific, straightforward suggestions for how to do that, with examples drawn from our own extensive research and experience as well as insights from effective leaders we've interviewed across different organizational settings and professions, both domestically and internationally.

You'll learn how to deal more effectively with the reality and inevitability of failure. We'll offer you a practical, seven-stage framework, the Failure Value Cycle, which you can use to apply these lessons in your organization, starting tomorrow. Along the way, we provide practical exercises for you and your team to better understand key issues and put these insights to work.

There are more specific ways you can benefit from our book, depending on your particular responsibilities and interests. We trust you can find them yourself after scanning the following dozen profiles, whether you run a large established organization or a small to medium-sized business, are starting a new venture, or are simply curious about our topic:

- **If you're in charge of your organization,** you'll benefit from insights of successful peers who are leading or have led global Fortune 100 enterprises, high-potential startups, thriving mid-size businesses, important government organizations, and highly respected nonprofits, to name a few. They'll share lessons learned and suggestions for how you can more effectively address the fear of failure as well as leverage the power of the other F word to drive innovation and growth.

  In our Failure Value Cycle, you'll learn specific steps you can take to bring out the best in the people you are leading. You should see the payoff in greater candor among your colleagues as you consider the choices ahead of you and their risks. You should witness increased evidence of creativity across your organization as your workers get more comfortable with a less-punitive culture that embraces excellence while accommodating good-faith experimentation.

- **If you're in marketing or sales**, you deal with the other F word every day, unless you are converting and closing 100 percent of your target prospects (in which case, *you* should be writing a book). A marketing campaign or sales call that doesn't yield what you'd hoped for, while unfortunate, also indicates what you don't know, or haven't yet shown, to convince your potential customers you're the answer to their needs.

  Our book can help you be more effective on your next foray into the marketplace. Since you deal most directly with your competition and see firsthand new trends in the market, your insights are essential to the success of your firm. Imagine how much more your cash register would ring if you could improve your yield by just a few percentage points.

- **If you manage the technology/IT side of your organization,** you understand the accelerating and disruptive pace of change. Offensively, these changes can unleash opportunities for new, creative products and services, redefine how you leverage ideas and resources, and even redesign core business processes. Defensively, they pose brand-tarnishing risks like network security breaches, getting outflanked by more nimble competitors and startups, and being hampered by legacy systems and outdated technology.

   Stay tuned. Our Failure Value Cycle can help you align your agenda with the most important priorities of your clients, even if they don't know the difference between the Zachman Stack and a short stack of pancakes. Applied rigorously to your own domain, it can complement your existing tools to anticipate, identify, and preempt potential failures-in-waiting, whether occasioned by malevolent hackers from the outside or inadequately examined failure scenarios inside.

- **If you work in finance,** you're concerned with how your organization manages its resources to get the best results from its investments and spending. You're also keenly aware of the disparity between the strategic objectives and commitments your CEO has established and the limited resources you have to allocate. We can't promise you a silver bullet, but we can offer you silver buckshot to help hit your targets.

   We'll show you how to extract unexpected value from your organization's "garden mulch pile," the accumulated residue from past product, technology, or market failures. We'll provide examples of how others have increased their ROSI (return on sunk investments), whether in the form of reconfiguring product offerings or repositioning solutions for entirely new markets. We can help you get more mileage out of your investments in innovation and operational improvement by facilitating an environment in which potential failures get flagged more rapidly, and better ideas for future actions get discussed and critiqued more openly. You know better than most how relatively small improvements in your working capital or net portfolio returns can cascade into dramatic positive results for your organization.

- **If you're involved with strategic planning**, you're in the business of recommending and making bets about the future. While leadership is fundamentally assertion in the face of uncertainty, your role is to advise the heads of your organization about which direction and mix of actions offer the best prospect for success. You must constantly balance the possibility for the results you want with the probability of the risks you will encounter.

Our book will not replace your traditional arsenal (e.g., scenario planning, Monte Carlo analyses, SWOT charts, BHAGs [big, hairy, audacious goals], affinity diagrams, etc.), but we'll help you improve the range of possibilities you are considering and the value of their vetting by your colleagues. Simply stated, if your organizational culture does not tolerate failure, you are never likely to hear what your fellow workers really think, whether the issue is where the organization should be headed, ideas for new products and marketing initiatives, or what the real chances are for implementing a particular strategic agenda.

- **If you're an operations executive**, you know what it's like to try to convert lofty strategy into practical results. What's in this book for you as a head-down, roll-up-your-sleeves leader?

  We'll show you how overemphasis on operational improvement in the vein of Six Sigma and total quality management (TQM) programs can inadvertently jeopardize real strategic performance improvement, especially when it comes to reinforcing a culture of innovation. This is exactly what happened at 3M, one of the best-run, most highly respected organizations around. We'll help you change the conversation you have with your direct reports so you're better able to identify failures faster and embed best practices in applying the lessons learned.

- **If you're a key talent or HR executive**, you're already attuned to the cultural strengths and weaknesses of your organization. You know in your gut whether your company's office environment is closer to a *Dilbert* cartoon[1] or one of *Fortune*'s Best Companies to Work For. And you are keenly aware of the difficulty of both continually invigorating your workforce while improving their skills and finding the next generation of talent to drive your organization's future success. We're not going to solve your comp design or succession planning problems, but we can help you strengthen your fundamental workplace culture.

  Fear of failure greatly compromises an organization's ability to inspire, retain, reward, recognize, and replace great talent. We will show you examples of how others have successfully confronted this issue and how to best change the conversation and culture in your organization.

- **If you're an entrepreneur,** you already know failure is your constant companion as you try to keep your investors' support, motivate your team, gain a toehold in a competitive market, and, above all, convince customers you have something they need. We've been there. We know what it's like to bootstrap a venture, convince your friends and family it's worth supporting with their patience and money, and go about converting a dream into a bona fide business.

We can help improve your odds of success by balancing your tenacity and love for your product, strategy, and vision with the open-minded curiosity to be alert to the wisdom contained in the setbacks you and your team will undoubtedly encounter. We share the experiences of other entrepreneurs who have struck the right balance between confident leadership and wise insight in launching successful businesses. Consider them honorary members of your startup team.

- **If you're running a small or medium-sized enterprise**, this book lets you compare notes with others facing similar agendas. We understand how lonely and isolated your job can be and have reached out to leading players in the SME arena to elicit ideas on how to best address the challenge of failure as you build and grow your organization. We'll share examples of how they've done it and suggest other possibilities you might want to experiment with. Our Failure Value Cycle isn't just for the big guys; you can start using it today in your business.

- **If you're a board member or advisor**, you're already attuned to thinking independently about opportunities, risks, and failures; how to prepare for them; and how to respond. How have other organizations addressed these failure-related issues? What examples, frameworks, or failure-savvy practices have helped? What questions should you ask of leaders and teams? We'll offer specific suggestions of how other companies and leaders have tackled the other F word to improve their performance—examples that can strengthen your role as well.

- **If you're a student or still early in your career and aspiring to leadership roles**, prepare for a guided expedition across a fascinating landscape of organizations, cultures, functions, and settings in which failure appears and is addressed by men and women in the kinds of positions you see in your future. As you read about their experiences, ask yourself how you might do things differently. What other strategies or techniques could you use in the situation at hand? After all, we are all experts at creating failures, but it's much harder to expertly leverage the underlying value failures create. So try your own hand. Take a look at how we approach the other F word in our classes in the Appendix. We welcome your vicarious involvement, and you don't even have to pay tuition to Berkeley or Princeton to sit in. (Grading is pass/fail, of course.)

- **Finally, if you're just curious** about the phenomenon of failure in contemporary organizations, we welcome you on our tour of this fascinating frontier. It can be uncomfortable and unfamiliar terrain, but it can also offer unexpected resources and insights that may change how you think, how you live, and how you lead.

However, if you're the kind of executive who firmly believes fear is the best motivator of performance, please buy another book. The good news for you is you're not alone. Many organizations and the people working there live in an atmosphere of fear; if it's not overt then it's just below the surface. If that's your style, good luck. But if your first instinct when failure happens is to look for someone to blame, you might think of this book as a mirror: be willing to see your own fingerprints on the situation. And welcome to the family of the fallible.

OUR ROLES IN THIS BOOK

We will be wearing three hats during our time together. First, we will be your scouts, exploring the frontier of failure and pointing out valuable insights based on our research, teaching, and professional experience as well as the insights of others. Second, we'll be your challengers, inviting you to rethink your assumptions about the other F word. Third, we'll be your coaches, helping you identify a range of specific, practical actions you can take as a leader in your organization to make it more failure-savvy and successful. Not all of these suggestions will fit every style of leadership, culture, or organization; but we offer them as possibilities worth experimenting with on your journey to becoming a more failure-savvy leader. Think of them as a playbook of options, some offensive, some defensive; some plays work best with a less experienced team, while others are best left to seasoned veterans.

As professors, we've read lots of research studies and books about leadership, strategy, innovation, and growth. Many of those books, including classic bestsellers, rightfully urge their readers to think big and lead boldly. Jim Collins understandably wants more companies to escape mediocrity on their climb from "good to great,"[2] and a few do just that, at least temporarily. Clayton Christensen lays out a comparably daunting challenge in his two classics, *The Innovator's Dilemma*[3] and its companion, *The Innovator's Solution*.[4] Christensen throws down the gauntlet of disruptive innovation, those with far-reaching strategic impacts capable of creating and defining entire new industries or business platforms.

Venture capitalists also shoot for the stars. They can do very well if as few as 1 in 10 of their portfolio investments hits the big time, earning a huge multiple on their money. Those big wins can outweigh the underperformance of the other nine, including some otherwise fine businesses as well as outright losers.

Of course, it would be wonderful if every startup venture could become the next IPO darling of Silicon Valley, New York, Chicago, Paris, São Paulo, Hong Kong, Mumbai, or wherever you are; every enterprise could go from good to great; every leader could pursue and attain excellence; and every major company could re-innovate itself. These moon-shot objectives are inspiring and admirable, but they don't reflect everyday reality for most executives and organizations.

What most executives need now is help dealing with and improving the on-the-ground reality they face every day. We understand most of you may not have all the "right people on your bus," and your company may not need or be able to dramatically innovate, but you still have high expectations for the future and your role in shaping it.

We wrote this book with that in mind. We don't assume you are Batman or Wonder Woman, even though you might covet their superpowers. We don't presume your business has had a rocket trajectory like Facebook or Google, or that your organization is awash with cash like Apple. And we doubt your workforce is God's gift to exceptional talent, extraordinary commitment, and brilliant judgment. We wrote this book for you to read where you are now, with the team you have, in the business you're leading today and tomorrow. We encourage you to shoot for the stars, but our focus is preparing you to lead better while you're on the ground.

We've organized the book into four main parts, each addressing a major dimension of the other F word and the issues it poses:

- Part I. What: The Facts and Facets of Failure
- Part II. When and Where: How Failure Appears at Different Organizational Phases
- Part III. How: Using the Failure Value Cycle to Advance Your Organization
- Part IV. Now: Put the Other F Word to Work

Each chapter includes specific tools you can start using immediately, and closes with a handful of WIIFM takeaways.

The frameworks, tools, and resources you find in these pages will help you truly set yourself and your organization up for failure—the right way. If we aren't offering you new ways to think about failure and how to use it to advance your leadership agenda, please stop reading and accept our apologies for spending your hard-earned money. In that case, we will have failed *you*.

WHAT

PART

I

What

The Facts and Facets of Failure

Failure's like gravity. A pervasive, albeit occasionally inconvenient, fact of life—and one we absolutely depend upon. We ignore it at our peril because, like gravity, the other F word has the potential to simultaneously ground, elevate, and accelerate our efforts to drive innovation and growth. If we are wise enough to pay attention.

In this section, we orient you to the issues and facts surrounding the other F word, including the baggage the word "failure" itself evokes. Most new businesses, acquisitions, products, major IT projects, new hires—the list goes on—fail either totally or significantly. It's a fact of life we need to recognize and respect before we can harness its potential.

We define failure as "mistakes and unwelcome outcomes that matter." This encompasses both unexpected outside events that happen *to* us and those failures created or even invited *by* us, as in results from intentional experiments.

Failure is also a quintessentially personal, painful, and emotional experience, which is why it can be so hard to address. Its memory lingers and deepens our fear of failure going forward. In fact, both the memory and fear

11

of failure distort our ability to realistically confront and manage it rationally. Fear of failure is one of the biggest challenges you face as a leader trying to accelerate growth and ignite more innovation in your organization, whether it's a startup venture, a growing business, a major company, or an established firm in distress.

2 | The Other F Word

"Failure" Is Such a Loaded Word

FAILURE

Stand back from that word a bit.
Think about it.
What experiences or memories does it bring to your mind?
How does it make you feel?

Chances are the word "failure" triggers all sorts of negative connotations for you, and maybe a few positive ones. It's a very powerful word—often loaded with intense emotions, strong memories, and conflicting interpretations. Most of us don't like to talk about it, admit when it happens, or spend much time in its company.

Take a look at this (partial) list of synonyms and examples of failure[1]:

- Bankruptcy
- Breakdown
- Collapse
- Defeat
- Catastrophe
- Mistake
- Loss
- Misstep
- Crash and burn
- Bomb
- Botch
- Bungle
- Bust
- Zero
- Downfall
- Fiasco
- Flop
- Bad move
- Implosion
- Lemon
- Loser
- Mess
- Disaster
- Screw-up
- Stalemate
- Turkey
- Washout
- Wreck
- False step
- Faux pas
- Flash in the pan
- Lead balloon
- Sinking ship

From bankruptcy to sinking ship, there's not an upbeat word or phrase in the whole bunch! No wonder "failure" has become a linguistic pariah in many organizations; it's either not discussed or it's disguised with euphemisms, but that doesn't fool anyone. People know failure when they create it or see it.

As authors, we struggle with the other F word ourselves. When we were circulating our proposal for this book, one publisher reflexively turned us down because they thought having the word "failure" in the subtitle would guarantee low sales. (By buying this book, you've helped us show the failure in their logic, so thank you.)

Because for all its baggage, we think most of us are fascinated and perplexed by failure. We know it's part of our everyday lives and we even understand it has lessons to offer us. But we still don't like it. We wouldn't ask failure out for a date or invite it over for dinner.

We get that. That's why we're offering you this new perspective. Our focus is not on the myriad reasons *why* failure happens, but rather what you as a leader can do *about* it before, when, and after it occurs.

FROM VERB TO VERDICT: HOW FAIL*ING* BECOMES FAIL*URE*

Nobody wants to fail. Ever. It hurts. It's embarrassing. It's lonely. Organizations, too, hate failure. They penalize it, rationalize it, ignore it, and some try to cover it up altogether. One of the major problems with the other F word is that too often we shift instantly from describing a situation as a failure to describing the *individuals* involved as failures. And that tendency makes it especially difficult for people to think clearly and talk honestly about failure in the first place.

David Kelley, a co-founder of IDEO, the global design consultancy firm, doesn't even use the term "failure" anymore. When we caught up with him at the TED conference recently, he explained that after serving colleagues and clients over the years, he thinks "failure" is itself a failed word. The real issue, he suggests, is "fear of being judged." In other words, it's not failure itself that is the problem, but rather the *judgment* applied to those involved that poses the real challenge.

We also spoke with executive coach Peter L. West, who has worked with hundreds of executives, helping them improve their personal and professional effectiveness. West notes this tendency to jump from calling a situation a failure to describing an individual as one is all too common. He observed that in their eagerness to distance themselves from a "failure," executive teams sometimes behave like the proverbial mob hunting for the village ogre, pitchforks in one hand and torches in the other. They want to fix blame on someone or some group; and usually punish the unfortunate individuals by firing them or exiling them to some lowly post where their failures (and successes) will never matter. Not coincidentally, by assigning blame they often avoid the harder work of looking at their own contributions to the failure in question.

Peter also notes that in many organizations if you fail once, you are forever marked internally. Imagine wearing a scarlet F on your back for the rest of your career. One senior executive we spoke with shared with us his experiences after being fired as CEO of a publicly traded company. The executive recruiters who had previously hounded him with enticing offers suddenly wouldn't return his calls. After decades of success and increasing responsibility he found that this one very public failure had tainted his reputation and impacted his career.

No wonder people are so worried about the other F word and so reluctant to acknowledge their roles or talk about failures at all.

Let's offload some of that fear and the baggage that goes with it. This is a book about success, about harnessing the power of failure to better lead your organization. It's not about wallowing in failure or celebrating it.

We wish we had a better word for it, but "failure" at least has the virtue of directness. So let's begin this expedition into the frontier of failure, baggage and all.

We warned you we were teachers. We'll start with a quick quiz: a simple 10-question 10-minute survey of your own attitudes about failure and how you deal with it as an executive, team member, or entrepreneur.

Exercise: Assess Your Failure Leadership Profile

1. What is the strategic position of your business now?
   - ☐ In imminent danger of closing
   - ☐ In peril on several fronts
   - ☐ Not particularly vulnerable
   - ☐ Relatively strong
   - ☐ Powerfully dominant
2. If you had to choose between better *executing* your "today" business versus *experimenting* to find your "tomorrow" business, how would you allocate your resources between those two agendas?
   - ☐ 100:0 Execute today's business:Experiment to find tomorrow's
   - ☐ 75:25
   - ☐ 50:50
   - ☐ 25:75
   - ☐ 10:90
3. How do you view the relationship between innovation and failure? (Select all statements you agree with.)
   - ☐ Failure is an absolute prerequisite for innovation
   - ☐ If we want/need innovation, we have to accept the possibility of failures along the way
   - ☐ It is possible to manage or control failure in our quest for innovation
   - ☐ Failure is not required to innovate

4. Thinking back honestly on how you *initially* deal with failure in your organization, how would you describe your actions? (select all statements you agree with)
   ☐ I want to find who is responsible and hold them accountable
   ☐ I tend to avoid dealing with it unless it's serious
   ☐ I try to not make a public display of the situation inside my organization if at all avoidable
   ☐ I try to uncover the underlying reasons for the failure so we can learn something positive from it
   ☐ Other: _____

5. Do you think most people in your organization would agree with your answer(s) to Question 4? (pick *one*)
   ☐ Absolutely yes
   ☐ Probably yes
   ☐ Possibly yes
   ☐ Probably not
   ☐ Definitely not
   ☐ Not at all sure

6. On a scale of 1 to 10 (1 = not important at all; 10 = most important), how important do you see *fear of failure* as a challenge for your leadership? (circle *one*)

   Not Important   Most Important
   1-----2-----3-----4------5------6------7------8------9------10

7. How would you characterize your fundamental message about failure in your organization? (select *one*)
   ☐ "Failure is not an option."
   ☐ "Fail once, you're okay; fail twice, you should probably look for another job."
   ☐ "Failure is okay as long as we learn something valuable from it."
   ☐ "To err is human. We have a forgiving culture here, provided you acted competently and in good faith."
   ☐ "Fail often, fail fast. It's the only way we're going to get where we need to go."
   ☐ Other:
      "_____."

8. Are there examples in your organization of people who have been promoted or otherwise positively recognized, either because of, or in spite of, a significant failure and how they managed it? (select *one*)
   ☐ Nobody
   ☐ One person

(continued)

(*continued*)
- ☐ A couple people
- ☐ Several people
- ☐ Many people
9. On a scale of 1 to 10 (1 = very dissatisfied; 10 = very satisfied), how satisfied are you with the level of innovation, creativity, and initiative in your organization?

Very Dissatisfied   Very Satisfied
1------2-----3-----4------5------6------7------8------9-----10

10. To the extent you are dissatisfied with this level, why do you think your organization is not stepping up to the level of innovation, creativity, and initiative you would like to see? (Weight each possible factor so your total percentage equals 100.)
- ☐ _____% Fear of losing their jobs if things don't turn out well
- ☐ _____% Fear of losing credibility if things don't turn out well
- ☐ _____% Uncertainty about what needs to be done where and when
- ☐ _____% No apparent reward or recognition for success
- ☐ _____% No training or resources to support these activities
- ☐ _____% No apparent management emphasis on this agenda
- ☐ _____% Other: _____
- ☐ 100% TOTAL

Please put your pencil down. This concludes your test. (We put that in for old times' sake.)

While this is clearly not a scientific survey, we are not aware of any widely used instruments that focus directly on these failure-relevant issues, including the benchmark Multifactor Leadership Questionnaire (MLQ). You obviously don't need to share your answers with anybody, but we hope it gives you some clues about your own leadership approach to the other F word in various contexts.

Let's take a look at what your answers might suggest:

Q1. Strategic Position—If you checked the "imminent danger" box, you might have bought this book a little late. If you picked "powerfully dominant," we'd like to know more about the secret to your business success. Assuming you didn't check either of those, your answer should suggest the degree to which your business needs new thinking, strategy, positioning, and maybe a new team—and how soon.

Q2. Today:Tomorrow Balance—Presumably this reflects your answer to Question 1, and is an indication of the degree to which you are comfortable with the status quo and current direction of your business. Regardless of how comfortable you may be, we suggest a little humility about your present circumstances could stand you in good stead going forward. Think about what kinds of questions or assumptions are involved in your current business model and strategy. Consider what new customers or markets might make sense for you to target. Reflect on what your competitors are doing differently or what new startups are appearing in your traditional space. Any or all of those will probably suggest issues worth examining and then potential solutions worth testing.

Q3. Relationship Between Innovation and Failure—Your answer(s) here may give you some insight into your overall approach to the other F word in your organization. It's your default position, perhaps subject to change once you've finished this book.

Q4. Your Initial Failure Response—This question checks your consistency. If you answered it fundamentally differently than the philosophy you selected in Question 3, you might be perceived as disingenuous or even hypocritical by your colleagues. At the very least, a misalignment between the two answers might suggest a need for some further thinking about how your actions match your understanding. Don't feel bad about it. Most of us react poorly in the heat of the moment when failure occurs; and we've all been guilty of perhaps making things worse in the process.

Q5. Alignment with Your Team—This is a potential *Dilbert* situation. If your organization sees things fundamentally differently than you do, or is confused about how you are likely to deal with failure, chances are good your colleagues feel they are on uneasy ground. They are less likely to take risks, express their real opinions, volunteer their best ideas, or align closely with your fundamental agenda if they are uncertain how you will deal with failures along the way.

Q6. Fear of Failure—This one's tough to get a handle on, precisely because your employees are highly unlikely to acknowledge their fear to you. Instead of taking a shot in the dark, consider this question as an invitation for you to be creative in trying to ascertain the real culture in your organization. To the degree fear of failure is prevalent, you are unlikely to see much creative innovation from your people, and you may be on your way to a complacent culture rather than a highly competitive one. Conversely, if there's no real fear of failure, you may have created an environment where recklessness reigns.

Q7. Your Fundamental Failure Message—There's no right answer here, and you may have come up with your own short phrase that better captures your approach. Again, you might find it instructive to see the degree to which the message you think you are communicating is in fact being received with some fidelity by your organization.

Q8. Examples versus Scapegoats—This is a highly symbolic matter. Your team will be intensely curious about these situations, and is likely to vividly remember how you handled them. After all, it's easy for them to put themselves in the position of the individuals involved in a significant failure circumstance.

Q9. Level of Innovation, Creativity, and Initiative—This one speaks for itself. Think of it as your own call to action if you scored from 1 through 3. And if you scored in the 8-to-10 range, you might ask yourself how your toughest competitor or your best employees might answer the same question.

Q10. Your Possible Agenda—There's no shortage of things you can do as a leader to reduce the fear of failure in your organization and encourage greater initiative. That's what this book is all about.

* * *

With these initial insights in hand, let's take a deeper look into the nature and territory of failure.

3

The Gravity of Failure and Failure's Gravity

A UNIVERSAL FORCE

Most new products fail, most new businesses fail, most mergers and acquisitions fail, most big IT projects fail—and that's just a partial list of the endeavors on the most-likely-to-fail list. Add to that the endless array of less likely but still frequent failures: new hires or promotions that don't work out, ad campaigns that fizzle, stores that close, strategies that falter, new policies that backfire. You get the picture. In fact, when you think about all the failures we live with day-to-day, it's amazing anything significant or lasting ever gets done.

As we thought about this landscape of failure, we struggled to find an appropriate analogy or metaphor to capture its ubiquity, its pervasiveness, and, perhaps, its inevitability. Finally, we hit upon one: *Failure is like gravity.*

It is all around us all the time. It's an inexorable and unavoidable fact of life, one we ignore at our peril. It affects virtually everything we do or try to do. The gravity of failure limits and, in a profound sense, humbles us, whether we acknowledge it or not. But it's also the gift that keeps on giving, because it often contains the very seeds of the success we so desperately want—if only we can unlock its secrets.

As much as we might like to deny or defy it, we (and the organizations we work in) spend most of our respective lives immersed in failure, with occasional and temporary success along the way, if we're lucky. Too strong a statement for you? Consider the following facts:

- **Startups:** Between 50 and 70 percent of all new businesses in the United States fail within the first 18 months.[1]
- **Venture Capital–Backed Startups:** Statistics for this group are even grimmer: 75 percent of VC–backed startups, presumably the best-vetted cream of the crop, fail to earn back even their invested capital. More than 95 percent fail to meet investor expectations.[2]
- **Profitability:** Publicly traded companies are losing their mojo. Based on their return-on-asset performance, they are one-fourth as profitable as their counterparts were in 1965, according to Deloitte Research.[3]
- **New CEOs:** Two out of five fail to last 18 months. Even in the Fortune 500, almost a third of CEOs will be gone before their fourth anniversary on the job.[4]
- **New Products:** As many as 95 percent of new products introduced each year fail, including those with enormous research and marketing muscle behind them. New Coke, anyone?[5]
- **Mergers and Acquisitions:** Between 70 and 90 percent of mergers and acquisitions fail to add to shareholder value or meet their objectives.[6]
- **New Hires:** A recent three-year study among 5,000 hiring managers of major firms found that 81 percent of new hires don't work out.[7]
- **Sales:** Most sales calls are failures, as are most advertising impressions on TV, the web, or in print. Internet ads, for example, get clicked about once for every 1,000 views.[8,9]
- **Patents:** More than 99 percent of U.S.-approved patents fail to earn a cent for their inventors. Of 1.5 million patents in effect, only 3,000 of them are being used for something commercially viable (if they're being used at all).[10]
- **IT Projects:** An estimated 68 percent of major IT projects fail to meet their goals.[11,12]

And business is hardly alone. Failure's a fact of life in virtually every field of human endeavor and experience:

- **Love:** Almost half of new marriages end in divorce; just imagine how many more are in a state of deep unhappiness.[13]
- **Sports:** Even superstars like Michael Jordan (49.7 field goal percentage),[14] Ty Cobb (.367 batting average),[15] and Wayne Gretzky 17.6 shooting percentage)[16] failed more often than they succeeded.
- **New Year's Resolutions:** About 88 percent end in failure.[17]
- **Life:** 100 percent of human bodies ultimately fail. It's called death.

We not only live *with* failure; we live *in* it every day.

GRAVITY'S SILVER LINING

But before you despair, take heart. Gravity has both a positive and a negative character. It is one of the four fundamental forces known to physics (along with the electromagnetic force and the weak and strong nuclear forces). Experts argue that although it's the weakest of these four, in the words of one prominent scientist: "the central theme of the story of the Universe turns out to be gravity."[18]

It is the cosmic glue that holds our entire universe together. Without it, we quite literally couldn't live, walk, drive, fly, cook, or go to the bathroom. It makes hydroelectric power possible, and even allows interplanetary space travel by allowing spaceships to slingshot around planets, accelerating their journeys thanks to a boost from gravitational forces. In a fundamental sense, our world depends on gravity.

On the one hand, just as gravity is essential to life, failure may be as essential to other things we want and value, like innovation and growth. And as Icarus discovered at his peril with his wax wings, you need to be properly, not blithely, prepared if you're going to try to defy gravity. We can't ignore failure even as we crave success. We can learn to fly, but only when we respect gravity's pull. We can succeed, but only when we respect the grip that failure and fear holds on our plans and aspirations.

Two Real Space Cadets

If anybody should know something about failure's relationship with gravity, it's Franklin Chang Diaz, who shares the record for most flights to space. Physicist, engineer, astronaut, and company president, Diaz says, "I expect failure all the time. Things usually don't work out the way you'd planned, so you just have to learn to be patient, deal with problems as they arise, and move on."

On every one of his spaceflights, something went wrong. During one flight, the Space Shuttle *Atlantis'* cooling system broke down and the shuttle almost had to land in Africa carrying the nuclear-powered *Galileo* spacecraft in its cargo bay, not exactly a convenient backup location to Cape Canaveral in Florida, or Edwards Air Force Base in California. On another mission, a very delicate 13-mile (20 km) electrical conducting cable tethering the shuttle to an experimental satellite, broke, leaving his crew to figure out how to prevent the ship from becoming entangled with the equivalent of a 100-pound (50 kg) "space kite" and its 20 km string.

"You can't get innovation without failure," notes Diaz. As chief executive of his own company and board member of others, he sees fear of failure as a "huge challenge for leaders." Executives are simply afraid of making a mistake, especially when they're laying it on the line for investors—for fear they may lose their job. Not surprisingly given his career trajectory (pardon the pun), Diaz actually likes taking risks: "There's no risk like sitting on top of a rocket, waiting for someone to light the fuse." We'll take his word for it.

Diaz highlights his failure-savvy leadership style this way:

1. "I expect I will fail. It's the first thing in my mind, so I can condition myself psychologically to think about how I will react when failure does happen . . . After all, you don't have to prepare yourself very much for success."
2. "I try to ensure smaller failures from which I can recover rather than making big jumps from which I cannot. I can afford to twist an ankle or break a bone but not to kill myself."
3. "You have to be optimistic to be a leader. You have to sometimes walk into a room with the feeling you can overcome whatever obstacle is there, even if you don't have the answer right now."

4. "When my team faces a seemingly insurmountable mountain, I often tell them to look backwards—to see how far we've already come. This helps bring perspective that mountains seem tall when they're close, but small when they're far away."

Another astronaut, Yi So-yeon, knows something about insurmountable odds. As a young girl, she dreamt of becoming an astronaut, not an easy aspiration for a woman in Korean society. In 2006, she was selected and trained by the Korean government and Russian experts as one of two International Space Station flight candidates out of 36,000 applicants. In her book about her experiences, she talked candidly about the failures and setbacks she encountered, from difficulties getting funding for her PhD program to resistance by the government to approve her flight. As she said to us:

Failure is like a vaccine—it helps keep you from getting a disease that kills you, but it can make you sick and uncomfortable in the short term. You need pain to have glorious success.

FAILURE'S GRAVITY

Failure's not just like gravity in the *physical* sense; it creates its own gravity in an *emotional* sense. It often dramatically and negatively affects a person's self-confidence, esteem, compensation, job, and even career. Its effects on organizations can be equally significant, with losses of shareholder value, investor confidence, and morale.

The gravity with which most of your employees and colleagues view failure makes it an essential issue to address as a leader. Simply stated, while you can joke about the other F word, you should never take it lightly. We assure you, the people in your organization don't; and they are looking closely at how you deal with failure.

When we've talked with people about their experiences with a failed project or product, they frequently describe one common response by their organizations: isolation. Nobody wants to be associated with failure or those involved with it, for fear that the taint may jeopardize their own positions in the company. They want to distance themselves from it.

For the individuals involved in and even responsible for the failure, this can be not only an embarrassing, but all too frequently, an excruciating experience.

Your job as a leader is to understand the seriousness of these ripple effects and keep the team from falling into the equivalent of a black hole—a place where gravity absorbs everything around it, even light itself.

We don't suggest you necessarily celebrate failure. Nor do we recommend tolerating it as the norm in an organization. Accepting failure without learning from and leveraging it is a recipe for mediocrity. In fact, it is the very human effort to try things that may lie well beyond our reach that creates the preconditions for failure. In fact, we often set ourselves up for failure time and time again. And that's a good thing; it's what drives innovation, progress, and growth.

But the opposite of tolerating failure is just as unproductive. Castigating and humiliating those involved with failures is even less useful than denying it in the first place. "Failure is not an option" sounds great as a slogan, but it ignores reality in most circumstances. Failure is *always* an option, and if you want your organization to grow, become more innovative, and elicit the best from your employees, then failure will probably be a key driver.

We can fly because we understand and respect the power of gravity, an occasionally inconvenient but nonetheless essential force. Similarly, you can use the inherent power of failure to your advantage to inform, teach, and inspire your organization to lift its own level of performance.

4 | Defining Failure

Mistakes and Unwelcome Outcomes That Matter

For an issue this universal, it's not surprising failure has been defined in many different ways. Disciplines other than business have highly refined definitions of failure. Engineering and chemistry, for example, have entire practices and analyses around precisely defined failures.

Let's start with an official definition, courtesy of Oxford Dictionaries online:

failure |ˈfālyər|, noun

1. lack of success: 'an economic policy that is doomed to failure', 'the failures of his policies.'
   1.1 an unsuccessful person, enterprise, or thing: 'bad weather had resulted in crop failures'
2. the omission of expected or required action: 'their failure to comply with the basic rules'

2.1   a lack or deficiency of a desirable quality: 'a failure of imagination'
3.   the action or state of not functioning: 'symptoms of heart failure', 'an engine failure'
3.1   a sudden cessation of power.
3.2   the collapse of a business.

ORIGIN

mid 17th century (originally as *failer*, in the senses 'nonoccurrence' and 'cessation of supply'): from Anglo-Norman French *failer* for Old French *faillir* (see fail)[1]

This view suggests, right away, that failure is about missing something. It's a lack of success, an omission of some critical action, and—worse—it gets personal quickly. But it's time to take a fresh look at the other F word. Let's bring some light into the traditionally dark world of failure. One of the biggest challenges here is that failure can have both an objective as well as a subjective definition. When a plane crashes, a bridge collapses, or a disease like Ebola spreads because safety protocols were ignored, we can all agree a failure has happened. These are straightforward, objective examples of clear-cut failures. Similarly, in a zero-sum contest, everybody loses except the winner. But all of these examples mask the much larger number of circumstances in which failure can be in the eye of the beholder.

For example, perfectionists might see any less-than-perfect result as failure, not because it actually is one, but because it falls short of his or her expectations. Look at a few bronze medalists on the Olympics podium: Some are smiling broadly, others only slightly so, and some look like they're holding back tears. Their response to winning an Olympic medal—a feat most people would consider a huge accomplishment—is rooted in their expectations. In the business world, a corporate CEO might view a profitable year's growth as a failure because it doesn't achieve some strategic goal. Similarly, Wall Street can punish profitable companies for reporting earnings that, while respectable or even remarkable, don't meet some stock analyst's whisper number. But remember, in the words of French writer Jean Giraudoux, "Only the mediocre are always at their best."[2]

It's all about perception. In our discussion with startup guru Guy Kawasaki, he brought up Apple's Macintosh computer:

Is the Macintosh a success for Apple? Of course I would like to think so, having been the evangelist for this product. And it was a chief driver to launch Apple and have Apple become the most valuable company in the world. But by almost any objective measure, the Macintosh holds less than 10 percent of the global market share for computers, with Windows holding 90 percent share or more. When you look at the iPhone, iPod, or iPad, each one of those was more successful from a market-share and penetration perspective.[3]

Our definition of failure is simple: *a mistake or unwelcome outcome that matters*. Our view of failure includes both errors and events, but not just any mistake or outcome. According to our definition, failure only occurs when those outcomes matter to you, your organization, or the people you serve or who depend on you. It is a broad and admittedly subjective definition, but it becomes far more precise for each individual or organization once expectations are established. In this sense, not all mistakes and unwelcome outcomes are failures. Some are just losses and some are acceptable defeats. Losing a coin toss is not a failure, even if it means you have to buy dinner. It's just bad luck.

Whether an outcome is deemed a failure depends on your frame of reference, your objectives and expectations, your standards, and the consequences of a poor result. Failure always has both objective and subjective dimensions. Sometimes they are one and the same. For example, we might all agree that mistakes that cause loss of life, major destruction of property, or damage to the environment qualify as failures, as, presumably, do most violations of the laws or regulations society has established as standards of conduct.

Similarly, in an organizational setting, we might establish a set of aspirational strategic targets (e.g., profitability, growth, market share, customer satisfaction, etc.) that can set a measurable standard for separating failure from success. We could also set minimalist, admittedly less lofty, targets like covering the costs of staying in business. In either case, mistakes that jeopardize achieving those standards matter to your organization.

What matters to you may not matter to us, and vice versa. These more personal definitions of failure pose difficult challenges for you as a leader—precisely because they are hidden or unspoken. Yet they are no less real than the more overt definitions we might use in particular circumstances. To use the iceberg analogy, the publicly acknowledged failures you deal with are probably just the tip of the failures people in your organization feel every day. Don't confuse one with the other.

During our research and interviews, we compared notes with many leaders on this fundamental question of how to define failure. After all, if no one can articulate what failure is, how do we know what to do about it? Here's a sample of what we found:

- Warren Bennis, a friend and astute observer of all things leadership related,[4] talked about "consequential" versus "wrong turn" failures.[5] In his view, "Leaders make it clear there is no failure, only mistakes that give us feedback and tell us what to do next."[6]
- Bryan Roberts, a partner at Venrock, a leading venture capital firm, told us, "Failure is giving up; it's declaring that it's no longer worth pursuing a particular course of action."[7]
- Kef Kasdin, co-founder of Proterro, a pioneering biofeedstock company, and early-stage cleantech investor, shares her viewpoint: "Failure is NOT the opposite of success. It's just what's not possible at that particular moment. Understanding and adapting to why it's not possible opens the door to new opportunities for success (and failure)."[8]
- Bob King, former president of the United Automobile Workers union says, "I don't use the term 'failure.' I prefer to talk about 'problems and problem solving' and how we're going to solve key challenges."[9]
- Michael Hinshaw, CEO of MCorp and an expert on customer experience, sees failure as a "lost opportunity: whether financial, reputational, or personal."[10]
- Jennifer Granholm, former Governor and Attorney General of Michigan, says, "'Failure' is itself a failed word. It just doesn't help people very much. Why can't we come up with a word that focuses on learning through a bad experience, without being sophomoric about it—a term that doesn't accentuate the bad, but enables the good?"[11] Notably, her second gubernatorial term was during the 2008 U.S. economic crisis, when two of the Big 3 automakers filed for bankruptcy.
- Michael Sippey, former Vice President of Product and Design at Twitter, defines failure as "outcomes you neither expected nor hoped for."[12]

Whether or not you agree with these approaches or our working definition of failure—*mistakes or unwelcome outcomes that matter*—we suggest you give the matter some serious thought. Each of us has a mental image of what failure is and how it manifests itself. Sometimes these images are informed intellectually, other times they are stamped emotionally, and usually from a combination of both. As a leader, think about what your leadership definition is of the other F word. That's what will guide your actions and your expectations of others in your organization.

Exercise: *Your* **Definition of Failure**

It's time for a pop quiz: Try this simple exercise, right now.

Failure is:

_____
_____
_____
_____

Examples of failure in our organization include:

_____
_____
_____
_____

Now let's go for bonus territory. What have we learned from these failures?

_____
_____
_____

While you're at it, you might want to invite your colleagues to do the same to see how aligned your team is when it comes to the other F word in your business. You may well find it's the catalyst for a different kind of conversation in your company, a topic we'll return to in Chapters 9 and 10.

Henry Chesbrough, our University of California Berkeley colleague and father of the Open Innovation revolution,[13] has interviewed hundreds of executives as part of his research. He talked to us about how difficult it is for some companies, who generally think of themselves as innovative, to cite their notable failures and what they learned from those events:

It's hard to find any company these days who doesn't say it is "innovative." But when I ask executives about their failures, often they're not prepared to talk about those. If they have nothing to say, it's either because it's an off-limits topic, or because they don't have a process for managing failure. It's as if the message is "we want to innovate, but only if we won't fail."

If they do mention a failure, I ask who was involved with that situation and where those people are now in the organization. Is there "life after failure"? That tells you a lot about whether there is a genuine culture of innovation in a company. Being able to manage failure is the key to building that kind of culture.[14]

FAILURE IS TODAY'S LESSON FOR TOMORROW

As we've said, success isn't the opposite of failure; it's a sibling. The two coexist, albeit uneasily much of the time, but necessarily. Many great successes were derived from prior failure, probably as much as from prior success. In fact, one can look at the path of progress—scientific, evolutionary, economic, or otherwise—as the cumulative result of trials and errors, successes and failures. Think of any notable success, perhaps a new scientific discovery, technological breakthrough, or market-shaping business model. Now ask yourself what prior failures, discoveries, breakthroughs, blind alleys, or models led to that success. These enabling events may not happen immediately beforehand but they almost certainly occur, perhaps even decades or centuries earlier. As Julie Andrews sang in *The Sound of Music*, "Nothing comes from nothing. Nothing ever could."[15]

It is precisely this reciprocal relationship between failure and success that can help leaders come to better terms with the other F word. Failure isn't the opposite of success, it is more likely the precursor to it *if* we are lucky, enterprising, and have enough resources left to apply its lessons. Hence, our suggestion that failure is today's lesson for tomorrow.

Let's look at some prominent examples of this in action.

Have you ever wondered how WD-40 got its name? It stands for "Water Displacement, 40th formula."[16] That's the name straight out of the lab book from 1953. That's how many tries it took the three-person team from Rocket Chemical Company to create a working rust-prevention solvent for aerospace customers. That still-secret formula, in its familiar blue and yellow aerosol canister with the red top, probably sits in your garage, storeroom, or workshop today. Imagine if that trio had stopped in frustration after their 39th attempt. How many bolts, screws, car doors, hinges, and doors would have remained stuck had the researchers thrown in the towel at WD-39? Fortunately, Rocket had enough resources, including staff time, chemicals, lab space, and the like, to apply the lessons of the 39th failure to finally get it right!

Now, consider Henry Ford's iconic Model T. That was the successor to an alphabetic series of models and experiments starting with 1903's Model A and then skipping through Models B, C, F, K, N, R, and S before finally bringing the Tin Lizzie to market, revolutionizing American industry.

Finally, consider the story of Angry Birds, one of the most successful mobile games ever designed. It, too, is a story of many failures and near-misses—51 of them!—before Rovio, which was running out of cash to meet payroll, finally had a hit on its hands. They, too, were lucky and smart enough to preserve key resources to enable them to continue on that long and frustrating journey, which ultimately resulted in Angry Birds.[17]

Sometimes serendipity trumps strategy. The most valuable resource may be time: time to try the next iteration, time to tweak the features of a product, time for the team to properly reflect on what it's learning from the marketplace, and time for serendipity.

UNINTENTIONAL VERSUS INVITATIONAL FAILURES

It's easy to understand the connection between mistakes and failure. Leaving aside instances of mischief or malice, most mistakes are the result of carelessness and human error. We don't focus on relatively minor everyday goofs that have a trivial effect on your operations, and we suggest you don't either. Perfection is neither likely nor necessary in many aspects of business. Striving for it is a waste of your time most of the time.

Failures reveal mistakes. Most are unintentional, like Homer Simpson's "d'oh!" moments. That's why we usually think of failure in the defensive sense, as something we need to guard against so we can minimize its fallout. But failure can also have an offensive element.

Sometimes, we seek out circumstances in which failure is a likely outcome, even a desirable one. This is true especially when we are unsure of our logic, understanding, or solutions—when we are in the realm of exploration or experiment. To paraphrase Thomas Edison, one of America's most famous entrepreneurial inventors: *I have not failed. I've successfully found*

10,000 ways that won't work. Experiments are explicitly designed to test certain hypotheses and to learn better ways of tackling or understanding a specific challenge. We will return to this idea later. For now, we simply want to suggest that failure can be both unintentional and invitational. As a leader, you need to address both types.

WHAT ABOUT ACCIDENTS?

Some failures are the result of blunders, such as Netflix's disastrous introduction of its planned Qwikster service or the Federal Emergency Management Agency's (FEMA's) tragic ineptitude following hurricane Katrina. Although the World War II-era military acronym "SNAFU" has since made it into polite discourse, originally it stood for "Situation Normal, All Fucked Up."[18] And it is in the original sense that most of us use it today, so we will treat it accordingly.

But our working definition of failure includes, in street terms, both mistakes (fuckups) as well as unwelcome outcomes (in the vernacular, "shit happens" events). Why? Because many, if not most, of those circumstances—upon further examination—were far more foreseeable and potentially forestallable than they might first appear. We mean not just eminently predictable risks, but also the came-from-out-of-nowhere, disruptive "black-swan" events popularized by Nassim Nicholas Taleb in *Fooled by Randomness*.[19]

Should leaders be held responsible for anticipating and preparing for these seemingly highly random events? In many cases, yes. Just because the timing or magnitude of a particular black-swan event may be hard or even impossible to predict with precision, many happen with some regularity. For example, portfolio managers probably cannot predict when the next major economic upheaval will happen, but they should look for another job if they do not pressure test their proposed portfolio against precisely that type of scenario.

Or let's look at major cyberattacks. Target could not predict when, where, or how its computer systems might be hacked, but a successful hack attack on a trusted system was highly likely to happen at *some* time. It did during the holiday shopping season of 2013, when millions of customer records were compromised. Soon after, other high-profile companies like

Home Depot, Apple, and others were also hacked, when you could easily argue they should have been on higher alert, looking for vulnerabilities in their own systems.

One of the altars at which many corporate executives worship is that of long-term shareholder value, which is the generation of returns greater than their risk-adjusted cost of capital. In fact, many see that as their primary obligation. A few years ago, Deloitte Research did a longitudinal study looking at sudden losses of shareholder value for publicly traded companies from 2003 through 2012. They called these "value-killer losses,"[20] and they found that the biggest destroyer was not necessarily management ineptitude, but those nasty black-swan events like the credit crisis of 2008 and the ensuing Eurozone crisis that swamped key segments of the investment market. Here's what they said about how these events can expose and exacerbate other lingering risks:

> High-impact, low-frequency risks trigger most value killers. . . . industry- or economy-wide events such as the credit crisis or eurozone crisis drove the most value losses. These events often expose a company's biggest strategic, operational, or financial weakness, often triggering a further cascade of negative events for the company. While a black-swan event may trigger a value loss, its magnitude is often amplified by interdependencies among a variety of risks in an organization. Our latest research reaffirms the importance of thinking about risk events not just in isolation but in terms of how a risk event may trigger other events within a company and escalate into a massive value loss.[21]

In practical terms, the executives of the companies caught unprepared by those events left their investors (and, perhaps, their employees and customers) vulnerable to major threats whose timing may have been unpredictable but whose likelihood was anything but.

DEBUNKING THE "UNK UNK" DEFENSE

Sometimes leaders caught on the wrong side of history like to excuse themselves with the "unk unk" rationalization. They suggest they were victims of the *unknown unknowns* and should, therefore, not be held accountable for mistakes or decisions made in the midst of those "unk unk" circumstances, but the standard here is not about accurately or precisely predicting the future. As a corporate leader, you're accountable for anticipating beyond the predictable and probable. You need to consider the *plausible* events that could undermine or transform your organization's fortunes, especially when the consequences may be cataclysmic. These are the big-ticket failures that lie in wait.

We think most SH events fit squarely within our working definition of the other F word, and unless you care to play the business equivalent of Russian roulette, we suggest they fit in yours as well. We'll suggest several ways you can do this in Part III.

5 | Fear and Memory

Failure's Force Multipliers

We pay a heavy price for our fear of failure. It is a powerful obstacle to growth. It assures the progressive narrowing of the personality and prevents exploration and experimentation. There is no learning without some difficulty and fumbling. If you want to keep on learning, you must keep on risking failure all your life.

—John Gardner[1]

Let's be clear: Fear of failure is the single biggest challenge for leaders striving to make their organizations more innovative and resilient. To borrow a phrase popularized by former Secretary of State Colin Powell, fear is failure's "force multiplier." It distorts the likelihood of failure itself and often magnifies its impact—and it can actually set us up for the very failure we fear. Mark's father, Stanley Coopersmith, a pioneering psychologist and education researcher, captured this phenomenon concisely years ago: "Fear of failure is the best predictor of failure."[2]

Fear of failure even has a scientific name: atychiphobia (pronounced *attic-a-phobia*).[3] As much as we might like to deny or defy it, we spend most of the time living in and dreading failure, as individuals and organizations. It may well be the fear of failure that leads us to deny the likelihood of failure, ignore its consequences, or defy its power. In fact, we probably spend more time dreading failure than we spend actually *dealing* with it.

We fear what we believe often accompanies failure: being judged, isolation, guilt, demotion, retaliation, losing face, and even loss of a job. When one of our friends, a psychologist who works with patients with post-traumatic stress disorder (PTSD), heard we were writing this book, she asked: "Which is more important: one's fear of failure, the failure itself, or just plain fear?" To be honest, we don't know. But we do know fear of failure is a profound and pervasive phenomenon, observable at early ages in preschools and kindergartens; in every high school and university; and the factories, labs, and offices of every organization.

Leaders like to think of themselves as bold, willing to take the reins in difficult circumstances. Some might even confuse their boldness with fearlessness, but it's usually more complicated than that. Mark Twain understood this well: "Courage is resistance to fear, mastery of fear—not the absence of fear."[4]

FEAR OF FAILURE AND THE STATUS QUO

Ever wonder why *Dilbert* became one of the world's most popular cartoons? Because so many so-called leaders of organizations around the world create such a rich environment of hypocrisy between the ideas they espouse and the behavior they reveal. Nowhere is that disconnect more obvious than in the complacency trap in which most organizations find themselves.

We all know this trap. It keeps us locked in today's business, today's way of doing things, even today's way of thinking. And its border patrol is fear of the unknown, the new, the different, and above all, fear of failure.

There's a natural tendency to accede to the status quo, and therefore avoid risks and limit innovation. This may be directly related to where you perceive your rank in the pecking order of your sector. Our colleague Rich Lyons, Dean of the Haas School of Business at the University of California Berkeley, offered this observation: "Organizations that are not in the top tier are more willing to take risks to get there. Organizations already at the top have more to lose; they have more reputation to protect."[5]

FEAR: FAILURE'S MAGNIFIER

We've had many opportunities to teach and work with business and nonprofit leaders around the world. Most are trying to make their companies and countries more innovative and entrepreneurial to better compete and grow. Whether they are European, Asian, African, South American, or Middle Eastern, they encounter the same barrier American executives do: fear of failure that stifles creativity, curiosity, and the innovative spirit. In many of these cultures, recovering from failure is especially difficult; and therefore, the fear of failure is even more acute.

In fact, we think this entrenched, unspoken fear of failure is perhaps the single biggest barrier to countries trying to expand opportunity through innovation and entrepreneurship. It is more pernicious and powerful than inadequate laws, outdated policies, dysfunctional capital markets, ineffectual intellectual property protections, or poor education. It is the hidden killer of initiative.

So what are we, and it seems most other people in the world, afraid of? Is it failure itself, the perceived ripple effects of failure on other things we care about (e.g., reputation, job security, ostracism, saving face, pride, etc.) or something else altogether?

Why should we care about the fear of failing? Because we care about success.

Are Women More Fearless?

The issue of gender, the other F word, and fear of failure came up often in our interviews. It's a fascinating and complex angle to consider. A senior female executive we interviewed offered this observation about how women approach problem solving:

> Women are more dimensional in problem solving. They're not afraid to ask for directions, aren't afraid to ask for help. I will pick up the phone and cold call smart people if I think they can help me. I think women are more willing to open themselves up in that way.

As intriguing as this topic of gender and failure is, it will have to wait for another book.

FEAR: FAILURE'S STRONGEST ALLY

Fear's not necessarily a bad thing. It helps us make split-second decisions if we're facing a saber-toothed tiger, putting our hand in a fire, or getting caught in a speed trap. As human beings, we're hard-wired to react to fear. It's called the fight-or-flight response. And fear of failure can sometimes motivate an individual or team to take Herculean measures to avoid failing. As Intel's former Chairman Andy Grove so aptly put it, "Only the paranoid survive."[6]

Fear is the stick to aspiration's carrot. As a young friend of ours said, "My father always told us: 'Remember, second place is first place for losers.'" Unless someone's trying to fix a game, nobody wants to lose. Randy Komisar, a seasoned entrepreneur and venture capitalist with Kleiner Perkins Caufield & Byers, puts it this way, "None of us wants to fail. It's not okay to make failure acceptable. But when you do fail, you need to learn from it—and that turns the failure into a process that may lead to innovation and resilience."[7]

Fear of failure can be a positive force in sports, classrooms, and the marketplace. Google Ventures' Joe Kraus, another former entrepreneur turned investor, believes fear of failure helps ground vision with reality:

> Entrepreneurs who don't have any fear of failure are dreamers, and in my experience dreamers usually don't succeed. [Those] who aren't afraid to try, but who do have some fear of failure, are often the best entrepreneurs. This mixture combines an attitude of experimentation with an internal drive that helps these entrepreneurs succeed.[8]

But often fear wildly exaggerates the likelihood of failure and its probable consequences. In that sense, fear is a perverse magnifier of failure, and left unaddressed, can keep your organization stuck in neutral.

Doubt this? Think about your own personal attitudes about failure. Take a look at how the topic is handled in your workplace, your kids' classroom, or even your house of worship.

Exercise: Fear of Failure

Ask yourself this simple question:

What would I try if I had a guarantee I wouldn't fail?

Go ahead; let yourself go. We're not talking about your super-power wish list—invisibility, flight, or x-ray vision. We just want to give you a chance to write down a few things you'd really like to do, or at least try, but don't pursue because fear or other factors are holding you back. Here's a little space to capture your ideas:

_____

_____

_____

_____

_____

_____

_____

What'd you come up with? Most likely they were not minor improvements or tweaks on your day-to-day agenda. We'll bet very few even show up on your plans for today, tomorrow, this week, or even next month.

Your list indicates the degree to which fear of failure may limit your own decision making. Now imagine what your organization could be capable of if you and your employees could pursue new product ideas, new markets, or new business models in a more no-fault, no-blame environment.

Yes, fear is an essential part of the arsenal of survival for an individual, a species, or an organization. But that fear can also unduly magnify the likelihood of failure and prevent the kind of experimentation and discovery necessary to advance people's lives and organizations' goals. It can even lead to the very failure it fears.

This isn't a ticket for recklessness. Potential initiatives would still have to go through the gauntlet of analysis, debate, and budgeting to ensure proper vetting. But by reducing the fear factor, you can raise your organization's willingness to take on the innovation challenges it needs to grow.

We think a key to confronting and reducing fear's grip on your thinking and organizational culture is to recognize just how common failure is, even in otherwise successful, respected organizations. Failure doesn't play favorites. It is truly a democratic phenomenon, so get over it, and help your colleagues do the same. In the pages that follow, we'll give you some ideas of how to do just that.

Of course, not every organizational shortcoming can be laid at the door of fear of failure. Incompetence, bad luck, shortage of resources, and other factors play a role in creating ineffective or flat-out bad results. Fear of failure compromises the aspirations and expectations of people across your organization, eroding their sense of self-confidence and willingness to take risks. This is something you, as a leader, can do something about. We'll show you how in Part III.

Now, before we forget, let's talk about the memory of failure and how it plays into this discussion.

MEMORY: FAILURE'S LONG SHADOW

Fear of failure has its own magnifier: memory. In our inaugural "Other F Word" class at UC Berkeley, our MBA students talked about how failure seems to cast a much longer and larger shadow than the more fleeting glow that comes with success. When John asked them about that, most of the class said they could vividly remember the sting, isolation, and embarrassment of failures experienced many years before, but they had difficulty recapturing— and in some cases even recalling—the same level of joy, pride, and excitement experienced from much bigger successes. That echoes what we've heard from many others, including more seasoned executives like you. It just may be that the effects of failure have a longer half-life than success.

Psychologists call this "negativity dominance," the phenomenon of negative events creating more vivid and durable memories.[9] A key insight here comes from Daniel Kahneman, the Nobel Prize–winning Princeton psychologist and father of behavioral economics. Most of the decisions we make are based on our memories (including our fears based on those memories), not our actual experiences. In fact, Kahneman talks about the "experiencing self" and the "remembering self."

The experiencing self is a creature of immediacy, experiencing life in the moment but forgetting it soon after. It has a very short attention span—about three seconds, according to Kahneman. That's the psychological presence of any given experience. The rest is simply forgotten.

This is where the remembering self enters the picture, and it's also where things get very interesting with regard to failure. Kahneman's research is fascinating and frustrating from the perspective of a leader trying to shape a more failure-savvy culture. He suggests the experiences we tend to remember, especially those that have a defined ending, are those characterized by change.

Now consider this: How do most failures end? Usually in pain, embarrassment, isolation, ridicule, or worse. That makes a big impact on the remembering self. When John first heard Kahneman discuss this several years ago,[10] he recalls writing the following phrase in his notebook, underlining it, and then highlighting it again later: "We actually don't choose between experiences, we choose between memories of experiences . . . We think of our future as anticipated memories."

Wow! Consider the implications of that statement for our discussion of the other F word. If our memory of failure is seared into our consciousness (or subconsciousness, if you prefer), then failure itself becomes a particularly powerful influencer on our behavior. Our memory of experiencing it in our past reinforces our fear of it in our future. To be sure, it presumably competes with more positive memories of happier experiences, but it might not be a fair fight.

It's as if we are caught in the middle of a hall of funhouse mirrors, with one side distorting our memories of the past and the other distorting our anticipation of the future. No wonder this other F word is so difficult to get our arms around. It's quite literally difficult to deal with it in the moment because our attitudes and expectations are in different time zones, caught between memory and expectation.

This is really important stuff if you want to get serious about failure in your organization. What do you think is the "anticipated memory" of failure in the minds of your colleagues (and your mind, for that matter)? If they've experienced failure in your culture that resulted in blame, shame, demotion, or firing, how do you think they think about the future? Will they be willing to alert you to possible failures in the making or join a team to develop a new high-risk product?

If Kahneman is right, memory puts a big thumb on the scale of our behavior. The experiencing self has a short attention span, but the remembering self has a v e r y   l o n g   m e m o r y. The memory of past, painful failures can reinforce your organization's fear of failure, which, in turn, stifles creativity and compromises innovation. As a leader, your job is to help ensure a more constructive memory by paying attention to how failures end in your organization. We'll give you some practical suggestions for how to do that in Chapter 16.

For now, we'll close this chapter with an appropriate saying by that ubiquitous commentator, Anonymous:

Fear kills more dreams than failure ever will.

What Sports Psychologists Can Tell Business People about Fear of Failure

Psychologists have been studying fear of failure for decades, and sports psychologists have a particular interest in the connection between this fear and athletic performance.[11] Fear of failure can have its roots in childhood. It's a reaction to perceived threats, which in turn shift our focus from achievement to avoidance. Studies of students, athletes, and myriad others connect these avoidance behaviors with stress, anxiety, and a lower sense of general well-being, among other feelings.

Fear is a very understandable, natural reaction to a perceived threat. And perception is highly idiosyncratic, often working below the level of consciousness yet powerful nonetheless.

It's not necessarily the failure itself we fear, but its consequences. David Conroy, a prominent researcher at Penn State, suggests these five consequences play an important role: 1) experiencing shame/embarrassment, 2) devaluing one's self-estimate/esteem, 3) being uncertain of the future, 4) significant others may lose interest, and 5) significant others may be upset.[12]

Take a look at that list for a second. These are very natural human feelings. Ask yourself how they might manifest themselves in your workplace, recognizing you are likely a "significant other" to many people working for you.

Psychologists go further. Their research suggests overcoming fear of failure takes more than just increasing people's need and incentive to achieve. Those two factors seem to be independent of one another, and can result in four possible configurations between an athlete's fear of failure (fear) and need to achieve (need).

Athletes with high fear and low need are likely to withdraw from competitive situations if possible, whereas those with low fear and low need may be stuck in neutral, somewhat indifferent to competition.

Conversely, those with low fear and high need welcome competition and can accommodate failure rather comfortably if necessary. Finally, their high-fear–high-need counterparts embrace competition, but with a high degree of anxiety and they feel failure intensely.

The important thing here is to recognize how differently people react to the possibility and consequences of failure, whether on the playing field, on the factory floor, or in the executive suite. One size does not fit all, and Nike's "Just do it" suggestion isn't likely to work with many of your employees.

This research also suggests you have to deal with both parts of this equation—the fear of failure and the need to achieve—on their own merits. Don't expect improvement with one to yield improvement with the other.

PART

II

When and Where

How Failure Appears at Different Organizational Phases

Failure is nothing if not a constant companion. In the next three chapters, we'll give you an insider's tour of how the other F word manifests itself in three major organizational life phases, and—more importantly—what you can do about it:

1. **Start-Ups:** the exciting world of entrepreneurs seeking to launch new ventures and pursue their dreams to create value for customers, investors, and themselves
2. **Keep-Ups:** the vast and complex world of small and medium enterprises, where most businesses in the United States and around the world exist
3. **Grown-Ups:** the big businesses covered by the *Fortunes*, *Forbes*, and *Businessweeks* of the world

Each of these chapters follows the same format:

- **Story:** We put a face on this phase of organizational life
- **Key Facts:** A quick overview of the territory we're covering

- **The Other F Word and Start-Ups, Keep-Ups, and Grown-Ups:** How failure manifests itself in each life phase
- **To Do's:** Specific suggestions for becoming a more failure-savvy leader
- **Your Role:** Your fundamental persona for this phase
- **Takeaways:** Three or four highlights for you to keep in mind

6

Start-Ups

Launching Your Venture in the Land of Failure

Your Role: Passionate Convincer

Startups are like newborn lambs. Give them a chance and they will always try to find new ways to kill themselves.
—Duncan Logan, CEO and founder of startup accelerator RocketSpace

SMALL FAILURES CAN LEAD TO HUGE SUCCESS

In 2009 Kevin Systrom (soon to be joined by his co-founder Mike Krieger) raised $500,000 from Baseline Ventures and Andreessen Horowitz for his new venture, Burbn. He envisioned Burbn as an iPhone app that enabled users to "check in" to locations (similar to Foursquare), make plans, post pictures, and earn points. As they prepared to launch, after more than a year of work, Kevin and Mike gave the product a thorough review and also solicited input from their beta users.

The verdict: Burbn was just too cluttered. The insight: Customers loved the photo application. Armed with this input, Systrom and Krieger simplified Burbn. "[We] basically cut everything in the Burbn app except for its photo, comment, and like capabilities. What remained was Instagram," explains Systrom.[1]

Using the infrastructure and platform they'd already built for Burbn, the team created Instagram in two months. They made it easy to use and chose a distinctive square photo format similar to old Polaroid photos. Upon release in October 2010, Instagram became a huge hit on the iPhone, garnering more than 10 million downloads in its first year. In April 2012, on the first day it was available on the Android platform, it generated more than 1 million downloads.

That turned out to be a very good month for Instagram. A couple of weeks after its successful Android launch, the company raised $50 million, and later that same month, Instagram was acquired by Facebook for approximately $1 billion. We all should have months like this. At least once.

* * *

The Instagram story is the stuff of legends, not to mention the dreams of entrepreneurs. But the vast majority of startups create a very different kind of story. Most struggle every day to find less sexy sources of capital, assemble their teams without sophisticated stock option incentive plans, build products, and sell services far less high-profile than the next social networking site or big data analytics venture. So while we applaud (and live in) the Silicon Valley epicenter of U.S. venture capital–style entrepreneurship, let's also look at the rest of this territory to better understand how the other F word plays out across the broad spectrum of startups.

Just to give you a sense of the size and dynamism of this sector, consider this: Each month in the United States, roughly 543,000 new businesses are created. That's pretty impressive. But, at the same time, approximately the same number close their doors. Some disappear because the owners retire or lose interest, or the firms get acquired, but most shut down due to business failure.[2]

Key Facts

How big is this startup territory? Huge, both in the United States and internationally. Here's a snapshot to bring you up to speed:

- Almost 7 million U.S. businesses are launched every year, and a roughly equal number disappear annually for various reasons.[3]
- Startups raise an average of $73,406 from various sources, with almost half coming from personal savings or credit (35 percent), or family and friends (11 percent).[4]
- Although high-tech startups tend to get the most press, they represent a small minority of U.S. startups. Service-related businesses and retail account for more than two out of three American startups, followed by finance, insurance, real estate, construction, and wholesale ventures.[5]
- Venture capitalists invest in fewer than 1 of every 2,000 American startups (0.05 percent), but commit an average of $2.6 million to those they do support.[6]
- Angel investors reach more ventures than VCs, investing an average of $75,000 in slightly less than 1 percent of all domestic startups.[7]
- Startups show up actively in every state across the country, but recently the Western region has the highest rates of entrepreneurship. Interestingly, Montana, Alaska, and South Dakota recently had more startups per capita than our home state of California. The Western region was followed by the East Coast and Midwest regions. Indiana, Minnesota, and Wisconsin were the lowest-ranking states in terms of startup activity.[8]

The San Francisco Bay Area/Silicon Valley has the most robust startup ecosystem in the world as measured by funding, mindset, talent, and general entrepreneurial activity, but its slice of the global pie is shrinking as other startup hubs proliferate. This is based on rankings by The Startup Genome, an encouraging project seeking to better understand the whole startup phenomenon. Rounding out the top 10 are Tel Aviv, Los Angeles, Seattle, New York, Boston, London, Toronto, Vancouver, and Chicago. Other cities in the top 20 are Paris, Sydney, São Paulo, Moscow, Berlin, Waterloo (Canada), Singapore, Melbourne, Bangalore, and Santiago.[9]

Globally, the startup scene is both extraordinarily active and diverse:

- An estimated 150+ million entrepreneurs start up 100 million businesses each year around the world.[10]
- In developing economies in Asia (including India) and Latin America, new business creation is particularly prolific, growing at a far greater rate than in more established economies such as those in Europe.[11]
- Many entrepreneurs launch businesses out of necessity, especially in so-called factor-driven economies (think natural resources). For example,

39 percent of adults in Nigeria and Zambia are engaged in early-stage entrepreneurship.[12]

- In general, as levels of economic development and maturity increase, the percentage of adults participating in startup activity declines.[13]

THE OTHER F WORD AND START-UPS

Unfortunately (and fortunately, for reasons we'll explain), this vast territory of startups is also a failure-rich environment:

- Depending upon your definition, between 75 and 90 percent of startups fundamentally fail.[14] The Startup Genome project pegs the failure rate even higher at 92 percent![15]
- Startups face sobering mortality rates in their early years. According to one recent study, 25 percent of new ventures fail in Year 1, 36 percent by Year 2, and 44 percent by Year 3.[16]
- The survival rates vary widely by industry, according to the same study. For example, 58 percent of startups in the finance and real estate industries are in business after four years, while only 37 percent of those in information technology live that long.[17]
- In its 2014 "The R.I.P. Report – Startup Death Trends," CB Insights, a data analytics research firm, looked more specifically at failure rates among tech ventures. It found that 70 percent of venture deaths from 2010 to 2013 were in the Internet sector, an especially mine-laden domain for startups.[18]

Daunting odds indeed.

FAILURE'S UNIQUE FACES IN START-UPS

Startups have a distinctive relationship with the other F word.

First, startups by their very nature are new and fragile. Their core foundation has not yet been solidified, teams are being formed, products and services are still in development, revenues are nonexistent or nascent, and capital is typically scarce.

Duncan Logan sees dozens of startups every week. He is the founder and CEO of RocketSpace, a technology accelerator and co-working space in

San Francisco where teams of entrepreneurs grow their ventures. He observes: "It is a totally naïve founder who does not recognize that at some point—or at many points—during the startup process he or she will be so close to fundamentally failing, so close to death's door." He went on to add, "Very few entrepreneurs knock it out of the park on their initial product launch. Most fail large or small on day one. What's crucial is that the feedback you receive from the marketplace contains the ingredients for success. Drop what doesn't work, and use what does."[19]

Second, startup failures are more visible. Entrepreneurs can't hide failure nearly as well as more established organizations. Everyone involved in the start of a venture is pretty visible, as are the results of their efforts, whether in the lab or with a customer. Failure is up close and personal in this setting. With luck, the startup team can take advantage of this greater visibility of failure by adapting quickly and making the proverbial pivots necessary to stay alive for another day. So in this setting, the oft-quoted "fail fast, fail forward, fail often" mantra makes perfect sense.

Justin Kan has founded several technology and media businesses, including video site Twitch, which Amazon acquired in 2014 for just under $1 billion. He is now a partner at startup accelerator Y Combinator, where he works with new ventures every day. Looking back on his own startups, he recalls, "Most of the time we were failing in some way or another. You just may not get it right the first time. I learned to talk to customers and build what they wanted."[20]

Third, failures are more frequent. Startups probably make more mistakes more often than their more established counterparts—precisely because they are continually experimenting with new products and features, business models, marketing strategies, channels, pricing, and more. Whereas in the past startups needed to develop many capabilities from the ground up, today more and more tools and capabilities may be open-sourced or rented, such as Linux for an operating system or Amazon Web Services for web servers. This makes it easier and cheaper for startups to investigate many combinations and options, moving on quickly when failures teach them what they didn't know before. As Kleiner Perkins venture capitalist and *Getting to Plan B* author Randy Komisar shared with us, "Entrepreneurial success comes from figuring things out as you go along."[21]

Chris Michel, founder of Affinity Labs (a business that builds online communities), echoed that sentiment:

We were always failing as we tried to emerge from the "creative muck" of our everyday activities. We made mistakes, had products that didn't work, etc. But I tried not to convey a sense that we were afraid to fail, because we had to fail to survive. As a board member of established businesses now, I use that startup experience and find myself asking a recurring question: Are we trying not to fail or are we trying to succeed?[22]

Fourth, the effects of failure are more immediate in startups. Throughout the history of entrepreneurship, most startups by necessity have been pretty lean endeavors. It's the nature of the beast: An entrepreneur scrapes, saves, and borrows enough resources to quit his job, puts together a small team in Spartan surroundings, and tries to get a business off the ground. That was true long before today's "lean startup" label became popular.

In such an environment, startups are often one or two mistakes away from closing down. A late-paying customer, a delay in product launch, or the loss of a key team member can be fatal. They illustrate the immediate vulnerability of startups to the other F word.

Fear of failure looms large here, too. It remains one of the key barriers to greater startup activity,[23] even when opportunities abound and people seem to have the requisite skills. To put this in perspective, here in the United States (arguably the most startup-friendly country in the world), in any given month only 3 adults in 1,000 will start a business.[24]

START-UPS HAVE A COMPLICATED RELATIONSHIP WITH FAILURE

With the knowledge that catastrophic failure happens frequently for startups, let's not overlook the silver lining. In those startups that do succeed, failure typically plays a dual role in their success: first, to create the venture opportunity itself, and then to capture it.

"My Start-Up Was Launched by Your Screw-Up"

The primary reason startups exist and succeed in the first place is because they identify new or unaddressed opportunities to create scalable and valuable ventures. The fact that these openings exist at all may be characterized as a failure on the part of existing players in the sector to identify these opportunities, develop products, and service customers. After all, they presumably had the resources, reputation, customer relationships, supply networks, and talent to exploit those market opportunities in the first place. But for whatever reasons—inattention, misalignment with current strategic focus, complacency, etc.—the incumbents left the field vacant for the insurgents; and that's what keeps entrepreneurship such a target-rich, as well as failure-rich, domain.

The irony is that many entrepreneurs themselves developed their new venture ideas while working for their former companies, and in many cases offered or tried to develop their product inside their previous firms before deciding to leave. Amar Bhide discovered that a "substantial fraction" of Inc. 500 company founders got their venture ideas this way.[25] In other words, some incumbent companies actually groomed their own future competitors.

Let's look at a current example. Nest Labs, with its Learning Thermostat and other smart-home products, has taken its field by storm. Nest was launched by a group of former Apple product executives who were interested in the connected home. They left Apple to found Nest, which quickly became a favorite of consumers who wanted an easy-to-use smart thermostat. Nest also captured the fancy of Google, which acquired it in 2014 for $3.2 billion, with the former Apple engineers now accelerating Google's product development efforts. Nest was even able to outflank Honeywell, the historic leader in this category. Honeywell has since come out with its own smart thermostat, so we'll just have to wait to see how this market shakes out.

Another example is how AOL lost its early connectivity-driven web prominence to Yahoo! and its convenient homepage, which was then passed by Google with its dominance in search due to their better algorithms.

Screw Up Before You Grow Up

Paradoxically, startups often have to fail to survive and grow. Entrepreneurs have to optimize scarce resources across many fronts while building their ventures. Each of these also consumes resources of its own. The more people you hire, the more money and time they require. The more people and

equipment you have, the more space you need, and the more rent you pay.
In so doing, entrepreneurs often unwittingly invite failure in several areas:

- **Team:** the wrong people; dysfunctional chemistry; too many people
  too soon; or the wrong people doing the wrong things at the wrong
  time[26]
- **Funding:** inability to raise sufficient capital for product development
  and operations; overinvestment of scarce funds on noncritical activities
  far removed from ringing your cash register; waiting too long to secure
  the next round of funding to maintain momentum
- **Products:** falling and staying in love with your product too long;
  devoting too many resources to features of little or no value to initial
  target customers at the expense of strengthening core functionality
- **Business model:** believing too strongly in untested or unverified key
  assumptions about how your venture can make money and grow
  profitably
- **Customers:** confusing need with demand (will they buy your solution?); mistaking initial customer interest and usage with locating a
  scalable market that can be effectively addressed by your marketing and
  sales team (Geoffrey Moore's "crossing the chasm" problem)[27]

Entrepreneurs who make these mistakes have, in different ways, squandered not just the time and talent of their people, but also the life blood of
any venture: the working capital it takes to keep their doors open and pay
bills until they reach profitability.

Startups face a veritable gauntlet of potential failures as they evolve from
original idea to implementing operations and scaling. Any one of these
elements can derail an early-stage venture, and in combination they are
especially lethal. Particularly cruel is the situation where new insights have
been discovered through experimentation and hard work, but the startup
exhausts its financial runway before being able to apply the lessons learned.

Too Much, Too Soon

A perverse version of this issue sometimes happens when startups raise too
much money too soon. In these situations well-funded startups undertake what
the Startup Genome project calls "premature scaling," a key contributor to
startup death.[28] What's that? It involves investing too many resources in the
wrong things at the wrong time. It's the opposite of a disciplined bootstrap

startup focused more on the "start" than the "up." Significant funding at an early stage not only postpones the day of reckoning, it can seriously handicap the entrepreneur's single-minded attention to how the market is reacting to this new business concept. A faster-than-necessary cash burn rate can force a startup to close its doors, perhaps just as it was discovering the right products and business model.

Particularly well-funded startups may behave more like an established company in this regard. Think of this as the "Webvan Curse," in honor of the online retailer that burned through more than $1 billion in funding before going bankrupt.[29] According to Shikhar Ghosh at Harvard Business School:

> What funding does is cover up all the problems that a company has. It covers up all the mistakes, it enables the company and management to focus on things that aren't important to the company's success and ignore the things that are important. This lets management rationalize away the proverbial problem of the dogs not eating the dog food. When you don't have money you reformulate the dog food so that the dogs will eat it. When you have a lot of money you can afford to argue that the dogs should like the dog food because it is nutritious.[30]

Unfortunately, startup entrepreneurs make these mistakes again and again. In doing so, they violate what we might call the First Three Rules of Failure-Savvy Leadership:

- **Rule #1:** The best failure to learn from is somebody else's (learn by watching).
- **Rule #2:** The next best is to learn from simulated reality, games, or analysis (learn by playing and thinking). Rules #1 and #2 are relatively safe, helpful, and sometimes extremely valuable, but often not sufficient for deeper personal learning, especially as you enter unexplored territory. Scott Adams, creator of the comic strip *Dilbert* and author of his own recent book on failure,[31,32] calls this "learning lite." As Scott told us, "Learning from others' mistakes is the lite version of learning from your own. It's only 10 percent as effective." And that leads us to Rule #3.
- **Rule #3:** If you have to learn by doing (and you probably will), test first and prepare to be wrong.

These are the principles around which we organize our "Workshop for Startups" course at UC Berkeley. We want our students to squeeze as many potential failures out of their new venture ideas while they're in school, before they decide to put their savings, credit rating, and relationships at risk. If you're curious how we do this, check out our description in the Appendix.

TO-DO'S: IMPROVE YOUR ODDS OF START-UP SUCCESS

How can you reduce your venture's risk of a fatal failure? To start, answer three basic questions:

1. Why this solution for these customers?
2. Why now?
3. Why you?

Question 1: Why This Solution for These Customers?

In short, the answer to this question lies in using experiments to improve a product or service, create a better fit with the market, and develop a solid business model. Smart entrepreneurs understand the value of constant testing as they search for traction in the market. Given their limited resources, they have no choice but to be scrappy. You can borrow a page from the *Lean Startup* playbook, based on the thinking of our UC Berkeley colleague Steve Blank, and popularized in the book of the same name by one of his former students, Eric Ries. It's a fast-moving exploration and refinement process known as "customer discovery."[33]

Customer discovery is a highly iterative process. It involves a series of real-time, market-facing experiments where entrepreneurs share prototypes and MVPs (minimum viable products, which are essentially stripped-down versions of a product that still deliver the core value) with their customers. Based on customer reactions and feedback, entrepreneurs then quickly iterate and evolve their offerings, learning from negative and positive outcomes alike, as they improve their ability to meet customer needs and desires.

The customer discovery process also provides startups with valuable insights about what to do and what not to do in their go-to-market strategies and in their revenue and business models. Rather than strictly labeling outcomes as successes or failures, look at them the way a scientist might, even though most entrepreneurs are hardly working in laboratory conditions.

Borrow from the scientific method to create hypotheses, conduct experiments, and identify positive and negative results. Successful entrepreneurs obviously welcome results that confirm hypotheses, but also know that negative outcomes provide valuable input into the next set of hypotheses to test or experiments to conduct.

Or think like a sailor, who knows that his boat's course from A to B will likely involve many zigs and zags as the wind changes and currents shift. The telltale pennants on the mast are like the signals you should be looking for from your team and target customers. They tell you when it's time to change course. One cautionary note: be careful not to pivot too soon. Sometimes riveting beats pivoting, giving your concept time to win over skeptical customers.

This approach of rapid iteration and real-time market testing can enable you to compress your failure-to-insight cycle from years or months to weeks or even days. It can also be used to evolve your business model in an early-stage venture. From these inputs, you create a variety of different product offers, bundles, and prices, and also test various channels and partners. For those offering products online, a broad range of easy-to-use, inexpensive, and sophisticated tracking and metrics tools and solutions can help. They make it simple to conduct and analyze multiple A:B tests[34] and undertake complex comparisons of different product offers and configurations, leveraging real-time results to rapidly evolve offerings and business models.

Use these many outcomes and "small-f" failures to provide insights and help you avoid "big-F" Failures that can terminate your venture. You want to be a survivor. Don't vote yourself off your own island by falling too much in love with your original idea and strategy at the expense of listening to and learning from your real market and future customers. Treat it like a rough draft written in pencil, and expect lots of erasures before you get it right.

There are two other points to keep in mind before you think there's a magic formula for this effort. First, we suspect that iconic entrepreneurs who have brought *radically* new solutions or technologies that redefined markets or created entire new industries (think: Steve Jobs and Steve Wozniak with their Apple computer, Henry Ford and his Model T Ford, Akio Morita's Sony Walkman, and Bill Gates's operating system) would not have been disciples of the *Lean Startup* movement.

They famously relied on their own instincts and bold tenacity (and luck) to bring their breakthrough ideas to life without spending much time engaging with target customers beforehand. Henry Ford was asked why he didn't consult with customers while developing his revolutionary car. He allegedly replied, "If I had asked people what they wanted, they would have said faster horses."[35] Steve Jobs agreed, "A lot of times, people don't know what they want until you show it to them."[36]

So by all means, think lean, be scrappy, and pay close attention to how your potential customers react to your big idea, but be prepared to trust your gut and your vision as well, even though early on it may mean you'll have to be more missionary than mercenary in convincing them to see the wisdom of your ways. And if many of your customers start using your solution the "wrong" way, pay extra close attention to understand what they see that you don't. The answer might be right in front of you.

Second, your venture's success depends on many factors besides product–market fit and insightful customer discovery. How well your team can work together, whether you can design an appropriate financing structure to support your particular strategy, the strength of your intellectual property protection, and how effectively your competition responds to your entry into their markets are just as important determinants of your ultimate prospects, and need to be as carefully addressed.

Exercise: What Has To Be True?

Here's a useful way you can identify and align your core team around the fundamental issues or assumptions you need to test. Have each of your team members do this "What Has To Be True?" exercise separately, then compare and discuss your results so you can see whether you are all on the same proverbial page during this critical early stage. On a large sheet of paper (we prefer poster size for this exercise), ask each person to draw a circular target with three concentric rings, making sure the smallest one is still big enough to write in. Then divide the target into eight equal sections labeled Customers, Product/Service, Business Model, Team, Timing, Money, Competitors, and one open topic to fit your situation.

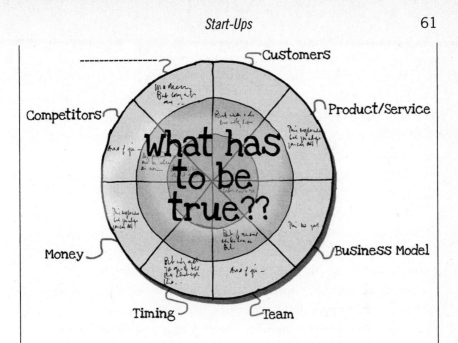

Ask each person to identify the *single* most important assumption that must be true for your business success in the center circle for each of these eight segments. In the next ring, ask them to identify one to three specific actions that could answer or confirm that core assumption. In the outer ring, ask them to write in any additional or wildcard assumptions they think are worth discussing and considering.

Give them overnight to complete their target. The next day, when everyone is finished, post the results side by side and ask your team to do a walk-by review, much like they might in an art gallery. Jot down notes to capture your observations along the way (e.g., points of convergence, disagreement, and uncertainty). You now have the ingredients for a focused and pragmatic conversation to reach agreement about your real strategic agenda: What are the fundamental assumptions that need to be confirmed in each aspect of your business, and how specifically will you attempt to do precisely that? Make sure you carefully listen throughout this process before you lock in on the final target.

Question 2: Why Now?

Getting your timing right can be everything. A great idea at the wrong time is just that—subject to an untimely death in an unripe market. While rapid testing may not be able to fundamentally change the outcome of a poorly timed introduction, it can provide early signs about market readiness, help you identify a better growth strategy, or consider major shifts in direction.

Take a look at Pets.com, one of the first and the largest online specialty pet food and accessories retailers. Julie Wainwright joined Pets.com as CEO in 1999 with the mandate to grow revenues, build the brand, invest in infrastructure to support growth, and take the company public. And she did just that, leading an IPO in early 2000 at the height of the dot-com boom, knowing the company would almost certainly need additional capital to finance infrastructure development and marketing (remember the Pets.com sock puppet?), and to underwrite ongoing operating losses until profitability was reached. When the public equities markets dried up shortly after the IPO, the company's strategy did as well. Pets.com ceased operations in November 2000.

Pets.com became famous because of its fast rise, and then infamous due to its even faster fall. What insights can be derived from this failure that might help future executives and entrepreneurs? We spoke with Wainwright in the San Francisco offices of her current venture, The Real Real, a fast-growing online luxury goods consignment retailer.

She shared that, in late 2000, she and the company's board opted to shut down Pets.com and return some of the IPO proceeds to shareholders, as opposed to trying to stick it out and see if they could make that cash last through what turned out to be a long and deep recession.

With the benefit of hindsight, it is highly unlikely that the company would have been able to survive the extended recession. Even so, when it came to the reputation hit, Wainwright acknowledges had they waited a few more months before shutting down the company, there would have been other online retailers and technology companies going out of business that could have claimed many of those early headlines. eToys.com closed three months later and Webvan outlived Pets.com by only seven months. Pets.com might not have become such a high-profile poster child for the dot-com implosion if it hadn't been among the first high-profile casualties.

As it happened, its experience demonstrated what might be called the first-mover *dis*advantage.

What if the timing of Pets.com had been different? In the late 1990s observers questioned the business model and logic of selling heavy and bulky pet food online. Fast-forward 15 years. Amazon and many other online retailers now sell 50-pound bags of dog food with fast and free delivery. The concept doesn't seem at all silly now. Timing and context can change everything.

With insights gained from her experiences leading Pets.com and other companies, Wainwright founded The Real Real in 2011. As opposed to building out a large and expensive infrastructure in advance of revenues (as was the strategy at Pets.com), she assiduously kept capital expenditures and costs low and has invested only as needed to build out company capabilities. In less than three years the company attained a run rate of more than $100 million in sales, with a business model that is fundamentally profitable.

As Julie observed, "I always think big, but this time I started small and learned from my interactions with the market. Entrepreneurs should always look for 'fast proof,' and the ultimate fast proof is when customers are willing to part with their money for what you are selling. That's what I found here at The Real Real, and I knew I had something big."[37]

Question 3: Why You?

Having a great team trumps many other factors in creating a successful startup. Terrific products, strong financing, cool offices, and a great website don't matter much if your team can't work well together. Developing a great team and establishing a healthy, productive organizational culture are two of your most challenging tasks in a startup. They are also more in your control than many other elements discussed in this chapter.

Here are a couple suggestions:

Mirror, Lenses, and Glue

Look in the mirror. Don't hire too many people that look like you. Your team should be able to see the world through different lenses professionally, intellectually, socially, and personally. This is not seeking diversity for its own sake, but rather building a broader and stronger team that will help you with different and useful viewpoints, capabilities, and approaches that will be valuable as you build your business. You're hiring people who are not your clones but your complements.

Experienced investors will tell you they fundamentally invest in the team. Of course vision and strategy are important but, when investors trust the team, that vision can evolve while maintaining their support. Your challenge is to build just such a team, one that is up for the adventure ahead. You probably have fewer than five major hires as you get underway, so think like a sports team owner on draft day and make every pick count. Think how each of them will complement one another's strengths and compensate for their shortcomings, especially when the proverbial shit hits the fan.

Your organization may not be big yet, but your culture is already forming. Every day, you and your initial team are building the foundation for the bigger company you want to create. Begin the right culture from day one. You're shaping the organization's spirit, integrity, and style of operating and communicating, including how you handle failure. That's the glue that binds your team together. Remember, culture starts with just two people, multiplies quickly, and is surprisingly fragile. Give it the attention it deserves.

Bias to Action and Relentless Dissatisfaction

In an early stage company, the most effective culture is one of execution. In startups there's no room for people who want to sit back and give advice. Clear metrics, accountability, and transparency are key. They make it easier to quickly recognize, minimize, and learn from small failures.

Bryan Roberts, one of the most successful healthcare investors in Silicon Valley, calls this "relentless dissatisfaction." He doesn't mean you should be the eternal pessimist; that can corrode morale very quickly, especially when times are tough. Bryan looks for entrepreneurs and board members who are constantly on the lookout for "what can go better and what's the next hill to climb" as well as the squeaks, friction, and goofs that suggest where things are not going smoothly now. A relentless focus on data and information combined with the independent thinking necessary to understand and correct those situations are valuable assets in a startup. They also temper a founder's self-confidence and hubris with the kind of humility and curiosity that can lead to continually improving business performance.

Michael Berolzheimer, founder of Bee Partners, a pre-seed-stage investment fund, agrees: "Failure to me means when an entrepreneur stops listening to the cues that differ from what he or she believes. That translates into an unwillingness to adapt and experiment."[38]

YOUR ROLE: THE PASSIONATE CONVINCER

As an entrepreneur you, by definition, pursue opportunities and take risks often without regard to the resources you control. This pretty much requires you to be a consummate communicator and convincer. It doesn't necessarily mean you have to channel your inner Steve Jobs and his famous "reality distortion field."[39] But it does mean you tell your story and present your venture in a compelling way that resonates with others and contributes to progress every day. Startup leaders hire great employees, close big sales, and speak with credibility and conviction to investors and partners.

You maintain employee morale, share big visions, celebrate small wins, and make everyone on your team feel like they are an integral part of something bigger than them. You are also an attentive listener, hearing the needs of different stakeholders and presenting your venture in a way that meets those needs. And you do it all with authenticity and passion. You lead the organization by providing others with words and actions they can use as they take initiative, and by shaping the culture, all at the same time.

Takeaways

1. **Build your tomorrow culture today:** This is your first chance to set the tone for the kind of company you envision. Seize it. Show, by personal example, how you will be a failure-savvy leader, dealing effectively with the other F word when it manifests itself, while helping your colleagues leverage its lessons openly and fearlessly. Expect it, embrace it, engage it, and, above all, apply its lessons to your venture.

2. **Focus:** Work with your team to clarify and test the most important assumptions or questions that need to be validated to get your venture to the next stage. Embrace the reality of the journey you're on; when you encounter failure, learn from it, wherever it manifests itself.

(continued)

(*continued*)

3. **Remember:** Only you own the final "no" on your venture. Starting a business is not for the fainthearted. Once you've made the decision to launch a venture, you will enter the "no zone." Prepare to hear that word directly and indirectly, bluntly and politely, over and over and over, from investors, bankers, potential customers, suppliers, possible hires, not to mention people even closer to you. As difficult as it is, try not to take those negatives personally. Think of them as questions you need to answer, assumptions you need to test. Then get back out there; one of those next contacts may be the "yes" you're looking for.

7 | Keep-Ups

Surviving and Thriving After You Meet Payroll

Your Role: Confident Juggler

Hell, there are no rules here—we're trying to accomplish something.
—Thomas A. Edison

FISHING FOR PROFITS

Northland Fishing Tackle was founded 40 years ago by John Peterson, a fishing guide in Minnesota who started making his own tackle to improve the fishing for his clients. Word of his great lures and accessories spread and soon a company was born. Located in Bemijdi, Minnesota, Northland grew over the years to offer thousands of different lures, baits, hooks, fishing line, and other accessories.

By late 2012, however, it became clear that the company's profitability was stuck in a long slow decline due to increasing costs and tough competition. Throughout this period, as the business deteriorated, Northland managers kept to the same basic operating routines hoping that the results would somehow improve, as opposed to developing new strategies to improve the trajectory.

Pat McIntyre was a Northland shareholder and board member. When it became clear that major changes were needed, he stepped in as CEO to address this slow-fuse failure. McIntyre and his team came to the conclusion that they needed to simplify an overly complicated product line, outsource manufacturing (in many cases to local suppliers), and upgrade their internal systems and processes. An ambitious agenda. In early 2013 Project Streamline was initiated to address these issues.

From Makers to Managers

For a 40-year-old company used to doing things "the old-fashioned way," this represented wrenching change. To guide the company and its managers through this evolution, McIntyre convened regular meetings to explain the new systems and processes, listen to and address employee concerns, share results, and publicly recognize those team members who were excelling in this changing environment. In meetings with his managers, he outlined specific metrics for each and aligned incentive compensation with those objectives. Then, the managers shared their goals with one another so they could help everyone hit their targets. This created an environment of collaboration and shared goals, and it broke down silos that existed even in this relatively small business.

A Great Catch

Eighteen months later, the hard work started yielding results. The product line was simplified, revenues were up, and, perhaps most importantly, margins rose dramatically while cash flow improved. As those initial programs evolved and additional programs were added, McIntyre and his team could clearly see the path to additional improvement in the coming years.

* * *

This IS business in America, and in most other countries in the world. It's the small business that delivers your newspaper in the morning, the franchisee donut or coffee shop that starts your workday, the lunch stand you eat at every afternoon, the cab driver you meet, and the movie theater or club you attend at night. And that doesn't include your dry cleaner, gardener, gas station, beauty salon, hardware store, florist, drugstore, or shoe repair shop.

But it is also the midsize businesses like your local grocery chain, accounting and law firms, manufacturing companies, regional retailers, distribution and warehousing firms, and many more, some with hundreds of millions of dollars in revenues.

For some of these businesses, the focus is growth and expansion, as they aspire to become a really big company. For others, innovation and strengthening their competitive position is at the top of the agenda. But for many, success does not necessarily mean growth per se. Managers of these companies often decide their businesses have grown up enough, thank you very much. Other factors—like being their own boss or having flexible hours—can be more important. Reinforcing this observation, a recent University of Chicago study suggested that only one in four small business owners wanted to grow their ventures beyond their current size.[1]

We call these companies Keep-Up businesses. Why? Regardless of their immediate priorities, their fundamental objective is to at least keep up with the competition, perhaps to keep up on key trends in their markets, and definitely to keep their doors open.

KEY FACTS

Let's take a quick tour of this vast landscape of Keep-Up businesses:

- Over 99 percent of the businesses in the United States are small and medium-size enterprises (SMEs).[2] That's 28 million enterprises! Small enterprises are defined as having up to 50 employees; medium-size firms between 50 and 250.
- Some couldn't get any smaller; they have no employees, just the owner. There are 22.5 million of these non-employer *solopreneurs*.[3]

- Altogether, American SMEs employ roughly 81 million workers—more than *half* of the nation's workforce, and closer to 60 percent if you consider all those solopreneur operations.[4]
- SMEs are even more prevalent in the European Union.[5] They account for 99.8 percent of all firms, and employ almost 7 out of every 10 workers.[6]

And this phenomenon is not limited to the developed world:

- McKinsey estimates there are 80 to 100 million formal so-called micro, small, and medium-size enterprises (MSMEs) in emerging markets alone.[7] (Micro enterprises are defined as having fewer than 10 employees.)
- Worldwide, SMEs are estimated to account for at least 95 percent of all registered businesses.

Family Businesses Rule

You're Not the Boss of Me! (Oops, maybe you are)

Home may be where the heart is, but it's also where the cash register rings. In fact, 52 percent of all small businesses in America are home-based.[8,9] Family firms represent 80 to 90 percent of business enterprises in North America.[10] In addition to all those 22.5 million solopreneur businesses, most of which are presumably family-owned, there are 5.5 million more family-owned employer entities.[11] And lest you think of them as the mom-and-pop corner store, families control most publicly traded firms in the world[12] and one third of companies in the S&P 500 (including Walmart, Koch Industries, Cargill, and Mars);[13] not to mention other behemoths like Samsung or Porsche. So "family businesses" run the gamut of business itself.[14]

By and large, Keep-Up companies drive Main Street business, without the hoopla of Silicon Valley, venture capitalists, IPOs, and all the rest. This category also includes many hobbyist or lifestyle businesses in which the owner-manager cares less about growth than simply having a creative outlet for his or her spare time interests. Despite this notion, most SMEs can't afford to take a lackadaisical attitude toward their business survival. Many are simply trying to survive to meet next month's payroll and keep afloat for another year.

Why does all this matter? Because, simply stated, these SME Keep-Ups are the primary drivers of not just the American economy, but also many other economies around the world. In the United States, they provide 75 percent of net new jobs, and create about half of the GDP.[15] Those jobs fuel the consumer spending that anchors the U.S. economy. Not to mention the fact this is where most American workers spend their time and apply their talents and ingenuity during their lifetimes.

Let's put some faces on these Keep-Ups to get a more personal feel of their leadership challenges and operational realities. Lena Requist is Chief Operating Officer at ONTRAPORT, one of the top 50 "Great Small Business Places to Work" in the country, and itself a provider of web-based

America's Cloneable Business Model

Would You Like Fries With That Franchise?

Franchises play an important role in the U.S. economy. They account for more than 10 percent of all businesses with employees, generating almost 3.4 percent of our gross domestic product (GDP). In 2013, they generated $802 billion in revenues and provided a livelihood for 8.3 million workers.[16] They account for roughly 10 percent of all new jobs in the country.[17] Small wonder. This business model offers aspiring business owners a tested business model with many prescribed elements designed to improve the odds of launching and running a successful, profitable enterprise, whether that's a local McDonald's or Burger King or a 7-11 or Subway.

Whatever your feelings are about the quality of those jobs or the wages they pay, there's no denying that franchises are a vibrant, vital component of the SME world. But success is elusive even here. The *Wall Street Journal*, based on data from the Small Business Association (SBA) on delinquent loans from 2004 to 2013, showed that more than 40 percent of Planet Beach, 31 percent of Huntington Learning Centers, and 29 percent of Cold Stone Creamery and Quiznos Subs franchisees failed to pay back their SBA loans.[18] On the other end of the spectrum, Jimmy John's, Little Caesar's Pizza, and Days Inn franchisees experienced default rates of 2 percent or less during the same period.[19]

customer relationship management platforms to other small businesses. She spoke about how their company often has to "deprogram" some of their new hires who come from larger organizations:

> Sometimes employees come in so afraid of failure and being blamed for mistakes. They can spend half their time looking over their shoulder rather than focusing on the job right in front of them. So we spend time "deprogramming" that baggage, because it's not at all the kind of culture we want here. I tell our folks, "Look, nobody's going to die if we make a mistake in our software business. If you do make a mistake, just ask for help. You don't need to cover it up—that's much worse."[20]

IT'S NOT EASY CHASING THIS VERSION OF THE AMERICAN DREAM

There is a fairly high mortality rate among early-stage SMEs, not surprisingly given the statistics we saw in the last chapter. Out of every 10 new employer firms, 3 die before their second birthday, and an additional 2 won't last until their fifth.[21] But the remaining 5 do pretty well, all things considered: Of those, 3 will last at least 10 years, and at least 2 will be in business 15 years or longer.[22]

If this group of business organizations could improve its odds of success ever so slightly, it would have an enormous multiplier effect across our society. But whatever their definition of success may be, to achieve and sustain it in competitive markets, Keep-Up company owners have to do a better job of confronting and leveraging the other F word in their businesses. Even keeping up with the Joneses requires agility and innovation.

This is a domain where failure gets personal very fast, both emotionally and, frequently, financially. These organizations don't have a lot of bureaucracy or layers that have to be navigated before things get decided and done. In a small organization, failure can't hide. Neither can responsibility; there just aren't as many people to point fingers at when things go south. Those 22.5 million solopreneurs, for example, don't have that convenient excuse. They just have to look in the mirror to see the most likely person responsible for the screwup.

Failure can also have a direct and often immediate impact on one's bank account. Fred Stuart, the CEO of ELMS Puzzles, a small business in Maine that sells and rents beautiful wooden puzzles to customers around the world, knows this firsthand:

> I came out of retirement to take over this business when my wife, Ellen, who founded ELMS, died. We were doing just fine until 2008, when the economy collapsed and the government shut down. Even though our customers are fairly well off, it's tough to sell expensive toys in today's uncertain market. We still haven't recovered. I've had to dip into my own pocket to keep our folks on the job. We're thankful for our rental business in the meantime.[23]

The fundamental challenges remain: how to build and motivate an effective team, how to keep products and services ahead of the competition, how to maintain and build customer loyalty, and the like. But they take on particular urgency in this setting, and while their character and configuration may change as businesses grow, failure and fear of failure remain constant challenges for leaders at every step.

However, these are also the kinds of organizations where the leader's own personality and style can make a direct, immediate, and visible impact on how his or her organization handles, learns from, and leverages failure in its efforts to reach the next stage in its life.

If you are one of the millions of Keep-Up business players, read on, whether you are reading this in your garage office, your corner office, or listening to it on your way to work. You will find many suggestions for how you can increase your odds of success in this incredibly important sector of our economy.

RUNNING THE "SIX C" GAUNTLET

If you're an owner or key player of a Keep-Up business, you probably juggle many roles. In fact, in any given week, you might wear most of the hats in your entire business. You face your own version of the murderers row Start-Up entrepreneurs confront. Six challenges can expose your company to failure:

1. **Consistency in operations:** Many SMEs struggle with lack of adequate data with which to analyze and improve their day-to-day operations. You may lack the routines, procedures, and training to create repeatable,

excellent customer experiences. You may not have the sophisticated management systems and manager depth that larger firms rely on to capture economies of scale, deliver high-quality service to customers, ship consistently excellent products, and deliver expected financial results to owners.

2. **Cash and credit in finance:** Sorry, Mom, but if there is any business segment where, as the saying goes, "cash flow is more important than your mother," this is probably it. Many Keep-Ups contend with thin financing and limited options. While not necessarily hand-to-mouth or month-to-month, you may have difficulties obtaining solid financing to fund necessary growth or improvement activities. This can leave you acutely vulnerable to adversity, whether in the form of general economic downturns, slowdowns in your business sector, natural disasters, health problems, or other events.

3. **Continuity in management:** Here's where you may face the dual problems of the second shift and the second generation. Do your employees know what to do when you're not there? When you own a business it's hard to take a day off and even harder to take a vacation. In other words, who takes over the business when you're tired and want to go home? And who's going to step up when you want to retire? These are both failure-prone challenges for many Keep-Ups, perhaps yours included.

4. **Complacency in outlook:** Just because you're small or medium-sized doesn't give you a hall pass in how you need to anticipate and creatively serve your customers. Ask any independent bookstore owner facing competition from Amazon and e-books, or a small-town retailer just after Walmart moves in down the road. Some did well, but most did not. Your competition in this global marketplace can come from across the street or across the ocean.

5. **Capabilities in people:** As a player in a Keep-Up business, you frequently don't have enough talented, trained people to handle things. The good news here, however, is the sheer array of new web-based resources available to Keep-Up executives compared to even 5 or 10 years ago. These range from accessing the crowd in the cloud (including firms such as 99 designs for artwork and website design, or Elance for contingent workers) to Square for credit-card processing, Task Rabbit for errands, and so much more. Keep-Up executives have access to highly competitive global resources. And so does your competition.

6. **Culture in context:** For better or worse, your culture in a Keep-Up reflects your personality, warts and all. If you have a tendency to micromanage, or confuse the business's need for coordination with

your need for control, you can inadvertently increase your odds of failure, precisely because you have the potential to embrace or alienate your colleagues. The great thing about Keep-Ups, though, is that you have the ability and control to create a genuinely great place to work. You have the wherewithal to emulate, design, and reinforce a workplace characterized by trust—where your people feel they have one another's backs, where they're heard and respected, and where they have a genuine sense of belonging to a team.

FAMILY DYNAMICS: CAN THEY HELP?

It's hard to imagine that the kind of family dynamics most of us have occasionally experienced around the Thanksgiving dinner table might actually play a positive role when it comes to how family businesses manage the other F word. Is it possible that the sibling rivalries, intergenerational tensions, and emotional intensity families create could actually be an asset here?

The evidence is mixed, but also intriguing, especially in multigenerational family businesses. The recruitment and succession challenges of these businesses are well documented, but investigations of how larger family enterprises perform relative to traditional corporations suggest a countervailing advantage.

It may be that family-owned businesses are relatively better able to withstand the vicissitudes of business, by taking a longer-term view of their performance expectations and de-risking their balance sheets in the interest of maintaining resiliency to deal with unforeseen adversity. A recent study by McKinsey found a distinctive pattern in the way these companies deal with risks:

> Successful family companies usually seek steady long-term growth and performance to avoid risking the family's wealth and control of the business. This approach tends to shield them from the temptation—which has recently brought many corporations to their knees—of pursuing maximum short-term performance at the expense of long-term company health. A longer-term planning horizon and more moderate risk taking serve the interests of debt holders too, so family businesses tend to have not only lower levels of financial leverage, but also a lower cost of debt than their corporate peers do. . . . [24]

We don't want to suggest that these businesses are in any way immune to the gravity of failure; we're simply pointing out that the dynamics of their ownership structure and multigenerational outlook bear further scrutiny if your business is trying to become more failure-tolerant.

At the very least, it appears that some of those families gathered around the holiday table have some things to celebrate as well as argue about. And they're not alone as potential models for how other SMEs might think about the issues of resilience and failure-savvy leadership.

THE GOLDILOCKS ZONE

The vast majority of SMEs, as we've seen, are truly small (even tiny) businesses. At the high end of the SME universe are roughly 200,000 medium-size U.S. firms (defined, in this case, as those with annual revenues between $10 million and $1 billion), according to data from the National Center for the Middle Market at Ohio State University. On average, they have been around for 31 years, and together, employ over 40 million people (tallying more than half of all SME employment and a third of all U.S. jobs), and they generate more than $3.8 trillion in annual GDP. That's equivalent to the fourth-largest economy in the world. These companies are spread across the United States.

Who owns these firms? Families own 31 percent; a mix of private equity and family money own 40 percent; and 14 percent are traded publicly.[25] For comparison, two-thirds of large firms are publicly traded.

And therein may lie their Goldilocks advantage. These midsize firms are big enough to have economies of scale and scope, professional management, and tested operational systems and procedures; yet small enough to be more nimble than their Fortune 500 big brothers. In the words of Anil Makhija, the director of the Ohio State Center for the Middle Market, they exhibit patterns between "small-like and large-like behaviors."

Unlike their much larger competitors, most leaders of these middle firms face less pressure to demonstrate short-term, quarter-to-quarter results for a fickle, demanding, and impatient stock market. Like many of their family-business counterparts, they are often more willing to invest for the long term despite the tough economy.

TO-DO'S: REV UP YOUR KEEP-UP

Given the myriad of businesses within this Keep-Up category, we won't even attempt a laundry list of all the things you might do to reduce the likelihood and impact of failure in your company. But we will offer two suggestions that can improve your ability to anticipate potential failures and possibly identify promising opportunities in the process.

1. Raise Your Periscope

We appreciate the importance of tenacious focus in businesses like yours. Keeping your eye on the proverbial ball is often a matter of survival for SMEs. The difficulty is that frequently the threats and trends you miss are on the periphery of your current business, just as happens with the big guys. Sometimes that can be a new technology, or a shift in the demography or tastes of a particular customer segment. It could be a new regulation that changes your playing field or an upstart venture that has just opened its doors to some of your existing customers.

These may be asymmetrical threats, but they can also represent opportunities for new markets, new alliances, or even new business models. The important thing is to guard against complacency, especially if yours is a market in flux. So what can you do?

Excellent resources for SMEs seeking to avoid potentially serious or fatal failures are available on your tablet or laptop. And in this case, size doesn't matter. There is a smorgasbord of free and innovative platforms, tools, and information available online that can enable you to renovate your business before someone else innovates you out of business.

Take just one example. Short of talent? Take a look at sites like InnoCentive and Kaggle that allow you to share your agenda with people around the world interested and available to help, sometimes with no more incentive than a chance to win a modest prize you offer for the best solution to your issue.

The good news is you don't have to do this alone, and it can even be a fun, welcome diversion from the disciplined, day-to-day focus you bring to your business. Consider asking some of your people periodically to scout for new trends and ideas that could be relevant for your business and customers.

This doesn't need to be fancy or expensive; sometimes all it takes is an invitation for them to share what they are already looking at, thinking about, or surfing on the web. Send them to a nearby industry or technology trends conference, watch a few TED Talks connected to your business and vision, chat with a local professor or journalist who works on issues related to your company's long-range agenda. The important thing here is to expand your and their peripheral vision.

Think about reserving 15 minutes in your weekly management meetings to talk about a topic that emerges from your "idea invitational." It'll be up to you to keep this both genuine and productive, but you may be quite surprised at the sparks of imagination it unleashes.

2. Start with Your Most Valuable Antidote to Failure—Your Customers

You may not have all the staff resources of a big business, but you still need to decide how you will devote some portion of your time, people, and resources to experimenting and exploring promising opportunities to defend, expand, or change key elements of your business. Start with your most valuable resource: your customers.

Spend in-depth time with one or two clients each week and ask a few of your colleagues to do the same. Listen to how they evaluate your business: its products, services, prices, attitudes, and ease of doing business. Think how you could deliver a whole other level of service and benefits to them—the kind of service you'd want if you were a regular at your neighborhood restaurant or grocery store.

Be willing to turn your existing view of your business inside out or upside down. For example, if you sell a product, what would happen if you sold your real benefit as a service, or vice versa? If you deliver a narrow application today, how could you complement it as a more complete package solution to your clients? If you sell, could you rent or lease instead? Are there aspects of your behind-the-scenes operations that might be valuable on their own to other customers? Turnabout is fair play, so borrow a page from Amazon's playbook. That is the kind of fresh thinking that led to Amazon Web Services, a powerhouse business in its own right.

The objective here is to be intentional as well as creative, and keep at it until you identify possible targets worth pursuing more earnestly. Once you do, decide what execution-to-experimentation split makes sense and set aside time with your team or advisors to stay on top of the experimental side of your new agenda, understanding that, if you don't, it will almost certainly become a casualty of your team's focus on today's business.

YOUR ROLE: THE CONFIDENT JUGGLER

Sorry to put it this way, but more than in any other organization, if you run or have significant responsibilities for an SME, the buck not only stops with you, it also starts with you and is printed by you. Your personal style and caliber of leadership matter here more than those of your counterparts in very large organizations. It's important for any leader anywhere, but the intimate close quarters of your day-to-day business put you in the spotlight even more than people with comparable titles responsible for thousands of employees and billions of dollars. You have a greater ability to put your stamp on your organization—simply, visibly, and personally.

Takeaways

1. **This Keep-Up business is your sandbox:** The power is yours to create an environment where your people thrive, where they respond well to failures and opportunities alike. Where your culture is collaborative and your people are naturally hard-working and supportive of one another. You set the tone with how you show up every day and how you work with each and every employee. Create an environment of trust. Communicate openly and often. As we have seen with the results from the Great Place to Work Institute, an environment of trust is the number-one indicator of what makes for a great place to work.

2. **Channel your role as the juggler:** Toss some more balls in the air. Identify new resources that will enhance the capabilities of your company. Experiment with free and innovative platforms, tools, and information now available online. They can enable you to renovate your business before someone else innovates you *out* of business.

(continued)

(continued)

3. **Unlock the power of your people:** Look at your current team; many of them will likely work with you for quite a while. Encourage and challenge them to come up with new ideas, try new things, develop different ways to meet your customers' needs, and grow your business. Have them visit other companies, including competitors and others both inside and outside your sector. Send them to conferences or networking events. Offer incentives such as modest prizes or recognition for the employee with the best solution to an issue. You might be surprised at how they respond.

8 | Grown-Ups

Dodging the Oxymoron of "Big Company Agility"

Your Role: Trusted Colleague

If you don't like your job, you don't strike. You just go in there every day and do it really half-assed. That's the American way.

—Homer Simpson[1]

FROM CONFIDENT, NIMBLE INNOVATOR . . .

From its founding in post–World War II Japan through the end of the 20th century, Sony grew from a small consumer products producer to become one of the world's most trusted and respected companies. After failing with its initial product, an electric rice cooker that did a better job burning rice than cooking it, Sony went on a 50-year run that transformed the consumer electronics sector with innovative, well-designed products such as the transistor radio, Sony Walkman, Compact Disc (CD), and Trinitron TV. Mark, one of this book's authors, was an executive at Sony during much of the 1990s, a time when Sony's global brand and prominence was at its peak.[2]

During its years of leadership, Sony exhibited a great capacity to learn from its failures to drive innovation and growth. One of these examples began in the 1970s when Sony's Betamax videocassette technology was competing with the Video Home System (VHS) standard in what became a videotape format war. By most measures, including better video quality and smaller size, Betamax represented the superior technology, but VHS prevailed. One of the crucial factors behind the VHS success was that its backers worked aggressively to develop licenses and release VHS tapes with pre-recorded movie content. Prerecorded movies were particularly valued then because there was no online digital distribution of content, cable networks were still evolving, and the only way for most consumers to see a movie was either in a cinema or on broadcast TV.

Years later, when Sony introduced its CD technology to replace analog cassettes and vinyl records, it remembered its Betamax failure. It entered into a partnership with CBS Records to release CDs of CBS recording artists on the Sony standard. This partnership—later made permanent when Sony acquired CBS records—helped ensure the success of Sony's standard and also accelerated adoption of Sony's CD players in homes and cars, not to mention portable devices such as the Discman.

Fast-forward a few more years. Anticipating yet another platform shift, from analog VHS tapes to DVD (digital video disc), Sony acquired film and TV studio Columbia Pictures to release DVDs featuring Columbia's vast film library. As you might expect, Sony's standard again prevailed. For Sony, those insights and decisions were worth billions of dollars.

. . . TO STUMBLING FOLLOWER

Today, Sony has fallen on hard times, suffering ongoing losses and a less relevant lineup of products. It's a shadow of its former self, eclipsed by the likes of Apple, Samsung, and LG. Carl Yankowski was the President of Sony Electronics during Sony's dominance in the 1990s, a time in which he oversaw substantial growth in revenues and profits. When we asked him how the company that created the Walkman and the Discman went on to lose its leadership to Apple and its iPod, Carl cited several reasons:

> Sony lost its way. The company shifted from having an external customer-centric orientation and turned inward. The different business units began focusing more on their internal organizations and divisional objectives. That led to a reduction in innovation overall, and certainly fewer new products that effectively integrated the capabilities of Sony's complementary content and electronics businesses. All this was exacerbated by rigid silos and lack of company-wide collaboration.[3]

Sony is not alone in having forgotten the powerful lessons from its past. It forgot how to press the rewind button on its own history.

* * *

Some of the companies profiled in *Good to Great* by Jim Collins and *In Search of Excellence* by Peters and Waterman have also fallen on difficult times or become extinct. Remember Circuit City, Atari, and Wang Labs? What might these companies have done to avoid their fate, while still enjoying their positions as market leaders? Or, as Rich Lesser, CEO at the Boston Consulting Group, asks, "How do you turn around the successful organization?"[4]

KEY FACTS

Grown-Ups occupy the land of BIG business:

- The 2013 combined revenues of the Fortune 500 were $12.2 trillion.[5] Compare this to the total U.S. GDP of $16.8 trillion.[6]
- Large businesses employ 38 percent of the U.S. workforce.[7]
- U.S.-based multinational companies employ over 21 million of those workers, more than 19 percent of the entire American private-sector payroll.[8]
- There are approximately 18,500 U.S. firms with more than 500 employees, and about 1,000 firms with 10,000 employees or more.[9]

Americans tend to be more ambivalent about big business than small business. A 2010 Pew survey found that 25 percent of Americans believe large corporations exert a positive influence on the way things are going in America, versus 71 percent who have a favorable impression of the influence of small businesses.[10] Seventy-eight percent of Americans feel that too much power is concentrated in the hands of a few large businesses.[11]

For comparison purposes, here's a global view of the Grown-Up landscape:

- There are 8,000 companies worldwide that exceeded $1 billion in revenue.[12]
- In 2010, 415 of the Global 500 were located in developed regions. By 2025, that number is expected to decline to 271, with China (120) and other emerging markets (109) representing the balance.[13]
- The top private employers in the world include: #3 Walmart (2.1 million employees), #4 McDonalds (1.7 million), and #10 Foxconn (800,000). The rest of the top 10 global employers are public-sector entities in the United States, China, England, and India.[14]

Grown-Ups are successful and substantial enterprises. They have created products and services that customers want. They've scaled their operations, in many cases globally, to address large markets. They know how to source products and people, and deliver goods and services as efficiently as possible. They have been innovative and resourceful over the years as they out-maneuvered and outlasted competitors.

NEWTON'S FIRST LAW

Grown-Ups are the aircraft carriers of the business naval fleet. Large and powerful, they are acutely subject to the second clause of Newton's first law: *A body in motion stays in motion with the same speed and in the same direction unless acted upon by an unbalanced force.* In simpler terms, a body tends to keep doing what it's already doing.

This inertia typically makes Grown-Ups better at incremental improvement than major innovation. David Pottruck, former CEO of discount brokerage leader Charles Schwab and author of *Stacking the Deck: How to Lead Breakthrough Change Against Any Odds,*[15] put it this way to us:

Companies and large organizations in general are set up for consistency, reliability, predictability, and risk minimization. All of the systems of the company, the planning, budgeting, operations management, performance appraisal, incentive awards, are all built around an incremental improvement process.[16]

Most leaders of Grown-Ups talk about the need for major innovation and growth. Many undertake mergers and acquisitions, which, as we have previously noted, have stunningly high failure rates.[17] Others launch major new product initiatives, with similarly disappointing failure rates, often in the 75 to 95 percent range.[18]

However, perhaps the biggest and most insidious failure for Grown-Ups may not come from competitors or unexpected events, but from within the organization itself.

THE IRONY OF "TOO BIG TO FAIL"

Whoever coined the phrase "too big to fail" should go back to high-school world history. Throughout recorded time, big things have failed—empires, nations, big businesses, whole industries, cities, even religions. In fact, when we look at the broad sweep of human history, it might be more appropriate to ask instead whether a particular entity has gotten "too big to succeed." Let us explain our logic here.

Scale is a fascinating phenomenon looked at through the lens of failure and innovation. On the one hand, it is the hallmark of success. After all, things get big because they must be doing something right. A small business like Apple becomes a global behemoth. A proverbial garage startup becomes Hewlett-Packard. A fledgling group of small colonies becomes the most powerful nation on earth. And the list goes on.

The founders of those large-scale successes should be rightfully proud, even posthumously. But here's where scale often becomes its own worst enemy. As organizations grow, they often ossify. What was once a hotbed of fervent innovation and excited creativity becomes a maze of sclerotic complexity and intramural squabbling. What was once an exquisitely customer-focused enterprise becomes obsessed with its internal culture.

In short, bureaucracy and complacency overtake experimentation and excitement.

This is not a new phenomenon. Empires—whether in business, philanthropy, or government—tend to overreach and lose sight of their core values and reason for being. Their peripheral vision becomes cloudy, leaving them to miss the early signs of new discoveries, ideas, technologies, and models that pose existential threats as well as opportunities to them.

Often the most mortal threat to established, large-scale enterprise is something you didn't see coming. It's the English longbow archers against the French armored cavalry at Agincourt in 1415. It's the guerrilla colonists against the British regiments in the 1770s, or the Vietcong against the U.S. Army in the 1970s. It's Michael Dell versus IBM, or Jeff Bezos versus the world.

If you're an insurgent revolutionary, this saga is an inspiration. But if you're an established incumbent, it's downright depressing. Time after time, large-scale, entrenched organizations allow themselves to be overtaken by much smaller, poorly equipped upstarts—whether in the form of a new business, a radical guerrilla group, or just the slow advance of changing tastes or circumstances that alter the face of industries over time as surely as erosion transforms the physical landscape.

THE RISK/REWARD PARADOX

Entrepreneurs almost by definition are *all in*. They are willing to risk their livelihoods and reputations to chase the possibility of huge rewards, knowing the odds are stacked against them. This math of expected returns is seductive, even when the distribution is very uneven. And this is definitely the portfolio math venture capitalists rely on when they expect as few as 1 in 10 of their investments to really pop, and perhaps only another 2 or 3 to generate some additional return.

Startup accelerator and investor Y Combinator (YC) has invested in more than 700 startups. Justin Kan, one of its partners, punctuated this point: "From a YC standpoint, 1 percent of the companies we invest in create 90 percent of the value."[19] With Airbnb and Dropbox, among others, in their portfolio, those returns look to be promising indeed. But as much as corporate CEOs may bemoan their companies' lack of innovative spirit and intrapreneurial zeal, it's not as simple as asking Grown-Ups to start acting like startups. They are rarely willing to go all in, even when facing mortal peril.

One reason is psychology: Failure and fear of failure are always personal to the individual, even if the consequences might be relatively trivial to the large organization. People's willingness or reluctance to think or try something new seems independent of the size of the organization in which they work.

The second reason is mathematics.

GROWN-UP MATH: THE BEAUTY AND TYRANNY OF THE BIG DENOMINATOR

The arithmetic for large organizations is fundamentally different. When a Grown-Up embarks on a major new initiative, it puts much at risk: its brands, sales, distribution channels, customer loyalty, recurring revenues, and ability to meet investor expectations. Large entities fundamentally have more to lose than smaller entities, and they also must address the inverse dynamics of the large denominator. Unless the initiative results in a major increase in revenues or attains other substantial goals, it will not fundamentally change the direction of the ship.

Mark, here: When I was at Sony, I co-founded a new business unit. We reached $150 million in revenues within five years ($225 million in today's dollars), and I thought that would be reason for celebration. Instead, I discovered the "illions" that matter for a global enterprise more often begin with a "b" than an "m."

This way of thinking becomes self-reinforcing. Executives whose compensation is aligned with investor expectations also have a large personal financial stake in producing expected outcomes. Exceeding those targets may result in incremental bonus dollars, but missing the targets can put bonuses at risk, not only for the executive in charge, but also for the entire team. So there is a natural disincentive to put current business at risk while developing new innovations and products.

It's one of the reasons some large companies despair of their ability to grow new businesses organically and instead look to mergers and acquisitions as their best options to get profitable scale impacts, despite ample evidence to the contrary.

> ## De-Scaling
>
> Henry Schein, Inc.—a leading worldwide distributor in medical, dental, and veterinary supplies—tries to tame the tiger of scale by consciously de-scaling. The company created over 400 P&L units to create a more entrepreneurial mindset, each run by managers who feel a sense of ownership and influence in their particular business. These units function within a company culture of interdependency and collaboration. The company does not get bogged down in detailed accounting for the financial exchanges between units, focusing instead on generating profits from customers in the marketplace. Schein's consistent growth and profitability are the envy of many in their industry.[20]

YOUR BIGGEST COMPETITOR MAY BE YOU!

Ask yourself the following questions:

- Do your coworkers truly believe that what they're doing is important? To them? To you? To your organization? To the world?
- Are they giving your company their all?
- Do they feel valued and appreciated?
- Do they show up for work each day filled with passion and purpose?

In 2013, Gallup polled 230,000 workers worldwide and asked them 12 basic questions about their workplace.[21] The resulting "State of the Global Workplace" report found that 70 percent of workers in America considered themselves disengaged from their jobs![22] That's hardly a ringing endorsement for our current management practices and leadership prowess, is it?

This reality was reinforced in a conversation we had with a former Microsoft executive who noted that, in years past, when Microsoft was innovating, growing, and dominating its markets, he spent 75 percent of his time and energy externally focused, engaged in his work with customers, partners, and markets. He loved his job. Years later, he had an epiphany when he realized that 75 percent of his time was now spent on internal planning and meetings. The thrill was gone and so was he, departing Microsoft for greener pastures soon after that realization.

The implications of this disaffection are stunning. More than two out of three American workers are *fundamentally* not engaged with the mission and purpose of their organizations. They're not likely to go out of their way to go above and beyond in their job. But as hard as this may be to believe, America may still have the competitive edge (or at least less of a competitive disadvantage). Worldwide, the employee engagement measures are even worse, with only 13 percent of employees globally feeling engaged at work. Trailing the pack: China at 6 percent and Japan at 7 percent.[23]

Imagine what it could mean if organizations unleashed the latent engagement potential of their workers in this increasingly global workplace. Whichever country or company among us that figures this out should have one of the most powerful, game-changing competitive advantages imaginable.

What Would *Dilbert* Say?

Obviously, many people believe they live in the land of *Dilbert*, one of the world's favorite comic strips because of its wry, insightful look at corporations, cubicles, and cultures. We thought we'd go right to the source, and spoke with Scott Adams, *Dilbert*'s creator, about why he thinks corporate workers are so disengaged. Adams had this to say:

> My first reaction is that if work didn't hurt, they wouldn't need to pay you. . . . You need to be at least a little bit unhappy to strive for the next better thing. If the workforce ever became 100 percent engaged, it might be the worst-case scenario.[24]

TO-DO'S: FOCUS ON THE BIGGEST ISSUE IN BIG BUSINESS

It's about trust. If you can create and sustain a culture of mutual trust in your Grown-Up organization, you should get more intensively engaged employees. Some businesses famously do just this, including Southwest Airlines and

Wegmans groceries. Businesses that adopt this trust and loyalty culture typically outpace their competitors.[25,26]

Where to start? Ask your people. Conduct your own internal survey. Investigate what it would take for your employees to find greater meaning in their work and believe they can make a difference every day. Have them help paint a picture of what an engaged workplace looks and feels like, and what communication takes place.

Drive Trust to Build Genuine Engagement

Most of you are probably familiar with *Fortune* magazine's annual "100 Best Companies to Work For" list. It is developed by the Great Place to Work Institute (GPTW), which polls more than 10 million employees every year in organizations around the world. Based on its quarter-century of workplace research, the Institute has identified *trust* between employer and employee as the number-one driver of what contributes to a great place to work and a more engaged workforce.[27] It is the tie that binds, and has consistently been the defining difference that sets apart those companies from their peers at every level, small, medium, and large.[28]

Here's how China Gorman, GPTW's CEO, highlighted this point for other CEOs in a recent interview:

> So how do you increase levels of trust as a CEO? You start at the top. You become a trustworthy leader. There are three fundamental things to do that will inspire people's trust in you. The first is to live up to your word. The second is to treat others with respect. The third is to be even-handed with people. Without demonstrating credibility, respect and fairness, no leader can expect his or her people to trust them.[29]

Roughly half of U.S. employees think their bosses are open and upfront, but almost a quarter don't trust their bosses to be straight with them, according to a 2014 study by the American Psychological Association.[30] Without transparency, trust is unlikely—whether it's between employees or investors.

Scott Delman is one of the leading, most successful funders of theatrical productions on Broadway, arguably one of the most failure-prone environments anywhere. He's won numerous Tony Awards including for *The Book of Mormon,* a production that continues to pack theaters. Scott shared with us that, when dealing with investors and partners, he "communicates early and often, typically leading with the bad news first." He's worked hard to build a reputation for being "candid and forthright, with no hedging or fudging." The result? Delman's investors frequently tell him how much they appreciate his brutal honesty and how forthcoming he is, and they "look forward to [his] updates, even if they deliver disappointing news."[31]

If you're cynical enough to not care much about employee trust or engagement for its own sake, do it if you care about results. Deloitte puts it simply: "Without effective [employee] engagement . . . it is virtually impossible to get better results."[32] If you want to align your employees' behavior around your strategic objectives, give them better reasons to become more truly engaged in what they do and why it matters to them as much as to you.

What sort of "performance" do most performance management systems reward? Do you agree with the following syllogism?

- Complex companies breed complex systems.
- Complex systems breed complex rules.
- Complex rules breed predictability and consistency.
- Predictability and consistency breed complacency, mediocrity, and incrementalism.
- Therefore, complex companies breed complacency, mediocrity, and incrementalism.

Whether you do or don't agree, it's hard to argue that big companies struggle with how to maintain a culture of excellence in the midst of systems that foster a culture of compliance. Even companies as innovative as Google and Apple face this challenge every day, as their internal budgeting, human resources, and reporting systems, policies, and procedures risk eroding the fundamental spirit of experimentation and irreverent exploration on which they were founded. It might just be that the bigger you get, the more likely you are to become your own biggest competitor.

Johan Aurik, Managing Partner and Chairman of the Board of the A.T. Kearney global consultancy, has a comparably irreverent suggestion borne of his own decades advising hundreds of organizations:

Kill most incentive and performance evaluation systems! They are a major source of big company mediocrity. They tend to reward consistency above all else, often at the expense of people's need for purpose, a sense of enthusiasm about the journey their organization is on, and freedom to contribute their ideas to that mission.[33]

Why? Because the metrics that seem to be an inherent element of virtually all these systems tend inevitably to reward precisely the kind of incrementalism that prevents large organizations from actually achieving the types of breakthrough innovations they need to remain vibrant competitors in fast-changing, fickle global markets that are driven by unpredictable technologies, emerging trends, key discoveries, and all-too-common disruptive black-swan events.

Maybe the answer is to get your innovators outside your host organization.[34] Borrow a page from Lockheed Martin's famous "Skunk Works" playbook. Clayton Christensen thinks this approach of extracting your innovators, at least temporarily, can be one solution to the classic innovator's dilemma. Other authors have suggested ways for organizations to become more ambidextrous, capable of both exploiting current opportunities while exploring new ones.[35]

Your organization, like most others, probably needs both improvement and innovation in varying degrees of urgency across its portfolio of activities. Whichever approach you opt for to encourage both better execution of today's business and experimentation to identify tomorrow's, you will nonetheless have to address this employee-engagement challenge. That, in turn, will place a premium on how you can handle both the fear of failure and its consequences in both pursuits.

Learn from Others' Mistakes, but Be Willing to Make Your Own

There are many who believe learning from the mistakes of others is the best approach, and we agree, to an extent. But if you're not actively investigating new opportunities and new markets, or not making your own mistakes in that process, then, by extension, you're destined to be a follower rather than an innovator. One of our colleagues noted that being a nimble follower may be an oxymoron if real innovation is what you need.

As companies get larger, it becomes that much more important for them to create their own innovation experiments with insiders and outsiders, where learning (and the failure that often precedes it) can be both personal and memorable. Of course, damage and risk exist, but a thoughtful and disciplined approach to experimentation can minimize fallout from failures and lead the way to new opportunities.

Google does this extremely well. Gmail, for example, was in beta mode for more than five years and supported more than 100 million users before the beta label was removed. Google kept the beta tag on it to help signify to users that the product was still evolving and wasn't quite where developers wanted it to be.

As companies try new things and experiment, they often fail, and this stresses trust in a culture. In many ways, failure creates the ultimate proving ground for trust. We don't necessarily need to know we can trust you when things are going great, but can we trust each other when things go poorly? We'll only know from experience or examples—and that's where your job as a failure-savvy leader comes in.

How can you instill an authentic culture of mutual trust? By showing your people how you deal with the other F word personally, professionally, and collegially.

Mark Hoplamazian, the CEO of Hyatt Hotels (which is on *Fortune*'s "100 Best Places to Work" list), talked about one of the innovation efforts launched at the firm's flagship London hotel. Based on feedback from transatlantic guests who arrived before check-in time, the general manager there wanted to try a very different organizational structure and process to improve the guest experience, including one major customer priority: rooms being ready when clients check in. He moved from the traditional department-by-department design, (e.g., housekeeping, engineering, in-room dining, etc.), with 300 colleagues in 34 different reporting units with 7 layers of hierarchy to 7 interdependent teams with fewer layers. The goal of the redesign was to improve the end-to-end guest experience from before arrival to after checking out.

Instead of a seriatim room-opening process (e.g., housekeeping enters, discovers a faucet needs tightening and a mini-bar needs filling, and refers to engineering or food service for attention), the hotel assembled an inter-departmental pre-arrival team that went room-to-room to handle everything in one fell swoop. This resulted in a 30+ percent improvement in room turnaround time, a feat that's right up there with Southwest Airlines' legendary seat-turnaround performance.

There were many failures along the way. Colleagues in the hotel were initially confused about the new procedures, handoffs occasionally got dropped, systems had to be retooled, and so on. There was friction among some of the department heads as they saw their traditional reporting authority, budgets, and metrics change. And, there was some turnover among the team in part due to individuals concerned that they could no longer see a clear career trajectory for themselves in the new regime.

Other hotel general managers were skeptical of the innovation, which had not yet translated into bottom-line improvement in the financial results for the London property. Hoplamazian saw this as exactly the kind of innovation-in-progress, failures and all, that the enterprise needs more of. The fact that London could achieve such a fundamental change in day-to-day core procedures and still maintain its financial results and guest satisfaction levels was cause for hope and reason for recognition.

Innovation's messy and unpredictable. You need to be able to encourage the process as well as the product. Hoplamazian is looking to change the "until I see results, I'm not going to try [something new]" culture. The number-two employee in charge of London has since been promoted, and the sponsoring general manager has been recognized company-wide for his courage in launching this effort, with the understanding that it is still a work in progress. This initiative also galvanized the London team, in both the front and back of the house, around an innovative idea. In the process, they gained a degree of self-determination and pride in having encountered and endured failures along the way, and serving as an example for Hyatt colleagues around the world.[36]

YOUR ROLE: TRUSTED COLLEAGUE

Every organization benefits from having a culture grounded in trust. But, especially in large organizations, there are policies, systems, and procedures (not to mention organizational charts, far-flung offices, and internal politics) that get in the way. As a leader, that's where you need to invest. Build environments where employees feel their input matters, where their coworkers have their backs, where experiments that don't work as expected are used as positive input for the next cycle of initiatives, as opposed to being hidden from view. Treat information like oxygen. Let it flow more freely up, down, and sideways in the organization. And use the power of stories to drive this culture home on a personal level, grounding these concepts in real-world examples, and illustrating how you and your colleagues have applied them.

Takeaways

1. **It's all about trust and employee engagement:** If you're like most organizations, you may be starting in the hole in that regard. The good news? There's lots of room to improve. So give your colleagues a reason to feel their work matters, that you genuinely respect what they do, and that you have their backs if things get dicey or they fail. Your goal: Get your team beyond just showing up; get them aligned with your common agenda and—bonus territory—start creating a great place to work in the process. The proving ground of trust is how you deal with the other F word, whether innovation, growth, or plain performance improvement is your aim.

2. **Startup math doesn't apply:** You're probably too big to pivot, but you can arc. Figure out where you think your company needs to be in two or three years (if you have that long) and start shifting gears *now*. Consider launching expeditionary forces to scout out the new territory, make friends with the people who already live and work there, learn the language. In short, get ready to move!

3. **Check your metrics and meetings:** What's your execution-to-experimentation ratio (i.e., the resources you're devoting to executing today's business versus exploring for tomorrow's)? Ask yourself how much of your internal meetings are spent discussing and arguing about inward-facing issues versus market-facing external trends, business models, and opportunities.

FAILURE **HOW** VALUE

How

Using the Failure Value Cycle to Advance Your Organization

You have several choices about how you handle the other F word. You can ignore it, rationalize it, excuse and forgive it, or even hide it. You can treat failures as isolated events or regrettable episodes.

But if you're serious about leveraging failure as a strategically significant resource to help you better innovate, engage your colleagues, and grow your organization, you need a serious, practical framework to do that.

In this section, we introduce the Failure Value Cycle, based on our research and the hard-earned insights from the prominent leaders we interviewed. It contains seven discrete but integrated stages in which, starting tomorrow, you can extract significant value from the failures you and your organization face—before, during, and after they occur.

Like any proper teachers, we'll offer you a practical report card you can use to grade yourself and your organization across the entire Failure Value Cycle. After all, we don't want you to flunk failure itself.

9 | The Failure Value Cycle

Seven Stages Where You Can Leverage or Flunk Failure

I try to avoid failure at all costs, knowing it's going to happen. But I view failure as necessary to attain real innovation. If you want to innovate, you have to take chances. If you take chances you will sometimes fail.
—Guy Kawasaki, best-selling author on innovation and entrepreneurship, and former chief evangelist at Apple Computer

Why, despite their strenuous efforts, do so many organizations fail at so many things so often? We think one major reason is very simple: They ignore the power and lessons learned from failure itself. They too often treat failure as an isolated, regrettable event, and miss the opportunity to address it systematically as a phenomenon on its own. They are understandably disappointed, frustrated, and even angry it happened. They may conduct a postmortem analysis to try to understand what went wrong and take corrective action.

And when failures get classified as *defects*, especially in companies versed in Total Quality Management (TQM) or similar disciplines, they will likely get a more thorough look to determine their possible systemic causes. But failure, like gravity, keeps showing up.

We suggest a different strategy. Think of failure not simply as an event or even as part of a process. Those are helpful at times, but miss a much bigger strategic opportunity. Instead, think of failure itself as a *strategic resource* for your organization, just like other resources you have figured out how to convert into value for your customers, employees, and investors. You have executives, departments, policies, and procedures to help you get the most from your other strategic resources—your people, money, physical assets, brand, customer relationships, and intellectual property, to name a few. Why not approach failure the same way?

Mark Zuckerberg, founder and CEO of Facebook, gets this:

> Don't worry about mistakes too much. The real question is how to learn from them. . . . What ends up mattering is the stuff you get right.[1]

We don't suggest you make room for a new kind of CFO (Chief Failure Officer) in your organizational chart, but failure has the potential to improve your business perhaps as significantly as some of those other resources you already manage. Besides, it's an asset you already own.

As we've suggested, failure's like gravity; it exerts its force across your entire organization all the time. To understand and leverage its true potential, you need to have a comparably broad and comprehensive approach of your own. After looking at hundreds of organizational failures across a wide spectrum of settings, we have identified a pattern: seven discrete stages in which organizations and their leaders can either successfully address failure or, to borrow a phrase from our classrooms, flunk it.

Utilizing our Failure Value Cycle will help you leverage the resource potential from failure across all seven stages. We designed it to be a straightforward framework: easy to understand, simple to remember, flexible to apply across different organizational types and life stages, and—above all—practical.

The Failure Value Cycle encompasses the far-reaching array of issues, challenges, and opportunities failure presents to your organization. To help you remember them (and with apologies to any pirates among our readers), we've labeled each of the seven stages with simple "R" verbs that capture their essence:

1. **Respect** the gravity of failure in an inevitably fallible organization
2. **Rehearse** the protocols to appropriately handle your most important types of failure scenarios, not just your usual disaster preparedness drills
3. **Recognize** the signals of failure earlier to buy time and minimize its long-term impacts
4. **React** effectively to failure, whether unexpected or self-initiated, when and as it happens
5. **Reflect** thoughtfully, quickly, thoroughly, and openly to clearly understand the underlying factors that led to the failure, and develop your plan to rebound
6. **Rebound** from the aftereffects of the failure, and apply its lessons to improve your post-recovery performance
7. **Remember** to embed your experience successfully, leveraging failure in the cultural memory of your organization

Expressed in graphic terms, this Failure Value Cycle forms a heptagon (a seven-sided polygon) and, as it turns out, this challenging shape is itself a good metaphor for the difficulty of managing all seven stages well.[2]

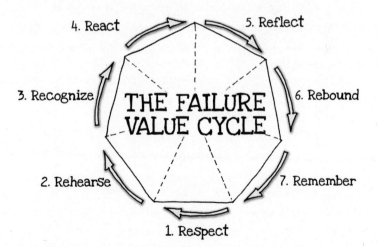

Each stage relates to the others, but also stands on its own as a focus for your attention and action. Some failures, like Target's previously mentioned handling of the 2013 Christmas hacking of up to 100 million customer records, illustrate how a widely respected company can flunk all seven stages completely. Other companies, including Apple, Home Depot, and JP Morgan, didn't heed that well-publicized calamity fast enough. They, too, receive a failing grade in several stages for suffering similar data breaches. Yet others, like Netflix and their bungled Qwikster service rollout, demonstrate "need for improvement" in several stages but an A in others as they respond effectively.

In the chapters that follow, we'll explain each stage in the Failure Value Cycle, and offer you examples of how leaders have either effectively addressed or flunked that stage. Most importantly, we'll suggest specific steps you can take to improve your organization's grade in that particular stage. These will address improvements in your company's culture, along with exercises or metrics that can help you assess progress in handling that stage. Together, they illustrate how you can become a more failure-savvy leader in the process.

It's not easy to get an A in every one of these stages. After all, failure is just one of many important challenges you have to juggle in your leadership capacity. It may not appear with the immediate urgency of today's cash flow or tomorrow's product launch, but failure is a highly valuable untapped resource for your organization—and fear of it is one of the most important obstacles to greater innovation and faster growth. To unlock that value, you need to find room for these seven stages at the management table.

Our framework is grounded on respect, which is where you and your organization should start.

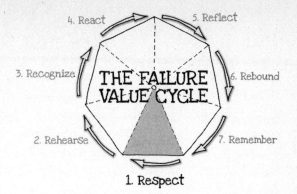

4. React 5. Reflect

3. Recognize   THE FAILURE VALUE CYCLE   6. Rebound

2. Rehearse 7. Remember

1. Respect

10

Stage One: Respect

Acknowledge the Gravity of Failure

Your Role: Straight Talker

BACK TO THE DARKROOM: KODAK LOSES FOCUS

The Eastman Kodak Company, founded in 1888, was based on George Eastman's vision of "democratized photography." The company became the global leader in consumer photography, creating a highly profitable business selling millions of inexpensive cameras such as the Brownie, introduced in 1900, and the Instamatic, which was brought to market in 1963. It also sold massive amounts of high-margin film, chemicals, and photo paper to support all those amateur photographers. Kodak commanded as much as 90 percent of U.S. film sales and 85 percent of camera sales as recently as the mid-1970s. In 1983, when *Fortune* magazine launched its list of most admired companies, Kodak was prominently featured.[1]

About then, however, the company started facing competition from Fuji in its film business, and later ran headlong into the growing popularity of digital photography, which undermined its fundamental business model. Kodak went into a long decline, eventually filing for Chapter 11 bankruptcy protection in 2012. Although it emerged from bankruptcy in 2013, by then Kodak was but a hollow shell of its former self. It was clearly not "a Kodak moment."[2]

What's fascinating is it could have ended so differently. Kodak actually possessed the key to the kingdom—actually *two* of them—complete with internal champions: one in its core chemical business with conductive film (the touchscreen surface of every smartphone and tablet), and the second in digital photography itself (to which Kodak owned the original patents). But leadership could not see past its current business model and ongoing decline. They failed to identify either of these as opportunities to reinvent the company and take it to even greater heights. They divested the chemicals business and let the digital product line languish. Ironically, at least with regard to the digital photography business, they missed an exquisite "Back to the Future" moment. After all, what was digital photography other than the latest incarnation of George Eastman's original vision of photography for the people? Too bad his successors didn't think to ask: "What would George have done?"

* * *

Aretha Franklin nailed it. It's all about R-E-S-P-E-C-T. If you don't give failure the respect it deserves, it'll come back to bite you again and again. You can't manage what you won't talk about, and if you don't talk about it, neither will your people. But all too often, the other F word is practically taboo in executive circles and management meetings. We hope to move failure from the realm of taboo to an important—dare we say *respectable*?—topic at the table.

Doubt the other F word is taboo in business? We did a little experiment to double-check ourselves here. First, we looked up the dictionary definition of "taboo." It's "a social or religious custom prohibiting or forbidding discussion of a particular practice or forbidding association with a particular person, place, or thing."[3] That seemed about right. Failure certainly meets this definition in most business settings. To confirm our suspicions, we thought about where that taboo might be apparent, and decided to look over the annual reports of major companies to see if the other F word was mentioned. Here's a sample of what we found:

- Walmart must've figured out the business equivalent of immaculate conception, because the word "failure" is nowhere to be found in its 2013 annual report. Apparently, the world's biggest company had no failures worth sharing with its legions of shareholders.[4]
- GE's lawyers at least flirted with the word, mentioning it twice in the fine print of the legal footnotes on credit risk in the back of the 2013 annual report.[5]
- Japan doesn't seem to like the other F word much either. It's mentioned just three times in Toyota's 124-page 2013 annual report.[6]
- It seems to be *verboten* in Deutschland, too. Daimler's 284-page 2013 annual report mentions it five times, always buried in the legal footnotes.[7]

This piqued our interest and we wondered how openly companies on the actual brink of collapse might have been discussing their own painfully obvious failures. For example, in the final annual report issued by Enron, just before it went up in flames, the word "fail" appears twice and "failure" never.[8] Maybe you can't expect a company run by crooks to play it straight, but what about upstanding members of the business community like Kodak or BlackBerry? The other F word made two cameo appearances in Kodak's 2012 pre-bankruptcy annual report, albeit buried in the financial disclosure footnotes. Perhaps Kodak's senior executives thought there was a better word to describe the collapse of one of the greatest brands and business platforms of all time.[9]

More recently, BlackBerry, a Grown-Up company on a "start-down" trajectory whose future is slipping away, was not so afraid of the word, mentioning it 32 times for those interested enough to read through the legal footnotes in its 2013 report to shareholders.[10] But nowhere did it directly discuss its core failure: not having an answer to the onslaught of iPhones and other smartphone devices in a category it helped define.

We understand no company wants to air its dirty linen in public, but executives and their teams might be more credible with their key stakeholder communities if they were a bit more transparent, not to mention straightforward, in discussing what's really happening in the companies they are reporting on. We hope yours is a more forthright company, so here's a challenge for you.

THE "ARETHA CHALLENGE": <u>CAN YOUR ORGANIZATION SPELL R-E-S-P-E-C-T?</u>

Why don't you try to find out whether failure is a taboo topic inside your organization right now? It won't be as simple as sending out a memo; you'll have to be a bit more circumspect about your curiosity mission. Perhaps you could ask someone else with a more direct pipeline to employee candor to be your interlocutor. Ask people when they last recall talking openly about a particular failure in the company. Find out what their perceptions were of that occasion. See how they assess the transparency of your organization's willingness to talk candidly about potential, present, or past failures that matter.

You may not always be able to precisely *measure what you treasure*, as the saying goes, but you can certainly talk about what really matters in creating value for your customers, colleagues, and investors, and what gets in the way of doing that better. More often than not, that is the other F word.

You could begin by using these six statements as conversation starters, assuming you can assure confidentiality to the people whose opinions you seek. Feel free to develop your own questions, as well:

1. Our organization is comfortable honestly talking about failure.
2. We have regular meetings or processes that incorporate learning from and leveraging failures, both big and small.
3. It's difficult to acknowledge failures or discuss them openly. Our culture treats failure as a taboo.
4. We openly share stories about previous failures, about what we have learned and why.
5. Our organization fairly treats people who have been involved with a failure, assessing their contributions and process and not just the results.
6. Can you recall a recent specific failure we've had that has not been adequately discussed and/or learned from? What was it?

If you get back evidence that yours is a failure-taboo culture, don't be too surprised if the next sound you hear is that of a whistle blown by some employee who finally got tired of internal systems or procedures seemingly focused more on suppression than expression. Leaving aside the question of the legitimacy of the complaint, you might ask yourself why somebody needed a whistle when a whisper or honest conversation might have sufficed.

Leaders who don't respect the gravitational nature of failure miss the opportunity to leverage it to move their organizations and teams forward. Worse, they set themselves up for behind-the-back criticism and deprive themselves of the candid input and feedback effective leaders so desperately need.

THE PRICE OF IGNORING

Denying failure is difficult enough, given its pervasiveness; trying to defy it can be worse. Take a look at the recent cheating scandal among U.S. Air Force officers responsible for safeguarding our nation's nuclear arsenal. It shows just how badly a "zero-failure" culture can go wrong, even in a high-stakes environment. In this case, the commanding officer at Malmstrom Air Force Base in Montana let it be known he expected every junior officer in his unit to score 100 percent on monthly proficiency tests, even though a perfect score was not required to pass the test. That certainly set the bar as high as it could go.

Unfortunately, it also led to rampant cheating, as officers tried to produce the scores he expected, for fear their careers would be derailed if they did not meet the 100 percent requirement. Almost half of the missile-launch officers and crew were either directly involved or knew about cheating and did nothing. To be sure, the Air Force itself has seen other examples of cultures of cheating within its ranks.[11] But at Malmstrom you had a command-and-control environment in which the command lost control of that environment in a misguided (pardon the pun, given the nature of the mission here) attempt to instill an excellence-only regime.

Now you probably don't have 450 nuclear-tipped missiles at your command, but you do have to set your expectations about performance. You have to decide just how high to set the bar, and, presumably, perfection is the highest standard you could ask for. In some circumstances, it may well be the most appropriate metric, but be alert for the consequences you can anticipate among your employees in striving to meet that standard.

FREE THE OTHER F WORD!

Yes, we know we're from Berkeley, and this heading may first conjure up images of protesters with placards harking back to the 1960s Free Speech Movement. But put those aside for now and think about how failure is addressed in your organization every day.

Your people are well aware of where and how your organization is failing right now, but if they can't talk about it openly, neither will you. In our speeches and conversations about the other F word with leaders and executives around the world, the number-one question we receive is: "How can we begin this conversation if our organization and culture are just not open to a discussion about failure?"

So your first action is to open up the conversation, and make room for failure. Bring it into your meetings and conversations, and out of the whispers around the water cooler.

Start with your colleagues. Try using the six statements we listed earlier in this chapter in the "Aretha Challenge." It's not profound or expensive, but it can be difficult and awkward if you've never done it before. Why? Because it starts with humility, an honest acknowledgment that you and your organization will fail from time to time in ways both small and large.

Make this conversation personal by sharing your own foibles and failures. Acknowledging your own vulnerability can directly strengthen the sense of trust and mutual support that differentiates also-ran results from jaw-dropping ones. Chris Michel, one of the entrepreneurs profiled in *The Intelligent Entrepreneur*,[12] put it this way:

> I try to start off with my teammates by telling them about some of my own screwups and failures. In retrospect, many are pretty funny to talk about. I figure if I can show them that I'm okay with talking about my own experiences, they may be more open in sharing theirs, so we can all do a better job together building this business—without the need to hide problems until they become too big to solve or to sit on ideas because they may seem too unusual to be taken seriously. It's the best way I know to create a real culture of excellence grounded in the most essential element of leadership: trust.[13]

Danae Ringelmann, co-founder of the global crowdfunding site Indiegogo, and one of our former students, deals with similar conversations this way: "As a leader, when something isn't working, we acknowledge it to the team if the team hasn't pointed it out already. We then ask the team for their suggestions for solutions. This transparency helps build trust and encourages innovation, both of which make for a healthier culture and better results."[14]

The message here is simple: Failure must be respected. Not the way we respect lightning (something powerful that can potentially hurt us), and not the begrudging way we might respect an enemy in order to improve our chances of victory. Respect failure as you would any force or phenomenon that has the power to influence an outcome you care about. Do this because failure is not only a fact of life, but also a necessity for progress. It is the essential companion of innovation and learning. In this regard, failure is not the opposite of success; it's its complement.

Here's an example of how one prominent CEO learned to respect the other F word through the power of simple conversation. Sara Blakely, the now-billionaire founder of women's undergarment company Spanx, grew up answering her father's daily question: "So, what did you fail at today?"[15] This was not done as a parental fault-finding mission, but as a recurring invitation for her to try something new and break out of her comfort zone. She learned early on that failing was not only okay, but could also open doors to new skills, insights, and experiences—lessons she carried forward in her decision to launch Spanx with not much more than a few prototype products and $5,000.

Blakely's experience shows the power of conversation as a way of shaping people's attitudes about failure. That attitude permeates her company as well. And that's where we suggest you start: Make room for failure in your conversations. It can be powerful, whether it happens around the family dinner table or in your office conference room.

DEVELOP A "RAISE YOUR HAND" CULTURE

Your team sees things every day—failures and opportunities alike—that are keys to a more dynamic and successful future for your organization. But they don't always act upon them. If people think they can't use the other F word in the open or can't discuss where the organization is failing, they're unlikely to acknowledge impending or actual failure until it's too late to do much about it. At the very least, opening up the conversation should generate greater transparency in your workplace.

Sheri McCoy, CEO of Avon, ran into this situation shortly after taking over the turnaround reins of the iconic direct-sales consumer marketing firm:

> I was in a town hall–style meeting with our sales force, updating them on, among many other things, the failure of a troubled major IT project I had inherited. During the Q&A sessions, one of our employees raised her hand and said, "We all knew that that IT thing was never going to work." But that word had apparently not gotten through the "clay layer" of our organization. I suggested to the audience that going forward we needed to have a "raise your hand" culture beforehand, where everybody [would feel] free to voice their opinions and ideas as they occur, up and down the management line.[16]

Start this conversation on day one. If you can, personally greet new employees on their first day at work. That's what our former student Scott Kucirek did as ZipRealty took off, going from a startup on the UC Berkeley campus to a publicly traded company. CEO Mark Laret does something similar at UCSF Medical Center, where he regularly joins new employee orientation sessions. It's a great time to plant the message about your culture, success and failure included.

If you can't meet face-to-face, try making a simple, short video. Why not create it yourself with your smartphone or camera, to give your new colleagues a more personal sense of who you are and what you hope to see and learn from them? If you need help, just ask your child or local teenager; they know how. It's fast, cheap, and easy. And because it's personal, it'll probably be more effective than the usual professionally produced PR-style video.

Open this other F word conversation to everybody in your organization. Nobody has a monopoly on wisdom or great ideas, and we all are experts at failing. Invite everyone to consider how they can best address and help each other learn from the failures they and their colleagues will inevitably create.

Don't be afraid to laugh at your own fallibility. It's likely others already are anyway. Think about how you might use actual relics or souvenirs from some of your organization's prior experiences in the failure zone. There's nothing like a physical example of a product gone bad or strategy that self-destructed to anchor your fundamental message: Failure happens to all of us, so let's get over it and learn from it.

The "Make Failure Public" Movement

If you'd like a more provocative example of how others around the world are tackling this issue, check out the FuckUp Night movement, which was co-founded in 2012 in Mexico City by Leticia Gasca, a former features editor at *Expansión* magazine.[17] These are monthly events in which three entrepreneurs each have seven minutes to share a notable failure using just 10 slides.[18] In only two years, these events have spread to other cities across Mexico as well as Mumbai, San Francisco, Paris, Melbourne, Stockholm, and more than a dozen other countries. Hundreds of startup veterans have joined the effort, as have thousands of attendees.[19]

FailCon, a San Francisco–based "embrace your mistakes" event has also planted its flag on five continents.[20] The one-day event, started by Cass Phillipps in 2009, also brings together entrepreneurs, investors, and interested observers eager to talk about the other F word and compare notes about how it shaped their strategies and careers. Phillipps explains its logic like this: "How can you predict what will work and what won't? Sometimes things just don't go as planned."[21]

We're not suggesting these kinds of venues or labels fit with your personal style, vocabulary, or organization, but hopefully you get the sense that you would not be alone in trying to change the conversation about failure and its significance in your own company.

If people inside start seeing you and your team comfortable with this kind of candor, it can become contagious. In fact, if you've never really opened yourself up to this other F word conversation, you may be deluged with the results. So be prepared to hear ideas, problems, complaints, and concerns you may not have heard before. Listen carefully and figure out which ones matter to the core agenda you're pursuing.

The goal here is not to obsess about failure, any more than it is to unleash the Chicken Littles in your organization. That misses the point. This is about opening a balanced dialogue around failure and how it can be more of a resource to help your company succeed. Many organizations flat out flunk this stage of the Failure Value Cycle. If you can start this conversation, you've made an early down payment on success in its last stage, where you can change the cultural storyline of your organization.

EXPAND YOUR VOCABULARY

As we noted at the beginning of our journey, the term "failure" and its cousins carry a lot of baggage. You don't want or need this conversation to be your organization's version of a "Failures Anonymous" 12-step meeting. It's not a group confessional; it's just a conversation about an important topic.

If you don't want to use the other F word itself, borrow a page from Bob King, the former president of the United Auto Workers. He talked about "problems that needed solving" as a way of depersonalizing situations and inviting his colleagues to take risks in creating possible solutions to those "problems."[22] Similarly, Avon's McCoy prefers to talk about "issues and challenges," which include both opportunities and failures.[23]

"Pivoting" and Failure

Henry Chesbrough, of Open Invitation fame, credits the lean startup community for popularizing the term "pivot," which can change failure "from something passive and negative [a screwup] into something more active and positive. A pivot is a simple recognition that what we're doing now isn't working, and we need to move to a different strategy with a higher likelihood of success."[24]

It may be helpful if you include some terminology and examples from other fields alongside familiar ones from your business. For example, try borrowing Thomas Edison's vocabulary; think and talk about your business as a portfolio of "experiments." After all, Edison is an icon of American business and ingenuity. A prolific inventor, relentless innovator, and visionary strategist, he knew that progress is driven by constant exploration of new ideas, combined with a ruthlessly candid assessment of what works and what doesn't—ideally in a setting that can connect those winning ideas to a practical way of bringing them to market.

Not surprisingly, he was intimately familiar with failure, and he brings us some of the best quotes about its importance. One of our favorites: "Negative results are just what I want. They're just as valuable to me as positive results. I can never find the thing that does the job best until I find the ones that don't."[25] That's the spirit—and the language—you need to unleash in your organization. It's the vocabulary of experiments.

Think about it for a second. When you hear about something called an experiment, do you instantly assume it will lead to success? Probably not. You view experiments as well-reasoned efforts to discover or learn something important, with failures or negative outcomes expected along the way. You want and hope for success, but you're willing to encounter failures you can learn from to get there. So, free the inherent power of curiosity and possibility across your organization. Start talking about your latest strategy, new product, or process approach as experiments that need the kind of support and insight Edison expected from his "muckers"[26] at his Menlo Park laboratory. Start where you are delivering a poor customer experience or rationalizing customer complaints.

Use analogies and examples from other disciplines, including other businesses. After all, failure knows no boundaries. You can use the scientific method and its vocabulary of hypothesis testing, but be careful about stretching this comparison too far. Business, especially startup business, remains far more art than science. Speaking of art, look at how visual artists use the concept of negative space as a way of creating insightful new works, or how architects build models to help them anticipate and address potential failures in their original drawing board designs.

These examples just scratch the surface. Think of how medicine uses postmortems and post-discharge sessions to better understand what worked and what didn't; how engineering has developed an entire discipline around failure analysis; or how designers use rapid prototyping to quickly test key assumptions before they get locked in.

Pick examples your people can relate to: a product that fizzled, an ad campaign that bombed, an acquisition that just didn't pan out, or a key customer loss. Use them to bring the issues surrounding the other F word to light. Remember: This should be a conversation, not a presentation. Your points should be powerful, but you don't need PowerPoints.

FROM SIX SIGMA TO ZERO STIGMA

It's easy to get carried away with the enthusiasm to eliminate defects and mistakes in your organization. That's understandable. After all, who wouldn't want fewer surprises that need fixing? It can be comforting to know your organization is staffed with yellow-, green-, and black-belt practitioners of the managerial arts of Total Quality Management and Six Sigma, ready to apply those skills to any operational challenge. But this is a book about how to leverage failure *throughout* your organization and at different stages of its development, not just in those parts that lend themselves to the TQM arsenal of improvement techniques (even if you could afford them).

In some sense, we're talking about something that could better be described as "Total *Fallibility* Management," specifically, how you as a leader can develop a complete repertoire for addressing and managing the full spectrum of challenges and opportunities presented by the all-too-human effects of the other F word. It doesn't matter whether they happen on the factory floor, in the research and development lab, purchasing department, marketing team, with your customers in the field, or in the executive suite itself. We're not looking for 100 percent scores or "five-9s"[27] quality across the board.

Before you begin your other F word conversations, give some thought to this idea of a "Zero-Stigma" failure culture as a counterpart to your performance improvement regimen. Of course, you should expect the best performance your people are capable of, and you should not tolerate mediocrity any more than you should encourage conformity. But if you can resist the impulse to stigmatize or scapegoat the people involved in a consequential failure, you may gain more in opening your culture to greater innovation and experimentation than you lose in immediate punishment and accountability. Depersonalizing failure can free it to become the more strategic resource you need to strengthen the results you care about.

There's obviously a delicate balance here. Be perceived as soft on failure and some of your people will slack off (or worse), but be ruthless in how you treat the individuals involved and you may pay a big price in shutting down candor and creativity. Think about the real long-term net impact you get from stigmatizing people as opposed to figuring out the underlying reasons for the failure itself and reinvigorating your team.

Here's a little thought experiment: Pronounce the word "failure" s..l..o..w..l..y. What do you hear? Fail-*your*. It's often *your* failure just as much as it was theirs. There's a good chance its real causes are not incompetence, negligence, or bad will, but something more systemic in your organization and operations—perhaps even your own leadership style—that bears further attention. It may help you start this other F word conversation on a humble note, which can help foster precisely the kind of trust that anchors a culture of excellence and shared accountability.

CHECKLISTS AND COMPASSES

Every organization has functions where failure is unwelcome and areas where failure should be encouraged or accommodated as a precursor to break-through innovations or performance improvements. Johan Aurik, Managing Partner and Board Chairman of A.T. Kearney, the global consulting firm, puts it this way:

> Ask why you are talking about failure. What role should failure play, if any, in your business? Not every organization wants to be, or should be, more innovative or creative for its own sake. For example, Rolls-Royce jet engines don't fall out of the sky, in part because Rolls-Royce does not, and cannot, tolerate failure in the design, engineering, and manufacturing of those engines.[28]

Take a look at your org chart from this perspective. Where would you like to encourage greater experimentation and innovation: in marketing, strategy, product development, HR, manufacturing? Where is failure unacceptable because the risks to life, health, the environment, or your company's reputation are simply too great? In other words, think of your organization as a portfolio of "Failure Zones," each needing its own guidelines in striking the right balance between execution and experimentation.

Some areas demand checklist-style management regimes to ensure little is left to chance, even though the individuals involved in those activities may have done them hundreds or thousands of times before. In other areas, a compass would be a better metaphor, precisely because you want to encourage greater experimentation and creativity in exploring new product ideas, considering new business models, leveraging emerging technologies, or capitalizing on new trends. Your other F word conversation should reflect the zone you're in.

If part of your organization deals with life-and-death issues, you probably want a zero-defect environment, to the extent humanly possible. A hospital operating room is not a place for haphazard procedures, nor is a nuclear power plant or big pharmaceutical manufacturing facility. But even these so-called "high-reliability organizations" are human. They screw up with some regularity, despite the best efforts of superb leaders and a performance-centric culture of excellence.

Highly routinized operations in your business may also be candidates for close-to-perfection expectations. This is the allure of the Total Quality Management and Six Sigma disciplines, which seek to drive out avoidable defects in manufacturing, accounts receivable, call centers, and the like. Companies all over the world have become devotees and even disciples of these management frameworks, with often impressive results to show for their efforts. General Electric under Jack Welch and Motorola under Bob Galvin became poster companies for this adaptation of W. Edward Deming's famous Plan-Do-Check-Act cycle. Motorola, for example, credited Six Sigma for generating over $17 billion in savings—clearly no small accomplishment.[29]

These efforts can be absolutely what the doctor ordered in certain parts of your organization. They offer a rigorous, analytical, data-driven, and teachable discipline to identify upper-case Failures and lower-case failures that can erode profitability and compromise brand reputation. In that sense, they represent a valuable arsenal of tools to harness the capacity of the other F word to reveal correctable shortcomings in your business.

But how many of the functions in your organization could, or even should, achieve Six Sigma perfection 99.99966 percent of the time? That's 3.4 defects/million instances. (Although, technically speaking, this represents 4.5 sigma for reasons too arcane to go into here.) And this quest for operational excellence is no guarantee of strategic success or company longevity. Motorola was purchased for patents and parts by Google. Six Sigma practitioner Ford faced its own near-death experience during the 2008 financial crisis. And 3M, a company with an extraordinary heritage of both consistent innovation and high-quality product standards, almost destroyed its innovative culture by overextending the reach of its Six Sigma regime.

So one size does not fit all. Thinking of your company as a portfolio of three kinds of Failure Zones will help you find the ideal balance between execution and experimentation for each one.

1. NO-FAULT FAILURE ZONES: FREEDOM TO EXPERIMENT

Consider creating "no-fault" Failure Zones in those parts of your organization where you are particularly focused on driving innovation and where the impact of failures can effectively be managed and contained. As you intensify your search for new products, services, and business models, recognize that failure will rear its head more often, and also will provide those crucial insights for innovation. So you might as well invite it, not fight it.

Maybe you're trying to launch a brand new business that nobody has figured out. Executive coach Peter L. West described just such a situation earlier in his career, when he worked for Cox Communications:

> We were launching the company's first internet business, at a time when nobody knew what those two words really meant. This was a "never been done before" situation. We expected failure. We had to try new stuff out and knew "shit's gonna happen." And it did, but we got the job done. It was a "just figure it out" challenge [versus] a "tell me what to do" kind of project. And because failure was expected, people were freer to think more creatively. It was a great antidote to the usual corporate norm of rationalizing cautious mediocrity.[30]

So one of your no-fault zones might involve your own version of a "never-been-done-before" innovation challenge or new venture exploration, situations in which you want your people to work without worrying or wondering what will happen to their jobs or careers if they encounter setbacks or failures.

Sometimes it's a crisis that unleashes the same kind of creativity and initiative. After a major storm outage, ask a utility crew how differently, more imaginatively, and quickly their organization behaved than in its business-as-usual mode. An army combat veteran we spoke with talked about how the multiple layers of the military vanished when things got dicey, and individual soldiers were forced to act on their own training and instinct. Either way, these are definitely not Six Sigma/zero-defects zones.

2. LOW-DEFECTS ZONES: BRING IN THE LOW-SIGMA TROOPS

These are the places in your operations where "good enough" is better than great, faster may be better than later, and prototypes trump perfection. In fact, they may be places where an unnecessary focus on completeness, much less perfection, actually works against your fundamental agenda. Take a look at the example Mark Hoplamazian, the CEO of Hyatt Hotels, shared with us:

> I have a phrase I like to use that I borrowed from the software industry: "Version 0.5 beats 1.0." We want to encourage our people to take more initiative in creating and testing their own ideas for how we can improve our guest experience and operating effectiveness. I'd rather see lots of early-stage prototypes that can be tested in real life now than wait for fewer but more polished initiatives that may not be any more successful, and in the process stifle the very creativity we're looking for.[31]

3. NO-FAILURE ZONES: WHERE PERFECTION IS THE STANDARD

These are the areas of your organization where the consequences of failure are extremely high, and failure needs to be avoided at all costs. They might include financial controls, data security, health and safety, ethics, or other areas where failure should simply not rear its head. Innovation and experimentation will happen less frequently or aggressively in these areas.

David Pottruck, the former CEO of discount brokerage Charles Schwab, was a strong advocate for innovation in his company. He understood innovation initiatives sometimes fail, and worked to create an environment where that was accepted. Nonetheless, his company operated in an arena with highly complex financial transactions where hundreds of millions of dollars regularly changed hands. He shared his attitude about accepting failure with us: "I was often asked by my people at Schwab 'Is it okay to fail?' There was not an absolute answer. Sometimes it was okay to fail and sometimes we just couldn't."[32]

Pottruck also explained his concept of "noble failure," which would fall into his "okay to fail" bucket. Under his definition, these were failures that were smaller in nature, where learnings could be leveraged, and did not imperil the financial viability or reputation of Charles Schwab.[33]

FIND THE VALUE-ADD

Results count; everything else is effort. The result you want from failure is insight that allows you and your company to improve next time around. So when you open and continue your other F word conversations with your colleagues, remember you're doing this not to celebrate failure but to liberate it as a resource to advance your strategic objectives. You want to extract genuine value from the failures you've created.

There's an old story about how Tom Watson, as president of IBM, dealt with this reality. Apparently, a top salesman had lost a lot of money (let's say $5 million) on a high-profile deal. When he was summoned to see Watson, he assumed he'd be fired. Instead, Watson greeted him by talking about their next big pursuit. When the sales rep asked whether he was being fired, Watson supposedly responded: "Fire you? Why would I want to fire you when we've just spent [$5 million] training you up?" True story or corporate legend, it captures the spirit of our suggestion.[34]

You're trying to build a culture that looks beyond excellence to include what it takes to get there. And we're not recommending trophies for trying or "everyone's a winner" medals in your company. Those trivialize the importance of the agenda at hand.

As Roche CEO Severin Schwan says, "We need a culture where people take risks, because if you don't take risks, you won't have breakthrough innovation."[35] More often than not, it takes resiliency and perseverance in the face of defeat, failure, and adversity. In a word, grit;[36] not the kind you get in your teeth, but the kind you feel in your gut when you pick yourself up from a setback and return to the task at hand with the renewed, almost defiant sense that this time you'll master it. Those times are what you will want to talk about. Failure's just the alarm clock that wakes you up to what you didn't know earlier. You want your people to see and respect it as such, talk about it openly, and share ideas about how to get the most from it.

That's the kind of R-E-S-P-E-C-T we're talking about.

YOUR ROLE: STRAIGHT TALKER

In this role you first acknowledge what everyone in your organization already knows: Failure happens . . . a lot. That said, you should highlight the distinctions between a failure-savvy organization (one that takes smart risks, knowing some will fail) and a failure-soft one, where too many excuses are permitted and rationalization reigns. This requires balancing performance and accountability, while still allowing experiments to fail and lessons to be learned without taking unfair casualties at every turn. Personal humility and self-effacing humor go a long way here, as do examples from the history of your organization where key players went on to their next project better prepared, and long-term results benefited from the insights from earlier failures.

Takeaways

Stage One: Respect

1. **Start the "other F word" conversation now:** Show your colleagues it's okay to discuss failure. The sooner you show them you're comfortable with talking about your own, the sooner you can unlock their insights.
2. **Keep it visible:** Make failure an explicit, visible, and accepted topic of your leadership and management agenda. You can determine your starting point using the culture exercise suggested in this chapter. Try a little self-effacing humor to soften the edge if necessary.
3. **Mix and match:** Tailor your failure accommodation conversation and metrics to the particular mix of performance/failure zones in your organization. You may well have *failure-free* areas involving life-and-death, hazardous, or ethical matters as well as *free-failure* zones where you want to encourage maximum creativity and innovation.

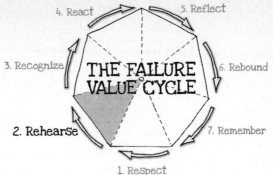

11

Stage Two: Rehearse

It's Not Just About Fire Drills

Your Role: Tenacious Coach

WHEN EVERY DAY IS GAME DAY

The Medical Center at UCSF (University of California at San Francisco) is one of the top hospitals in the United States, with 8,000 employees providing medical care and services around the clock. Hospitals like UCSF need to balance a particularly thorny set of challenges:

- Provide the best possible care to all patients, addressing their unique issues
- Drive innovation and incorporate new technologies and processes
- Coordinate the many handoffs between departments and caregivers happening every day for each patient
- Operate in an environment with complex, often contradictory, regulations, privacy issues, and third-party oversight
- Do all this 24 hours a day, 365 days a year

UCSF CEO Mark Laret shared with us his practical definition of failure: "the repeat of a process that results in an adverse outcome that might otherwise be preventable."[1] In this instance, an adverse outcome might truly have life or death consequences.

To limit adverse outcomes and provide the best possible responses, UCSF conducts frequent rehearsals across a broad range of possible medical emergencies along with potential disasters like earthquakes, fires, and large-scale accidents. Through this training, Mark and his team work to instill values that encourage the right kinds of decisions in every employee, from a department head to a janitor on the floor. He notes, "Disasters rarely happen on your preferred timetable. What's crucial is to instill in your people the right capabilities, ownership, and values to enable them to respond in the best possible way."

* * *

AN OUNCE OF ANTICIPATION IS WORTH A POUND OF IMPROVISATION

If your crystal ball told you there was a high likelihood something was going to happen, you'd probably prepare for it. Just as if the weather forecast was for rain, you'd probably grab an umbrella. Even though we do take steps like these in day-to-day life, when it comes to planning for failure, most organizations ignore the warning signs.

As we discussed in Part I, it's highly likely that failure will find you, probably sooner rather than later. And if you're actively seeking to drive innovation and growth in your organizations, that probability rises. We've already explored how you can think of your own organization as a portfolio of "Failure Zones." Now, let's look at two different types of high-performing organizations and see how they prepare for and deal with failure:

- *High-Reliability Organizations* include airlines, nuclear power plants, and hospital operating theaters. In these places, it's expected that the organization will perform with high consistency, reinforced by frequent rehearsals and checklists to limit variability. In addition, they may rely on redundant systems and controls or next-in-command understudies.

- *High-Resiliency Organizations*, like competitive sports teams, startup ventures, jazz combos, and consulting firms, have the ability to encounter a broad range of scenarios and handle them with relative facility and skill. They reinforce their resiliency with flexible team structures, adaptive strategies, and often-extensive practice and simulations to augment the experience of team members.

Most organizations have, or should have, a mixture of both types of capabilities.

You might be wondering about the many other businesses, governments, educational institutions, and similar organizations that fall between these two extremes. Except for the occasional disaster drill, most of these organizations don't practice to build skills or plans that will help them survive, and possibly thrive, when faced with a range of other more likely failures coming their way. This observation gets to the essence of our Rehearse stage. Success in this stage means identifying at least some of the types of practical failures that might be realistically encountered by your organization. You then build relevant simulations, team activities, and other types of practice to prepare for these types of events.

When we think of practice it's easy to think of sports. As parents we recall all the hours of practice when our children swam, ran, played baseball and soccer, and more. For professional sports, it's much more intensive. When athletes practice, they typically do so under the watchful eye of coaches, who provide feedback and instruction. The ultimate goal of practice in this environment is to prepare team members to be ready in the moment, when the coach is not on the playing field to provide guidance and offer second chances. After all, the baseball pitcher does not have time to consult the coach when a line drive is hit straight at him. For his or her sake (and ours, especially if that pitcher is our son or daughter), let's hope all those hours of practice pay off.

KEEP YOUR CROWN JEWELS SAFE

Start by identifying the crown jewels that form the foundation of your existence as a viable business. Every organization has a few assets on which its entire existence depends. For Arthur Andersen, one of those was client trust, and once they had squandered that hard-earned, precious asset after chasing the then-enticing Enron accounting business, the firm vanished almost overnight. For Lehman Brothers, it was resilient liquidity to withstand a financial crisis, and once that was gone, so was the 160-year-old firm, swamped by the all-too-foreseeable economic storm of the late 2000s.

Your organization's crown jewels might be in a vault, like the legendary Coca-Cola formula, or embedded in a secret or patented way of doing business, like Fair Isaac's FICO credit-scoring or Google's search-to-advertising algorithms. It could be your unique culture, anchored in a powerful way of doing business that generates employee and customer loyalty, like at Wegman's grocery stores. It might be a key person, like Apple's Steve Jobs or the Cleveland Cavaliers' LeBron James, or Argentina's national soccer team captain, Lionel Messi. Or, it could be some form of legislative or regulatory treatment that gives you your compelling advantage and longevity, like a utility's franchise or a pharmaceutical company's patents.

Exercise: What Are Your Crown Jewels?

Identify the crown jewels of your organization, both overall and for your particular business unit. Ask your colleagues to do the same. Here's a partial list of factors to consider: brand, customers, partners, products/services, design, business model, team, internal processes,  manufacturing, distribution, sourcing, location(s), legal/regulatory status, competitive positioning, technology, and intellectual property.

1. _____

2. _____

3. _____

4. _____

5. _____

Whatever your crown jewels are, start thinking about how your organization can keep them safe. How will you protect those existential assets, tenaciously monitor any threats to their value, and prepare appropriate contingency plans in the event they are compromised or, worse yet, destroyed? No amount of careful due diligence in designing other failure-protection measures can likely make up for a loss of these core assets, whatever form they may take in your organization.

HIGH-RELIABILITY SETTINGS WHERE YOU CAN'T AFFORD TO FAIL

Aviation requires high reliability. One of our UC Berkeley colleagues, Kurt Beyer,[2] is a former naval aviator. He flew fighter jets off aircraft carriers, and it's hard to imagine a more precise activity than that. One minor mistake can easily result in, as Kurt puts it, "the loss of a $42 million airplane and possibly someone's life." He adds, "The consequences of failure are so high that you have to avoid failure at all costs. Yes, you have to learn from mistakes when they do happen, but you absolutely don't want them."

His training regimen was intense and included a massive amount of rehearsal:

> For each hour in an airplane cockpit we spent 100 hours in simulators. In the simulator they always tried to make us fail as much as possible. We were always learning, rehearsing. If you fail the rehearsal as a naval aviator, you get grounded because the higher the complexity of the system, the more likely it is that something will go wrong. That's why rehearsing—both for what you expect and also for what you don't—is so important.

He also shared with us what happens when pilots and the Navy discover new ways for something to go wrong:

> Every accident results in an investigation to identify what contributing factors were mechanical and what were under human control. A findings report is generated, learnings are codified, and they are incorporated into our training and rehearsal, so we can practice the issues leading up to the failure and reduce the likelihood of a repeat occurrence.

REHEARSING WHEN HIGH RESILIENCY IS WHAT'S REQUIRED

The social media and messaging company Twitter was founded in 2006. It grew out of a project launched at a podcasting company called Odeo, which ultimately failed itself. But Twitter was one Plan B that definitely did not fail.

Twitter began as a simple 140-character messaging service focused on the mobile marketplace that made it easy for users to broadcast what they were doing at any moment. It soon grew beyond a basic social messaging platform as major international events, such as the Arab Spring uprising in Egypt in 2011, displayed Twitter's strength as a global communication tool with potential for meaningful impact.

Michael Sippey[3] was Twitter's Vice President of Product and Design as the company grew and went public. We talked with him about how Twitter evolved so quickly to become a significant player in social media, create new offerings, and develop a viable business model. One area Michael credits was the way Twitter runs constant experiments to test new product ideas and investigate different opportunities. Twitter then conducts regular "experiment review" meetings where individuals and teams:

- Present their hypotheses about products, customers, markets, competitors, and more.
- Provide an overview of the experiments they undertook to test these hypotheses.
- Share the results of these experiments, including extensive deep dives into the data and metrics associated with them.
- Lead an open discussion of results and insights with the whole group.
- Subject the entire discussion to peer review and additional investigation.
- Document the project in order to memorialize results so that the organization could benefit not just in the current timeframe but also in the future.
- Participate in a clear discussion of next steps to answer who, what, and when.

Not only were excellent insights generated and new product features developed, but this exercise also trained team members at large to be thoughtful in how they plan their own product experiments.

Additionally, Michael found he could drive deeper investigation and more thoughtful results by putting constraints on some of the scenarios. As he said:

> If you set some basic guardrails for your teams on how you want them to think about a problem, including you not being afraid to say "Remember: Our core business is X," you can actually force more depth of thinking and creativity in these key areas of focus, as opposed to imposing no constraints or limitations at all.

Checklists, especially in the product development process, can serve a similar purpose. Items considered "table stakes" are already accounted for in the checklists, leaving as white space the unchecked opportunities that come next.

Finally, Michael suggested ways for everyone to participate in these types of exercises, from the very experienced to newcomers on the team:

> You want to put the right people on the right problem, balancing their skills with the complexity and risk of the problem being solved. You want to put newer staff on smaller features, so they have the freedom to experiment—and potentially fail—without spending too much time in development, or putting the user experience at risk. We were always working to create a culture of learning and experimentation, so that teams can try new things, learn from failure, and celebrate success.

Exercise:
Apply the Un-Golden Rule

How do you prepare for failure when in many cases you don't know what's coming or where it's coming from? Try this "Un-Golden Rule" exercise: "Do unto yourself before others can do unto you." Ask your colleagues and teams the following questions:

- Where are we most vulnerable?
- If our fiercest competitors knew our secrets, where would they focus their efforts to take away market share?

(continued)

(*continued*)

- What strategies and tactics are our competitors currently using that seem to be working?
- If we were to start a brand-new business in our sector, what new products, services, business models, etc., would we offer?

Create different scenarios. Break up into teams. Make it a competition. See what strategies you and your team come up with that your competition might use against you. Then go out and prepare for the ones that seem most important to your future.

THINK OF YOUR EXPERIMENTS AS "PRE-HEARSALS"

We've mentioned Silicon Valley's "fail fast" mantra. It's become a cliché in many circles, but like most clichés, it contains an important insight. Failure itself is not the objective. The faster you can learn from failure, the better your chances of success.

That's why this issue and language of experiments can be so important. Here's how Joe Kraus[4] of Google Ventures explains it:

The best way to integrate failure positively—and this may sound trite—is to fail fast. Run many experiments quickly. If you develop a strong foundation and tradition of rapid experimentation, then you can deal with small failures much more effectively, in part because you know you will be running another experiment very soon. If you do not run many experiments, then you can become more invested in the success or failure of any one, and it may take on an unreasonable importance.

Experiments can be a productive antidote to smug, overly confident enthusiasm about your company's current strategy and positioning—if you're willing to undertake them as a regular component of "business as usual" in your company. They're your forays into uncertainty, the draft plays you may want to develop as part of your evolving playbook, whether you're on defense or offense.

YOUR ROLE: TENACIOUS COACH

Most people don't look forward to practice—it seems boring almost by definition. It's where you grind it out to get better and stronger. Swimming laps for hours, fielding grounder after grounder, playing musical scales again and again—some of that repetition may be inevitable.

Your job is to encourage, demonstrate, train, and constructively criticize. As coach you can make practice more engaging and effective, especially if you've established goals that truly motivate your team. Create scenarios and role-playing opportunities. Pit team against team in friendly competition. Make these simulations real, engaging, and personal.

Finally, be ready to reward, recognize, and praise your colleagues when you see the fruits of these rehearsals in their handling of a subsequent failure.

Takeaways

Stage Two: Rehearse

1. **Figure out your organization's *failure horizon*:** What are the most likely failure scenarios you may face? Don't forget potential black-swan events that could jeopardize your company's crown jewels. They are more likely to look like your screw-ups afterwards.
2. **Avoid the hearse; take rehearsals seriously:** There's a reason teams have both offensive and defensive playbooks—they want to win. Too many businesses die before their time because they don't respond effectively to threats or opportunities fast enough. Make rehearsals and "other F word" exercises engaging and part of your organization's regular routine. Mix them up with friendly competitions in addition to needed repetition. Think what would happen if the next time you had the equivalent of a business-centric fire drill, someone was waiting outside with fresh cookies or ready to lead a quick workout session.
3. **Cross-train:** Exercise the checklist capabilities that contribute to high reliability along with the compass skills that enable high resiliency. Develop rehearsals and practice activities that cut across divisions, silos, and ranks. Physical fitness trainers know that introducing new and varied exercises is the best way to develop a healthier body. The lesson is just as apt when it comes to developing the organizational capabilities of your people and teams.

(continued)

(*continued*)

4. **Channel your inner Andy Grove:** Intel's former CEO wrote a classic book, *Only the Paranoid Survive*, which illustrates how shocks and failures can come from any direction. Look to your competitors and other players in the sector. Where would you attack them? Investigate whether you have similar vulnerabilities or weaknesses. Where would they attack you? Create scenarios, run drills, and prepare for those potential attacks or failures. These should be realistic, emotionally engaging "What do we do *now*?" exercises that feel more like an intense computer game or pilot simulation than an abstract consultant–designed "What if?" exercise.

5. **Embrace the language and culture of experimentation:** It can open up the creativity of your people, reduce the corrosive effects of their fear of failure, and yield vital insights for your future strategy.

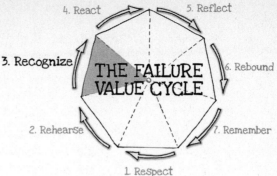

12 | Stage Three: Recognize

Pick Up the Signals of Failure Earlier

Your Role: Watchful Monitor

FROM BIG BANG TO BIG DATA TO BIG INSIGHTS

In early 2014, We Heart It, an image-based social network for the teen and young adult market, identified a group of new and unwelcome accounts on the site. The company encourages social expression and inspiration through the posting of images, similar to Tumblr and Pinterest. It was in a rapid growth phase, adding a million users a month, when President Dave Williams and his team noticed the intruders.

These new accounts were set up by hackers. Automated bots were attempting to hijack the We Heart It community, redirecting users to other sites and degrading the quality of content. Whenever these accounts were shut down, the bots would pop up elsewhere on We Heart It with different

131

profiles. This malicious activity presented serious risks to the growth and long-term health of the community, and to the company overall.

Dave and his team turned to a new, big data venture, Wise.io, for help in identifying the hacker patterns. When seeking to detect faint signals within a high-noise environment (like a globally popular, high-use social network), where better to turn than a business founded by whip-smart UC Berkeley–based astronomers used to scanning galaxies for minute signals among massive amounts of data? Working together, the teams sifted through millions of records to identify and isolate the unwanted activity. Equally important, they created automated tools and incorporated machine learning so their detection algorithms could constantly evolve and keep pace with the hackers.

Dave then shifted modes from defense to offense, and started utilizing big data to drive growth. Using some of the same techniques he was employing to protect against spammer attacks, We Heart It identified a number of common characteristics of high-quality and more profitable users. Dave and his team utilized that information to accelerate their marketing, customer acquisition, and onboarding activities, driving company growth and profitability. And it all started because of an attack by hackers.[1]

* * *

If there's one thing worse than failure, it's not recognizing failure or identifying it too late to do anything about it. Big data can be a powerful tool to help you avoid those unfortunate results. We Heart It, of course, is not alone in using big data defensively and offensively to recognize important patterns. Facebook identified similar patterns of correlation and causation in its new users. Known as "10 friends in 7 days," Facebook used this insight to drive onboarding and communications with new Facebook community members in order to develop more valuable users.[2]

Big data is not the only answer. Assuming you now acknowledge (if not appreciate) that failure is your constant companion, what's the next stage in making your organization more failure-savvy? Develop an effective monitoring capability to earlier detect signs not just of strategically significant failures in the making, but also of emerging opportunities for your future business.

This poses the classic signal-to-noise challenge familiar to most executives trying to monitor their organizations' complex activities in fast-changing environments. If only we could all be as sensitive as Obi-Wan Kenobi[3] to those "disturbances in the force" that act as distant harbingers of worse things to come. But we're not, so what *can* we do?

PICKING UP FAILURE'S EARLY SIGNS

Stay alert, be proactive, and think of this stage the way a doctor diagnosing a patient might. You are looking for early symptoms of an as-yet-unidentified condition. Look for any signs of change, patterns that may be out of the ordinary. These could indicate some type of oncoming failure, whether it's externally caused or internally generated.

Organizations' complacency, mythology, and structure often prevent them from detecting early signs of failure soon enough to mitigate its impacts, which all too frequently pose an existential threat. In Target's case, executives ignored apparent warnings that its data security systems surrounding customer credit card information were vulnerable to hackers. GM ignored troubling signs of its ignition problems for years before finally coming to grips with the failure.

Failure, always just over the horizon, will find you whether you are looking for it or not. It's far better to see it coming than be blindsided by it. Think of this Recognize stage as your early-warning alert system. Extending the radar horizon buys an organization both more intelligence to see what's happening and the ability to respond sooner. The most innovative organizations actively scan the horizon beyond their core operations, customers, and markets. They do so less to forestall failure than to better anticipate where failure might occur, and thus avoid more serious consequences.

Companies that fail to recognize the early warning signs leave themselves vulnerable to short-fuse surprises in addition to slow-fuse threats that may take months or years to play out, but are nonetheless detectable long before that. In fact, it is the strategic myopia and complacent cultures of many currently successful businesses that create opportunities for aggressive entrepreneurial ventures to create new, market-changing, and incumbent-destroying businesses within easy sight and reach of those bigger, entrenched Goliaths.

This isn't just the situation in fast-changing tech industries, such as where RCA failed to recognize Sony, which failed to recognize Apple, and so on. It also happens in retail, as seen after Borders' demise under the relentless siege by Amazon, or Sears and JCPenney's failure to appreciate the changing retail environment. Was it that difficult for newspapers and magazines to recognize the threat, as well as the possible opportunity, of upstarts like craigslist, eBay, or free web news sites? The list goes on and on, each a tribute to the importance of organizations doing a much better job of monitoring their horizons to recognize the early signs of change in their present operating environments.

Here are six important actions you can take to improve the acuity of your monitoring and avoid flunking this Recognize stage.

1. Don't Let What's *Now* Blot Out What's *Next*

No doubt you've faced the dilemma of how to balance your focus on running today's business while continually monitoring threats and opportunities that could shape tomorrow's business. Unfortunately, most organizations flunk this stage of the Failure Value Cycle. The history of business is littered with the skeletons of enterprises that allowed their business foundations to erode in the face of gutsy insurgent startups offering new solutions for customers or new business models for investors. Think no further than Kodak or Polaroid in consumer photography, Digital Equipment or Wang in computers, Northern Telecom or BlackBerry in telecommunications, Circuit City or Borders in retail. The graveyard is full of these casualties.

The executives in these companies were not stupid. They just didn't connect the dots on their radar screens soon enough or decisively enough, or they clung too long to outmoded products or business models. And many paid the ultimate business price for those failures. This is the evolutionary process of creative destruction and progress in capitalistic markets, as articulated by the economist Joseph Schumpeter.[4]

By admitting the logic of that concept, do you accept there's no hope if you are a successful incumbent yourself? We think not. But you'll need to recalibrate your environmental radar system to do a better job than your predecessors to avoid becoming roadkill for the next wave of innovators in your markets.

2. Listen for the Running Water

Here's a lesson from nature you might keep in mind. Consider the busy North American beaver, a paragon of efficiency and hard work. As you may know, this industrious creature builds lodges surrounded by protective moats, all made possible by dams it builds by gnawing down nearby trees. Apparently, this animal is second only to man in its ability to manipulate its environment to its purposes.[5]

Ever wonder what triggers the beaver's dam building and dam repair efforts? It turns out it's the sound of running water. That makes perfect sense both offensively and defensively, if your family's security and livelihood depend on creating a quiet pond in which to build your lodge. If there is running water, there might be an opportunity to construct a new dam to make it a pond; and if the pond's serenity (its status quo) is disturbed by the sound of running water, the dam needs repair.

What does running water sound like in your business? It's likely happening on, or just beyond, the perimeter of your current business. From a defensive standpoint, you should listen for changes like these:

- New startups employing emerging technologies or different business models to make their first inroads with your current customers
- Competition from other regions or sectors now entering your markets
- Reduced levels of customer satisfaction or other key metrics such as customer churn, complaints, returns, or decreased average revenue per user
- Key internal resources leaving, such as an unwanted uptick in your employee turnover, a loss of a handful of especially valuable up-and-comers, or even the weak but discernible signals of a decline in morale or confidence

From an offensive perspective, the sound of opportunity might be represented by:

- Regulatory changes that open up new markets
- Technology or efficiency gains that reduce costs
- Failures on the part of competitors such as product recalls or scandals

Whatever changes occur could be the early signals of turbulence in your own pond. The more actively you monitor the perimeter of your current business, the more likely you will spot the fraying edges of your current offerings and strategy, not to mention new competitors beginning to take advantage of that incipient weakness to create their own empire at your expense.

That, in turn, can buy you time to prevent your lodge from being compromised. These are your signals to act—both defensively and offensively!

Repair the dam of your business. Protect the moat around what's most valuable to it. Get moving while that sound of running water is still a trickle, and you may be able to avoid your worst fears. Scan competitors and others inside and outside of your sector for new initiatives and vulnerabilities. What are they doing that might impact your business, and how could you prepare for that? Are there capabilities or strategies you can adopt? Vulnerabilities you can exploit? The graveyard of Fortune 500 firms is full of companies from just the past 25 years that failed to heed these kinds of signals.

Or you may need to find a new pond and build a new dam. Tomorrow's business is probably not located where you are today. Someone else is likely already trying to build it. Why not you?

3. Put a Bounty on Potential Failures in the Making

This is a good time to think back to Stage One: Respect, and your organization's crown jewels. Those are readily identifiable with a little conscientious effort and honesty. Now, we're dealing with potentially peripheral events before they become trends or even significantly urgent in their own right. This involves identifying the kinds of events or metrics that, while remote, can be serious, even in an isolated circumstance.

Here is where your own employees, suppliers, and customers can act like big data signal detectors of their own. There were employees, including lawyers, at GM who learned of the early deaths and injuries connected with the company's faulty ignition system. Had that early learning been acted on right away, perhaps that scandal would not have reached almost 3 million cars or cost the company more than $1 billion in recalls and settlements.

Ironically, scale may actually help you identify such vulnerable failures in the making earlier. Let's look at Twitter. In the five years from 2009 to 2014, the platform went from 2 million tweets per day to 500 million tweets per day. In her recent TED talk, Twitter's Vice President of Trust & Safety, Del Harvey, summed it up this way: "Why spend so much time searching for potential calamities in innocuous activities? . . . [G]iven the scale that Twitter is at, a one-in-a-million chance happens 500 times a day."

In effect, Harvey and her team have telescoped time, since they can see emergent blips on their security radar before they may metastasize across the Twitter community or show up on other platforms. They have developed sophisticated procedures to identify potential threats, contain them, and neutralize them before major damage can be done. As she explained: "I visualize catastrophe. And that's hard. There's a sort of inherent cognitive dissonance in doing that, like when you're writing your wedding vows at the same time as your prenuptial agreement."[6]

Big data techniques can help you in this early detection undertaking; but you don't always need something so sophisticated. Sometimes, the solution can be much more straightforward, as we'll see in these examples from shoes to SEALs.

4. Identify Small Failures Soon Enough to Avoid Big Ones

Zappos, the online shoe and accessory company, has learned that despite its best efforts to recruit only the most excellent candidates for its training program, a certain number of those recruits will fail and customer relationships will suffer as a result. So to identify such selection failures early, Zappos makes what has come to be known as "The Offer" soon after the start of its intensive training program every new recruit must take.

Zappos actually pays its new hires to quit. After week one of the paid four-week training period that immerses every new hire in the company's culture of customer-obsession, Zappos makes The Offer. It's quite simple: If you quit today, Zappos will pay you for the time you have trained plus a $1,000 bonus, no questions asked.[7]

This is a clever hiring and onboarding strategy, and a good example of preemptive action on the perimeter of one's business, in this case, early hires. Why? Because if a new hire is willing to take the company up on The Offer, he or she presumably has priorities inconsistent with the sense of commitment needed to succeed in a culture that calls for laser-like dedication to the Zappos mission. Not to mention the significant cost of a bad hire. About 10 percent of new call-center employees take the money and run, and company managers are relieved every time it happens, because Zappos is determined to ensure there's good alignment between what makes individual employees tick and what makes the organization tick.

A much more grueling example comes from the U.S. Navy SEALs' "Hell Week," five and a half days of sleep-deprived, intense operational training in extremely challenging environments. The offer in this case is the daily invitation to ragged recruits to just ring a bell, drop out of the training immediately and have some doughnuts and coffee. Roughly three out of every four recruits ring that bell, leaving their erstwhile colleagues to carry on the SEALs' mission with even fiercer dedication.[8]

You can apply similar strategies across other areas of your operations. Consider inviting not only your employees in on the action, but also your retirees, suppliers, and loyal customers. Most are on your side of the table, so use them. Why wait for your competitors or disgruntled customers to find your failures in the making?

Every organization has failures just waiting to happen, and what's worse is that many people inside those organizations already know where they are. They just don't say or do anything. Is it a culture of complacency, fear, not-my-job, or all of the above? Without turning everyone into a premature whistleblower, smart leaders need to encourage initiative and communication when projects start going off the rails or have minimal chances of success.

How can you encourage that type of thoughtful reporting and transparency? Provide incentives for those who step forward. Recognize them. Reward them if appropriate. Promote them. They're your allies in creating a more failure-savvy organization.

5. Invite New Voices and Explore New Venues

Every organization and leadership team likes to believe in itself. The problem is that many stop listening to others. They stop paying attention to contrary and inconvenient opinions, and forget that they don't have a monopoly on wisdom and insight. In Jonathan Winters's terms, they "get to believing [their] own stuff."[9]

Start by looking around the table and listening to the sidebar conversations at your next management team meeting. Does much of your team look and sound a lot like you? Do you talk about the same newspapers, magazines, movies, or websites? How about customer conversations, analyst reports you've read, and trade shows and conferences you've attended? If everyone's tuned in to the same channels, it might be time to mix things up.

Recruit new team members that contribute a broader variety of backgrounds, experiences, and perspectives. Challenge your team to investigate new sources of information, including competitor websites and sales materials, products they've seen firsthand, analyst reports in adjacent industries, non-U.S. markets relevant to your core capabilities, new technologies and ideas from conferences or the blogosphere, and others. All of these contribute to the richness of an organization and its ability to recognize the early signs of failure.

Jed Katz is Managing Director at Javelin Venture Partners, a venture-capital firm managing $335 million. It has invested in more than forty early-stage tech companies. As he shared with us:

We see 100 pitches a month. In probably 80 percent of them, we can quickly identify a key reason or two why they will likely fail. We share these observations with the entrepreneurs and may invite them to come back once they have addressed them. Occasionally they adjust their strategy and come back, and we have seen some successes from there. In most cases, though, they continue down their current path and are not successful.[10]

As a key part of some of the executive education programs we run, we often serve as de facto guides of scouting parties to investigate new ways of thinking and leading. We accompany groups of executives and visit companies (often in Silicon Valley) that are driving innovation and disrupting entire sectors and markets. In many instances, these companies are in fundamentally different sectors from those of our participants. Nonetheless, our guests often identify surprising practices and approaches they can apply in their companies.

Ask yourself and your team to specifically identify what other industries, companies, disciplines, customers, or markets might be relevant to the underlying strengths of your company and its longer-term vision. Draw inspiration from other disciplines and perspectives—from anthropology to biology to sports and beyond—to find out how they can help you shape your business. Read, talk, and visit as much as you can to see what they're up to and how that affects your current and prospective business portfolio.

The scoreboard of business is not pretty. Far more losers exist than winners, and the standings in any particular league are highly volatile. Yesterday's pennant winner is today's cellar dweller. So don't just celebrate success that comes from business and your way of doing things *today*. Reward people and ideas that are exploring *tomorrow's* business possibilities and the failures that go along with that. We call this the *"future quo."*

Encourage fresh looks at your company's *dis*comfort zones. Every company has them—those areas, topics, or markets that are uncomfortable to think about, talk about, or do much about. We're not talking about sacred cows here; let them roam around for a while. Instead, we're talking about the territory occupied by potential new products, new customers, new ways of doing business, new strategies, and new insights about emerging trends that may be reshaping the landscape of your business.

Unfettered exploration is one of the reasons behind Google's famous 20 percent guideline (itself an update of 3M's original 1948 policy), which has given many of its employees the freedom to work on projects or ideas of their choosing for up to eight hours of their workweek. Even though some insiders refer to this time as "Sunday," it has nonetheless sent a strong signal across the culture that experimentation driven by personal, not just corporate, curiosity is welcome. And Google has reaped major rewards from that 20 percent time, including Gmail itself.

We understand you have to focus most of your resources, time, and talent on operating and improving what you do right now and in the near term for today's customers and investors. But the graveyard of business is filled with companies who kept trying to improve their current businesses while ignoring the gathering forces of technological, demographic, and operational tsunamis that eventually overwhelmed them.

You need to incent your people to not only improve the status quo, but to fundamentally change it. That means creating *future-quo* incentives—in public recognition, promotion opportunities, and money—that will unlock the enormous power of creativity and ingenuity lurking in the minds of your employees. It doesn't require or expect everyone in your organization to be an insider entrepreneur, but it does create a field of no-fault exploration of ideas that might just hold the key to your future.

Your company's future is like a frontier, full of uncertainties, surprises, discoveries, and risks. Like any frontier from the Wild West to outer space to the human genome, it will take intrepid scouts to map its contours, find trails through it, and learn its language and even secrets. You may need to charter scouting parties of your executives to explore ideas, technologies, business models, and markets beyond the perimeters of your current business. Expect them to bring back their observations, not as field-trip reports but as potential interpretations of what they've learned in terms of how it might affect your organization.

YOUR ROLE: WATCHFUL MONITOR

In this role you are part sentry and part scout, protecting your perimeter but not being limited by it. You're attentive and always on alert, both defensively and offensively. Like the beavers listening for the sound of running water, you are attuned to the trickles that may signal potential threats or promising opportunities. Is your dam in need of repair, or is there an even better pond nearby? How do you enlist others as sentries and scouts to identify what's changing in the landscape and why? What tools and training do you provide to enable them to be effective in this role? The sooner these potential failures and opportunities are recognized, the faster you can mobilize your organization to address them.

Takeaways

Stage Three: Recognize

1. **Protect your crown jewels first:** Make sure you have monitors in place for not only the moat, but also the countryside. Anticipate how your protected defenses can, in the words of network security expert Bruce Schneier, "gracefully fail"[11] while still safeguarding the foundation of your enterprise.
2. **Expand your peripheral vision:** Get your people to imagine, surf, read, and think about what is developing beyond the perimeters of your current business. Look for startups, new technologies, emerging business models, changing demographics, and incipient trends that may contain latent threats or promising opportunities. Listen for indications that your colleagues' conversations include a diverse range of ideas, terms, and issues.

(continued)

(continued)

3. **Engage your whole network:** Involve not only your employees but your suppliers and probably customers as well. They are your friendliest scouts and most informed monitors of potential failures in the making. Be prepared to recognize their contributions. You want their eyes and ears helping you develop a more failure-savvy organization.

4. **Be alert for the early signs of your "future quo":** We coined this term to stress the importance of moving from today's reality to defining tomorrow's vision. Done well, this Recognize stage can give you ideas for doing that, and begin experimenting in the best ways to get there, understanding that failures will be encountered along the way.

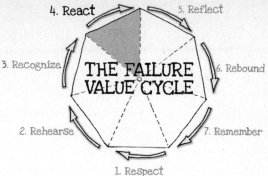

4. React

5. Reflect

3. Recognize

THE FAILURE
VALUE CYCLE

6. Rebound

2. Rehearse

7. Remember

1. Respect

13 | Stage Four: React

Deal with It!

Your Role: Team Captain

NEW YOGA POSITION: BEND OVER, INSERT FOOT IN MOUTH

Yoga and active lifestyle apparel brand Lululemon Athletica made headlines in 2013 when its high-end yoga pants proved to be a bit too sheer. As the company attempted to correct the problem, its next generation of pants had problems of a different sort, with the fabric pilling prematurely.

In response to these ongoing issues, Lululemon's founder, Chip Wilson, offered the following comments in a television interview: "Frankly, some women's bodies just don't actually work [for yoga pants]." And he went on, "It's more really about the rubbing through the thighs, how much pressure is there over a period of time."[1] This interview followed earlier comments Mr. Wilson had made in which he indicated a major reason some Lululemon yoga pants, which cost around $100 per pair, had become see-through was as a result of women buying yoga pants in sizes that were too small for them.[2]

Wilson's remarks led most observers to the opinion he was blaming his customers for problems with Lululemon products rather than taking responsibility on behalf of the company. The stock price of Lululemon Athletica, which had traded as high as $80 per share in mid-2013, was trading below $40 within a year.

* * *

Organizations may respect, recognize, and even rehearse adequately, but still flunk when it comes to actually coping with failure when it occurs, as it most assuredly will. They fail the call to action at the time when they are forced to make quick, strong decisions and allocate resources in response to the failure scenario of the moment, often with minimal and imperfect information. Confusion reigns, the organization is in upheaval and, in the meantime, the situation is not getting any better.

Critical to this challenge is the ability to rapidly diagnose the dimensions of the failure being encountered to determine the appropriate response. We lack a practical vocabulary for businesses to classify or triage different kinds of failure, something that can more easily match events to appropriate response protocols. At the very least, organizations should develop a process to quickly ascertain whether a scenario calls for a senior executive's immediate attention. Critical, strategically significant, existential threats or opportunities fall into this category. Less pressing issues can be handled through other channels.

Without a practical way to diagnose or even describe different types of failure, executives can misread the circumstances and react inappropriately in the moment, exacerbating a failure's impact. This compromises their ability to turn failures from unfortunate events into more manageable (and valuable) resources to improve their businesses.

Other organizations and fields have developed such tools. Meteorologists know what kinds of warnings and actions are appropriate for a Category 5 hurricane versus a Category 2; architects and engineers know how to adapt designs for earthquakes of different Richter magnitudes; and firefighters know the drill for handling a 2-alarm as opposed to a 5-alarm blaze. That common understanding enables them to respond appropriately rather than improvising in those different circumstances.

Most businesses don't have those kinds of action-shaping diagnostics and, as discussed earlier, all too often have not adequately rehearsed for the different situations those diagnostics might define.

This React stage generally unfolds quickly; in most cases it is the briefest stage in our Failure Value Cycle. Information is uncertain, expectations and responsibilities are often unclear, and the window of opportunity to step in and respond effectively may be short. With all these moving parts and tight timeframes, no wonder so many organizations flunk this stage.

Having effective outcomes in this stage is predicated not only on recognizing failures early, but also properly classifying them with regard to scale, scope, and type of failure. This is where the work in the Rehearse and Recognize Stages pays dividends, creating valuable organizational muscle memory. Finally, a strong set of shared values helps promote consistent responses and can facilitate otherwise difficult decisions, as seen in Johnson & Johnson's textbook handling of the Tylenol tampering scare in 1982.[3] That case also shows how the right reactions can have a multiplier effect. J&J's actions enhanced the reputation of the company for hundreds of millions of consumers in the United States and around the globe.

Other examples, like the Lululemon episode, demonstrate how poor leadership in a failure moment can exacerbate the situation and alienate otherwise loyal customers. In fact, a particularly poor or inappropriate response can do more damage than the original incident, compounding one failure on top of another. Lululemon's Wilson not only made it very clear that he did not want certain people as customers, but his insensitivity and lack of consideration turned many of his previously loyal customers against the brand.

British Petroleum's (BP's) response to the Deep Horizon underwater oil spill in the Gulf of Mexico is another example of how to flunk this stage of the Failure Value Cycle. BP initially downplayed the amount of oil leaking, compromising its credibility from the very start as coverage of the disaster broke. The company then attempted to deflect responsibility by blaming its drilling contractor Transocean Limited, while "offering their full support," implying BP was not really at fault. "It wasn't our accident," CEO Tony Hayward said on the *Today* show, "but we are absolutely responsible for the oil, for cleaning it up." While this may have been technically true (BP owned the oil but not the rig), it did little to engender trust or goodwill.[4]

Failure's Forms: Triaging the Failures Leaders Face

There are myriad causes of failure. This book doesn't attempt to catalog that list, nor is this chapter about root-cause analysis of failures. That's a vital tool for understanding and, done well, it can yield incredibly valuable insights. Our focus in this stage is not after-the-fact forensics, but before-the-act preparations and as-it-happens responses. As we've seen, failures can be both unintentional (things that happen to you) or invitational (things you seek out yourself in discovery). In either case, you need to know what kind of scenario you are dealing with in order to understand how to best prepare for it, deal with it in the moment, and learn from it afterwards.

For incoming failures, think of the analogy of a hospital emergency room. What are the elements of that environment that enable it to deliver urgently needed care, attend to the needs of non-emergency patients, deal with concerned friends and family, coordinate complex diagnostic and therapeutic procedures, comply with mind-boggling regulatory paperwork, and so on—without straining the doctors, nurses, and staff each day?

Training, rehearsal, and experience all play a role to be sure, but triage is a key threshold element. Triage is the ability to rapidly assess what patients need and channel them into appropriate work streams, enabling real emergencies to get immediate attention and ensuring everyone receives the best care possible. Done properly, it's a powerful tool that can optimize how an organization responds to a variety of incoming challenges. Done unevenly, and it can create failures of its own. For example, a recent study of 122 U.S. hospital emergency rooms found that "over triaging" (sending non-trauma patients to higher-cost trauma centers) resulted in a 40 percent increase in unnecessary costs.[5] So triage itself needs to be triaged and managed carefully.

Effective failure triage depends on a robust method of classifying different types of failure and a comparably resilient portfolio of rehearsed protocols to deal with them, including details such as who does what, when, how, and where in different situations. Think about how you and your team would triage the most significant and frequent failures you are likely to face, and how you would handle them.

HOW REHEARSALS CAN HELP YOUR REACT REFLEXES

Rehearsals can dramatically improve your ability to react to specific failures. Morgan Stanley's experience on 9/11 is one dramatic example. Among many heroes that day was a man named Rick Rescorla, who was in charge of security at Morgan Stanley, which had its main offices in the World Trade Center's Tower 2. A decorated Vietnam veteran, Rescorla, and his team, had anticipated the building's potential as a terrorist target before it was the site of a 1993 truck bombing. They also recognized the potential for an airplane being flown into the buildings. When Rescorla's recommendation to relocate Morgan Stanley's offices was not followed, he took it upon himself to design and rigorously rehearse emergency evacuation procedures with the company's entire 3,000-employee staff, which took up 22 floors of the building.

James Stewart described Rescorla's preparedness in a profile in the *New Yorker*:

> At a command from [Rescorla], which would come over the intercom system, all employees were instructed to move to the emergency staircases. Starting with the top floor, they were to prepare to march downstairs in twos, so that someone would be alongside to help if anyone stumbled. As the last pair from one floor reached the floor below, employees from that floor would fall in behind them. The drill was practiced twice a year. A few people made fun of it and resisted, but Rescorla tolerated no dissent, demanding military precision and insisting on a clearly defined command system. As he told [his security consultant and Vietnam war friend], he was simply following the "Eight 'P's," a mnemonic that had been drummed into them in the military: "Proper prior planning and preparation prevents piss-poor performance."[6]

Rescorla and four members of his security team were among thirteen Morgan Stanley employees who died on 9/11, but thanks in large part to his "Eight 'P's" rehearsals, over 2,600 employees and 250 visitors survived.

This is a memorable example of the power of rehearsal in real situations when there's little time to react and reflect. In the case of Morgan Stanley's 9/11 evacuation, 14 minutes between the moment the plane hit Tower 2 and the building's collapse. It's also an example of how these Failure Value

Cycle stages depend on and interact with one another. The more honestly you've respected the risk, the faster you've recognized a failure in motion and the better rehearsed you are for that contingency, the stronger your reaction reflexes are in times of crisis.

RESIST THE KNEE-JERK REACTION TO SCAPEGOAT

Every organization will face its share of failures, some more than others. Many of those situations will call for some response by the executives in charge. What should they do? How should they hold people accountable?

Chad Holliday, Chairman of Royal Dutch Shell, board member of Bank of America, and former CEO of DuPont, has seen many such scenarios. He talked with us about the tendency of high-profile, publicly traded companies, in their zeal to demonstrate to investors that they're taking action, to sometimes jump to the wrong question first: *Who should we fire?* While that may sometimes be an appropriate response, it's usually not the right *first* response. The company must take the time to carefully review what really happened, how, and why. In Holliday's experience, that analysis often reveals an organizational, process, or decision-making mistake worth correcting, rather than a fireable offense.

Moreover, if your first reaction is to blame someone for a failure, you shouldn't be surprised when others around you stop volunteering their opinions, ideas, or time on future risky endeavors your organization may need to survive and thrive.

ASK THE "RIGHT NOW" QUESTION

When a failure happens, organizations and leaders can quickly lose control of the situation, especially when it is public and highly visible to customers or other stakeholders. It's important to act swiftly, but not so rapidly that you respond to the wrong sets of inputs, move in the wrong direction, or make the situation worse. You first need to develop as honest an assessment of the situation as possible.

Since failures comprise a broad spectrum of situations, a crucial immediate question to ask is: *What do I need right now from customers, employees, investors, and the media?* These might include the safety of your customers or employees, better information about the situation, more time to respond, helpful (or at least patient) media coverage, or trust from key stakeholders. Clarifying your needs and objectives at the start of this stage helps inform and prioritize your actions during its fast-moving pace.

ACKNOWLEDGE AND APOLOGIZE

When a failure occurs, it's important that leaders be visible, available, and responsive—to show you are actively working to resolve the situation.

How you acknowledge failure plays a huge role in what happens next. Whether it's tens of millions of bottles of Tylenol possibly tainted by tampering, credit card data compromised by hacking, or Lululemon yoga pants that are too sheer, customers and other stakeholders look to your organization's leadership for information, guidance, and credibility. Effective leaders provide information in a straightforward manner to meet the needs of those who are affected, along with the media, and rebuild trust. This also lays the foundation to help stabilize the situation and build a platform from which you can move forward.

Where appropriate, your acknowledgment should be accompanied by a sincere apology. Even in cases where your organization may not be directly responsible, an apology acknowledges the problem and demonstrates your commitment to help address the situation, which can instill goodwill and drive collaboration. After all, a successful reaction preserves and leverages customer loyalty and understanding as much as possible.

Our colleague John Kador has extensively investigated the role and effectiveness of apology in business. In his book *Effective Apology*, Kador points out that "leaders who don't know how to apologize effectively are seen as liabilities to the organization." He goes on to conclude that "apology is not cost free but it's less expensive than denial, stonewalling, and defensiveness."[7]

WHAT ABOUT "FAILURE IS NOT AN OPTION"?

"Failure is not an option!" That's one of the most memorable phrases about failure in American culture.[8] It was popularized in the 1995 blockbuster movie, *Apollo 13*, which depicted NASA's frantic efforts to rescue the Apollo 13 crew after their moon rocket malfunctioned mid-journey. The stakes could not have been higher.

In the movie, Mission Director Gene Kranz is shown interrupting a rising chorus of worried voices from his engineers, desperately searching for solutions, with the now-famous phrase, "Gentlemen, failure is not an option!" The phrase captured the can-do spirit of NASA's early days, and became so connected to America's relationship to failure that it's worth a closer examination. In real life, Kranz apparently never uttered those now-famous words during the Apollo 13 mission.[9] The phrase is a Hollywood screenwriter's fiction.

Fortunately, in the case of Apollo 13, NASA did indeed figure out an ingenious way to return those three astronauts safely home.

In fact, NASA's early culture was grounded in a very healthy *respect* for failure. It *recognized* that failures were inevitable, and designed systems and processes with that reality in mind. Mission Control constantly *rehearsed* astronauts and flight engineers for failure, and in the face of unexpected failure, NASA *reacted* deliberately and coolly. Afterward, it *reflected* fearlessly, applying the lessons learned to *rebound* to new heights. To round out this example of our Failure Value Cycle, no organization was more committed than NASA to *remember* the sometimes tragic and always dearly won lessons, incorporating the details into the evolving and living cultural identity of the organization.

In recalling this period for an oral history project, NASA's original flight director, Chris Kraft, stressed how the early NASA team looked for failure at every opportunity and how doing so made the team stronger: "Everything we did was based on decisions on failure, rather than success." NASA engineer Bill Tindall explained, "[Given] the kind of work I was doing, they called me a professional pessimist."[10]

So NASA's Mission Control, far from being the no-failure-tolerated zone shown in the movie, was in reality an environment that embraced failure, where both worriers and warriors operated in tandem. The former felt free to voice their doubts; the latter were relied on to make big decisions and be accountable.

Failure is *always* an option. Denying that essential truth blinds us to the weaknesses of our own strategy, obscures the holes in our common wisdom, and underscores the perils of premature consensus. In fact, many years later, following the fatal Columbia and Challenger shuttle explosions, an internal review discovered NASA's culture had fundamentally changed. Unlike earlier in its history, people who identified potential risks and failures had been ostracized, discouraging further investigation into potential problems. In both fatal space shuttle accidents, the contributing issues had been previously identified but were neither aggressively pursued nor clearly elevated up the chain of command, as they may have been in NASA's earlier incarnation. The failures that ultimately occurred were catastrophic.

HONOR YOUR HONEST FAILURES

Recall our discussion about Daniel Kahneman's research on the importance of *endings* of experiences and how they can shape memory, which in turn influences behavior.

Failures occur for all kinds of reasons. Some happen because of incompetence or carelessness; those deserve to be dealt with sternly because they were avoidable. Many others occur despite the best efforts of dedicated, talented people who did everything they could but did not ultimately succeed. Those are honest failures, and deserve different treatment altogether. Finally, many failures result as a combination of these two types of behaviors.

Often, initiatives, concepts, or products that initially fail go on to become huge successes; for example, Pfizer's "Compound UK-92,480" became Viagra 1.0. But in many cases, it is other organizations that profit from the failures of their predecessors. Whether due to timing, execution, technology, or a host of other factors, examples of failed forerunners and winning successors abound, including failed social network Friendster and successful Facebook, defunct search engine AltaVista and industry leader Google, and flop retailer Webvan and e-tail king Amazon.

This is another important reason we say your biggest competitor may well be *you*. Your best talent and best ideas may just walk out the door if you can't figure out how to generate and develop new ideas internally, create a rewarding culture in which your employees can pursue new business concepts, or harvest lessons from the failures along the way. Imagine if those early innovators like Fairchild, IBM, or Xerox had captured the value of some of their most groundbreaking ideas, inventions, and failures—not to

mention the key employees involved—for themselves. There might not
have been an Intel, Microsoft, or Apple.

YOUR ROLE: TEAM CAPTAIN

People are looking to you for leadership, confidence, and authority,
especially in this stage. Why? Because your organization or team is under
the stress of failure, whether it was unexpected or the unfortunate result of an
experiment you initiated. People will watch you carefully to see how you
fairly balance accountability with supporting your team. If you fall into the
trap of scapegoating or blame, expect to pay a far bigger price when your
colleagues keep quiet and take orders in the future.

　　Be prepared to step up and lead. Show that you can handle the need to
acknowledge the situation, support your colleagues, and guide an effective
in-the-moment response.

Takeaways

Stage Four: React

1. **Resist the temptation to try and solve the whole problem:**
   The objective in this stage is to stabilize the situation, create a
   window for a more comprehensive response, maintain your
   customer goodwill, and build a foundation to better process
   what just happened. Then, you can assemble your Rebound plan.
2. **Communicate effectively:** This starts with listening and gathering information to gauge the full extent of the failure. Then,
   quickly communicate your message, addressing the people who
   are affected and the media, as necessary. Don't try to ignore the
   failure altogether or rationalize it without acknowledging its
   impact. Worse yet, don't deny it ever existed or cover it up.
3. **Apologize as appropriate:** Over the years, you have built up
   goodwill with your customers and partners. This is the time to call
   upon that. Be genuine and be humble. Make an honest commitment to resolve the situation. You might be pleasantly surprised at
   what happens.

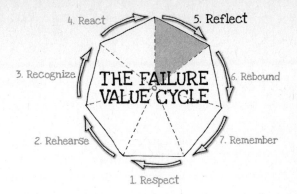

14

Stage Five: Reflect

Turn Failure from a Regret to a Resource

Your Role: Inquisitive Student

SEARCHING FOR THE WHAT, WHEN, HOW, AND WHY, BEFORE THE WHO

Since its founding in 1998, Google has changed the way the connected world interacts with information and one another. From online search and Gmail to maps and self-driving cars, Google has been fearless in its pursuit of new concepts, new businesses, and new business models.

In addition to the many internal businesses Google investigates and launches, in 2009 it launched Google Ventures. Since then, Google has invested in more than 250 companies, not only in information technology but also in other sectors such as cancer treatment, transportation, and energy use.

Joe Kraus, a serial entrepreneur himself, is one of the lead investors at Google Ventures, a position he took on after Google acquired one of the companies he founded. We spoke with him to gain deeper insights into how Google approaches risk-taking and failure. In Joe's words:

> Google processes failure extremely well. For example, there's a regular meeting at Google that is the most impressive forum I've ever seen to address the issue of learning from failure. At these meetings, a variety of experiments in search are explained and the results are presented. The most amazing thing is that everyone separates the success or failure of the experiment from the failure of the person. There is no penalty for failing. This attitude is incredibly liberating for those involved, and produces far less anxiety, because a failure of an experiment—or a *negative outcome*, to use scientific-method lexicon—does not have negative implications for the individual.[1]

A much smaller firm, ONTRAPORT (like Google, also a "Great Place to Work" company), does something very similar in its "retrospectives" process. Its business helps other startups accelerate the automation of their ventures' customer relationship platforms and related services. Lena Requist, ONTRAPORT's COO, talked with us about one of the many cultural traditions that have made her company a notable workplace. After every major project, the team holds a candid, no-holds-barred review of what went right and what didn't. The ground rules are pretty clear: The focus is on what, how, where, when, and why—not who.[2]

People are free to talk about the failures without worrying about personal repercussions. It's not a no-accountability environment: just more of a no-*fault* one. Lena says that while sometimes new hires may be a little anxious about the process, after a short time the retrospectives become a "no big deal" part of how the place does things.

When to Ask *Who?*

There is at least one setting in which the "who" question should be asked first, and that's when you are choosing your team for after-the-fact reviews or before-the-fact decision making. Here's where true diversity (not just in the demographic sense) can really help. Think of diversity as Roger Penske did when he invited United Auto Workers union members to join him in the turnaround of Detroit Diesel. Think of diversity in terms of intramural teams drawn from departments outside those primarily responsible for a particular issue. Chad Holliday did this at DuPont when he invited non-product-development people in the company to help examine the possibilities for its annual smorgasbord of 250–300 new product candidates.

This diversity issue was emphasized time and again during our interviews with leaders from big business, startups, small business, government, and nonprofits. Here's how A.T. Kearney's Johan Aurik put it: "You want real diversity of *thought* around you that reflects and shares the overarching goal your culture is trying to achieve."[3] This type of diversity will certainly not inoculate your organization from failure, but failure-savvy executives stress how it can improve your odds of success.

* * *

You've had a failure, and you've reacted for better or worse. What comes next is the moment of truth that indicates your level of failure savvy. It's easy to talk about the benefits of failure in the abstract, and even prepare your organization for it, but when it actually happens—after money's been spent, public commitments made, careers and reputations put at risk—that positive rhetoric is often the first to go. Finger-pointing, frustration, and anger too often replace thoughtful reflection.

Some executives' first instinct after a failure has occurred is to blame the people involved, often publicly. Disappointment leads to a culture of blame and shame—blame from the top and shame for the team. But when the failure is serious enough, the CEO often takes the blame as well, as happened with the firing of Target's CEO after its 2013 holiday data breach.

In their haste to distance themselves from failure and those associated with it, many organizations and their leaders flunk this essential stage of the Failure Value Cycle. It's impossible to engage in meaningful reflection without assuming responsibility. The Reflect stage is where real leadership is needed, especially in organizations that pride themselves on high performance and accountability for results. Failures that result from incompetence, inattention, or negligence need to be dealt with sharply. But what should you do about failures that happen despite the best efforts of a talented and dedicated team?

TAKE CARE OF YOUR INJURED FIRST

We suggested earlier that failure is like gravity, a pervasive fact of life. When it happens to you, it can feel like you've fallen into the most intense form of gravity, a black hole. Entire organizations can get sucked into it, too, leaving many employees stuck in the failure rather than constructively applying the insights it just delivered. The sooner you can attend to the people most directly involved and acknowledge the emotional dimension of a team's failure, the faster you can get back to business.

There haven't been many studies of this pre-reflection recovery phenomenon, but there is one in particular that caught our eye. In 2011, a team of researchers from Indiana University published a report looking at the aftermath of project failures in scientific research laboratories, a setting where failure is common.[4] They were interested in understanding the process through which the individuals and teams involved bounced back after those failures, particularly with regard to their willingness to "continue to support the organization." The people they talked to described failure like this:

- "Really painful . . . we were all equally depressed."
- "Altogether disappointing."
- "We had people that were nervous wrecks, breaking into tears."

These people were scientists, the academic epitome of rational, fact-based thinkers. They expect negative outcomes from their experiments along with positive ones, and yet it's still a difficult experience when it happens.

Learning and recovering from failure are not instantaneous. It takes time. In the researchers' words, "while time heals wounds, . . . the 'wound' is shallower for those who perceive their organization to normalize failure."[5] So, rebounding can be faster and easier when failure is accepted as an inevitable part of the organization's role and activities.

This is the acid test for whether yours is a real "learning organization." It's easy and important to celebrate success, but it may be more important to help your company meaningfully learn from failure. As CEO of Roche, a worldwide pharmaceutical leader, Severin Schwan practices this with champagne celebration lunches for notable research project failures:

I would argue, from a cultural point of view, it's more important to praise the people for the nine times they fail, than for the one time they succeed. . . . You really have to take care of the nine guys who worked as hard, had as bright ideas, and unfortunately failed, and therefore, in this sense, you should celebrate failures, nine times more than success.[6]

But not everyone has the same resilient perspective as Nobel Prize–winner Ivan Giaever, who said this about the process of experimentation: "To me the greatest moment in an experiment is always just before I learn whether the particular idea is a good or a bad one. Thus even a failure is exciting, and most of my ideas have, of course, been wrong."[7]

RECOVERY AND REFLECTION GO TOGETHER

Most of you are probably familiar with Elisabeth Kübler-Ross's landmark, five-stage model of grief: denial, anger, bargaining, depression, and acceptance. Obviously, organizational failures are not equivalent to the death of a loved one, but think for a moment and remember how your most recent experience with a significant failure felt. Depending on how much you had invested in a project, failure can bring about feelings similar to grief.

We've talked with students and hundreds of employees about their experiences with a failed project, product, transaction, or strategy. Here's our conclusion: Most individuals and teams trying to recover from failure may need to go through a version of the Kübler-Ross's grief process.[8] In the wake of a failure, participants' hopes have been dashed, their reputations may have taken a hit, their future job security may be compromised—those are major losses. The individuals involved need some time to recover before they can rebound from, and deeply reflect on, the experience.

Step back and think about how your organization makes room for this kind of post-failure recovery process. You may need to give teams and individuals time and perhaps even tools to help them go through these phases:

- **Denial:** Acknowledge the failure; don't ignore it or rationalize it away.
- **Anger:** Move beyond the initial instinct to assign blame. Share responsibility for the outcome, however disappointing it may be.
- **Bargaining:** Come to terms with the consequences of the failure rather than denying them.
- **Depression:** This one's particularly tough because it involves acknowledging emotional and psychological vulnerability. This can be a difficult

thing to do in most organizations that may mistakenly pride them-selves on cultures that deny those very human responses to failure and loss.

- **Acceptance:** This does not mean your organization tolerates failure, much less incompetence or mediocrity, as the norm. It requires you and, more importantly, the individuals involved in a failure situation to move past it, ideally sooner rather than later.

Don't worry. You don't need a staff of "failure counselors" on call. And this process need not take weeks or months. But you should be aware of it and pay attention to how your organization allows teams and individuals to cope with those losses, even if you use Don Shula's "24-hour rule." Shula, the winningest coach in NFL history, gave his players and coaching staff one day to either fully celebrate a great victory or mourn a painful defeat. After that, it was 100% focus on the game ahead. As he said: "Success is not forever, and failure is never final."[9]

ADDRESS THE RIPPLE EFFECTS

We presume you'd like to know why things went wrong, and to get solid answers and valuable insights, you need to focus on the failure's ripple effects on four groups:

1. **Ground-Zero Insiders:** those directly involved in the effort that went south
2. **First-Ring Outsiders:** customers, suppliers, and others directly affected by the failure
3. **Second-Ring Audiences:** investors, the media, regulators, and others whose expectations may have been raised by the project
4. **Watchful Insiders:** vitally important individuals throughout your organization who, while not directly involved, are likely to be keenly aware of how you respond to the situation

The concerns of each of these groups have to be addressed on their own merits before you can plunge deeper into the root causes of any failure.

Each ripple-effect group has been affected by this failure, and can offer valuable insights into its origins and implications for your organization's future. Take the time to address each on its own terms before you embark on the kind of intensive, candid reflection we suggest for this stage.

You'll note that we call this stage Reflect rather than *analyze*. Analysis, rigorous and otherwise, will undoubtedly be required, including tools like root-cause analysis, fishbone cause-and-effect models, and other techniques. But your focus, at this point, should be on genuine introspection, with a willingness to look at this failure scenario through fresh, unusual vantage points. This isn't like creative brainstorming, but it does require a similar tolerance for ambiguity and unexpected insights that can help you shift behaviors going forward.

1. Ground-Zero Insiders: Console and Thank

We start with a basic presumption: Nobody *wants* to fail. It's particularly painful for the insiders, however fascinating it may be for rubberneckers on the outside. People are naturally disappointed, concerned about the impact this will have on their immediate jobs and longer-term career outlook, and reluctant to talk about it. No doubt you have experienced this yourself, whether in an organizational context or a personal one.

Consolation matters here. Unless this failure was the result of negligence or incompetence, your job is to acknowledge the genuine effort of the individuals involved and share with them your own disappointment with the outcome, while resisting the temptation to point fingers publicly.

2. First-Ring Outsiders: Admit and Atone

Chances are good that a failure worth understanding has probably caused ripple effects with key parties outside your organization. Customers or prospects may have been disappointed, or even antagonized. Certain suppliers may be frustrated by their experience with this effort, and they undoubtedly have their own ideas about why and how this failure occurred. But before you elicit those perspectives, you need to acknowledge and respect their experience with this particular situation.

Atoning may sound a bit strong here, but somehow you need to convey your organization's regret at the outcome and demonstrate a genuine desire to make it right for the outside parties involved. Sometimes all that takes is a sincere apology. Other times it may take a bit more, perhaps an offer to discount a future purchase or provide some other benefit to preserve the relationship. Whatever it takes, make sure it represents an authentic expression of your gratitude for their continued involvement with your company.

3. Second-Ring Outsiders: Explain and Reaffirm

In some cases, your organization's failure may be even more public. Perhaps you announced this initiative with great fanfare in the media, highlighted it with your investors, or touted it to key government organizations involved in your business. Whatever the scope of these external audiences, you need to attend to them honestly and directly so they understand you're aware of the situation, addressing it appropriately, and appreciative of their understanding.

This is not about spinning a bad story. Too many companies make that mistake and corrode their own credibility in the process. Instead, addressing the second ring is about simply explaining what happened in terms that matter to each of these audiences, and then showing how you and your team are applying the lessons learned to improve your performance going forward. You don't need to air your dirty linen here, just show that you're still in charge of the laundry.

4. Watchful Insiders: Send the Right Signals

Word-of-mouth is an amazing phenomenon. It operates at the human equivalent of the speed of light. Rumors are spread and observations shared across organizations faster than any HR publication can ever catch up with. That was the case even before e-mail, Twitter, and Facebook accelerated word-of-mouth to reach viral speed.

Don't kid yourself. Most failures inside your organization rapidly become common knowledge. Company insiders are already in the loop, looking for any signal about how you handle it. Your actions will have an effect on their own willingness to engage in other activities with a risk of failing. They'll be looking to see if you own up to your responsibility or scapegoat some member of the core team. They'll be anxious to see what happens to the failing team's members: Do they keep their jobs or get exiled to your organization's equivalent of Siberia?

Your actions, words, and gestures will quickly and broadly reverberate throughout your enterprise . . . more than you think. Stop for a moment. Consider the broader question of how you want your organization to think about and deal with innovation, experimentation, and risk in pursuing its strategic agenda. The sooner you master an effective repertoire to move from the aftermath of failure to deeper reflection about its reasons and lessons, the better. Analysis is necessary, but not sufficient to succeed in this stage of reflection. Remember the Kodak story.

JUDGMENT TRUMPS ANALYSIS: THINKING BEYOND THE EVENT

Assuming your organization can avoid trapping itself in scapegoating and finger-pointing after a failure occurs, this is the time for careful thought. But beware a second trap: looking at every failure as an event rather than a process, much less a vital resource. Many organizations don't yet have repeatable procedures for analyzing failures in the first place, leaving them to deal with each ad hoc.

Here are three things to focus on in your reflection:

1. **Frame:** The scope of the failure needs to be appropriately defined because it will determine not only what issues to consider, but also what tools and metrics should be used to analyze them. Look at the episode through both internal and external lenses. Look for interdepartmental issues that can give clues to systemic problems. For example, a failure by your sales group may have its roots on your manufacturing floor; or a blown strategy may highlight gaps in your intramural communication channels and culture. Treat the failure first as an organizational failure rather than that of a team or individual; it's up to your team to figure out how they can avoid repeating it. Then, do a 360-degree walk around the situation through the eyes of your customers, suppliers, partners, investors, regulators, media, and the public—before you close the books on this Reflect stage.
2. **Invite:** Incorporating uninvolved parties on your Reflect team can often provide fresh perspectives those involved can't see because they're just

too close to the scene. Done right, this can also reinforce a collaborative culture of mutual trust and facilitate sharing of best practices across your organization.

3. **Diversify Your Analyses, Then Decide:** No amount of analysis can substitute for solid judgment in determining why what happened transpired and how your organization can best benefit from the lessons learned. We have no doubt that Kodak and Polaroid had very smart people analyzing their competitive market dynamics and assessing emerging technologies, but they simply reached the wrong conclusions from that work. There's no easy substitute here for a mix of rigorous analysis, candid discussion, and openness to diverse points of view. It's not a guarantee against groupthink or bad calls, but it can reduce the odds of them happening.

The Reflect stage is not just about diagnosis; it's also about determining the next direction your organization should take, now that it's better informed by this experience. And there are new resources that can help you do just that.

BIG DATA AND THE CROWD IN THE CLOUD

The advent of big-data analysis, made possible by increased computing capabilities, bodes well for how leaders can better learn from failure and leverage its power to drive innovation and accelerate growth. The beauty of big data, when it works, is that it can help you ask—and possibly answer—questions you didn't know to formulate. It can dive into massive amounts of data that would otherwise swamp traditional analytical techniques to discern correlations and linkages as yet undiscovered by your team (as we saw in the We Heart It example in the Recognize stage).

Prompted in part by the appeal of the Open Innovation revolution sparked by our UC Berkeley colleague Henry Chesbrough, many organizations around the world are inviting outsiders to help them address key challenges and shortcomings. This strategy goes beyond forensic analysis of failures and can be applied to many situations in which the inviting organization is looking for a second opinion, a fresh insight, or even a new scientific approach to an important item on its strategic agenda.

For example, Boehringer Ingelheim, a global pharmaceutical company, partnered with Kaggle, a collaborative data-science community, to invite scientists around the world to develop a model to better predict the biological response of molecules. The prize? $20,000. The result? Over 9,000 entries from more than 800 scientists and non-scientists alike. The winning algorithm is now used in the company's drug development regimen.[10]

Open Innovation companies are opening their doors, asking for help to solve some of their biggest problems. Rather than view this as an admission of failure, they see it as an invitation to success, acknowledging but not belittling their own limitations in search of more innovative, creative, and effective solutions to particularly thorny challenges.

Failure isolates; success unites. If you can overcome the immediate emotional reactions to it and do the deeper reflection we recommend in this stage, the reasons for this particular failure will become clear. More importantly, you'll see an increased willingness by your colleagues to undertake risky assignments, alert you to potential failures-in-waiting, and even more candidly share their best ideas for improving your organization's performance.

YOUR ROLE: INQUISITIVE STUDENT

Your job at this stage is that of an eager student thirsty for knowledge. You need to understand the underlying reasons for this particular failure, learn from the insights gleaned in the process, and improve your odds of success going forward. To do this you'll need more than the stereotypical, facts-only line of inquiry, because facts by themselves have a way of being more malleable than concrete, especially when viewed through a post-mortem lens.

Think about this stage as an exercise in the kind of "Zero Stigma" leadership we discussed earlier, rather than Six Sigma perfection. Focus on curiosity instead of culpability. Conducting your investigation in that spirit is more likely to yield the kind of candor, creativity, and conversations that result in the deeper understanding that can best inform your future decision making.

The type and sequence of questions you ask matters. So does your tone. Determining what happened, when, where, how, and why, is much more important than naming who to blame.[11] Too many organizations substitute blame for insight, limiting the insights and value that they extract to course correct and improve. That may be easier than exposing underlying limitations in the organization or leadership itself, but this is a better time for mirrors than scapegoats.

Takeaways

Stage Five: Reflect

1. **Take time:** Recognize that failure often contains the best insights into what you should do next—if you are patient and persistent enough to really probe it. Failure is reality's way of showing you you've been conducting an experiment.
2. **Insight trumps blame:** Look at the lessons of failure in a more no-fault environment. Removing blame from the equation allows a more objective assessment of the factors leading up to the failure, what you can learn from it, and how to develop the best strategies and tactics to proceed with new innovations and programs.
3. **Probe for deeper understanding:** Don't confuse rationalization of *what* happened with rational analysis of *why*. But don't let purely fact-based, rigorous analysis substitute for personal, candid conversations about the situation and why and how it happened.
4. **Get on with it:** This Reflect stage is not an invitation to wallow in a failure or to fall into paralysis by analysis. You need to understand what really happened, then determine how to best get back into the game and play a little better.

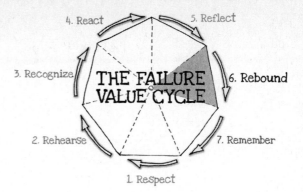

4. React   5. Reflect

3. Recognize   THE FAILURE VALUE CYCLE   6. Rebound

2. Rehearse   7. Remember

1. Respect

15 | Stage Six: Rebound

Retake the Initiative

Your Role: Field General

In 2011, Netflix announced it was splitting its popular movie rental business into two different services: a DVD rental service named Qwikster and a streaming movie service under the Netflix name. For customers who were currently enjoying both services in one subscription, this change would be accompanied by a significant price increase. In just a few months, Netflix lost nearly a million subscribers and three quarters of its market capitalization as its stock price plunged from almost $300 to $65 per share. Rumors flew that Netflix would be acquired and no longer be a dominant independent player in the media distribution business.[1]

So what did Netflix do?

First, it reacted in the moment. Since this failure was of its own doing, Netflix CEO Reed Hastings and his leadership team issued an apology to its customers. *TheStreet*'s Jim Cramer credited the team for this action and for limiting customer backlash, "The mea culpa of management was dissed by

Wall Street, but the customers loved it. The customers came right back. That wasn't in the playbook."[2]

Netflix then shifted to the Reflect stage in our Failure Value Cycle, as it determined how to respond over the longer term. The company assessed the damage, the competitive landscape, the fast-moving changes in media distribution, shifting user habits and preferences, and its customer base's willingness to pay for services, among other factors.

This turned up key insights about the continued rollout of high-speed media delivery services, the rapid adoption of tablets and larger smart phones, and increased customer frustration with even higher cable pricing. Recognizing there were major opportunities to further build the Netflix business, the company entered stage six of the Failure Value Cycle: Rebound.

It simplified its pricing, at levels that compared very favorably with the cable networks. It repositioned itself well beyond DVD rental and movie streaming with new original programming such as *House of Cards* and *Arrested Development*. And it invested heavily in infrastructure to provide premium levels of service. By the way, it also canceled Qwikster.

By late 2013, just two years after the Qwikster fiasco, Netflix shares were trading at an all-time high and the company had grown to more than 30 million subscribers, surpassing HBO as market leader. Toward the end of this comeback, Ted Sarandos, Netflix's Chief Content Officer, had this to say: "The goal is to become HBO faster than HBO can become us."[3] At least by some metrics, Netflix accomplished that goal.[4]

* * *

There's no doubt about it, a number of things have gone wrong. A failure of one sort or another has knocked you and your team off course. Hopefully, you *recognized* the failure before it became life threatening; *rehearsed* for that eventuality, and *reacted* as best you could. You've *reflected* on what went wrong and engaged in a deep but prompt analysis of contributing factors and current environment. Then, you developed a revised strategy. Now you need to get back on track, with the benefit of the lessons you just learned. Enter the Rebound stage.

The saddest failure is running out of the resources to apply the lesson of the prior one. That's why this Rebound stage is so vital. This stage includes Netflix-style comebacks that play out over months or years as well as shorter-fuse crises that may take minutes or hours. Lives are at risk, property needs to be protected, or your cash flow is hemorrhaging. You can't afford to dawdle or wallow in the failure. At this time, the imperative to rebound may overtake the opportunity to reflect on what has just happened (at least temporarily), depending in part on your own reflexive reactions in the moment. The importance of the prior Respect, Rehearse, and Recognize stages becomes clear, even if the time spent on reaction and reflection is compressed.

Success in the Rebound stage depends on how insightfully you reflect on the factors that contributed to the failure, including those within your control versus those that were not.

Finally, your employees, and perhaps others as well, will pay close attention to what happens to those team members involved in the failure. If malfeasance, laziness, or incompetence was involved, then tough action is appropriate. But if they were hard working and well-intentioned, taking risks on behalf of your company's own agenda, they deserve better treatment; and making them part of the solution makes sense. After all, they know the land mines better than anyone else. They will appreciate it and others will notice, and your actions will contribute to the very loyalty, intelligent risk taking, and hard work you probably need to accelerate innovation and drive growth.

SHORT-CYCLE VERSUS LONG-CYCLE REBOUNDS

Now ask yourself: Which scenario are you more likely to face: a terrorist attack, fire, or earthquake (for which you presumably already have procedures and drills); or a hack into your computer system, product collapse in the market, loss of a strategic customer, or major project failure? Your Rebound playbook needs to reflect your answer.

When engaging in Rebound planning (as opposed to post-failure damage control), you usually have the benefit of a more forgiving timetable. You and your team can carefully consider what has happened, why, and identify your best course of action to either recover or redirect your efforts. These kinds of rebounds may take months or years. Consider examples of company turnarounds like at Apple when Steve Jobs returned to its helm, Starbucks when founder Howard Schulz came back as CEO, or General Motors and Chrysler's comebacks after their own near-death experiences in the last decade. All rebounds to be sure, albeit in slower motion than our initial Netflix example.

GET BACK IN THE GAME

You've tended to the wounded. Now you face the next big question: How will you apply the lessons of this failure to strengthen your strategy going forward? Including the long-arc trajectory comebacks exemplified by Apple, IBM, Starbucks, and the like, you have five fundamental choices in this stage of our Failure Value Cycle:

1. **Tenacity:** Sometimes you need to *rivet* rather than *pivot*. Stick to your guns and chalk the adversity and failures up to beginner's bad luck. This option is strong, particularly if you remain deeply committed to the product or project at hand, and are convinced you can persuade others that you're right. Some solutions simply need time—not every success comes overnight.

2. **Tweak:** Make a minor adjustment to your previous course to take into account the insights you gathered from this particular failure scenario. Much like a sailor trimming his sails on his present tack from point A to point B, you make the small changes you need to get back on track.

3. **Turn:** You've determined that a more abrupt change is in order, and it can't wait. You need to turn a corner, which may take quite a concerted effort given the momentum created by your previous actions. This will take more planning and communication than a simple tweak, and it will probably take more time.

4. **Turnabout:** In this situation, the failure you've encountered calls for a fundamental reversal of direction based on what you've just learned from your environment. You may have had a product collapse, a customer revolt, or a stunning countermove by competitors that has dramatically altered the assumptions on which your previous strategy was based. This may not call for full-scale retreat, but it is nonetheless closer to a 180-degree shift.

5. **Throw in the towel:** Here, you decide to leave the field, not necessarily in surrender but simply because it no longer makes sense to pursue your previous strategy. Given the major revelation contained in the failure scenario you've just been through, you simply need to pull the plug on a product, project, or other initiative in order to refocus your resources on more promising activities.

Our goal here is not to discuss all the possible permutations of rebound strategies that may be appropriate to every situation. We simply want to give you the flavor of the kinds of decisions and consequent actions you need to be prepared for during this stage of the Failure Value Cycle.

Whichever course of action you choose will call for clarity from you worthy of your colleagues' confidence in your leadership. Whatever your new Rebound strategy is—whether it is a tweak, turnabout, or a decision to throw in the towel—your team will be looking for your guidance and eager to understand your logic in providing it.

You may have to project more confidence than you feel about the new course of action and its likely prospects. No doubt there are several choices available to you regarding timing, targets, metrics, and team assignments. But you probably don't have the luxury of prolonging or postponing the difficult decisions to wend your way through every alternative. Your colleagues await not just your decision itself, but the enthusiasm and self-confidence with which you announce and implement it. They want you to display decisiveness and conviction as you develop and explain your Rebound strategy.

But be careful. In their urgency to get beyond the failure *du jour*, some organizations come down with amnesia. They act as if a failure never happened, even to the point, in worst cases, of actively covering it up. To borrow an observation from criminal law, the cover-up is often worse than the original crime itself.

Your Rebound is likely to be only as effective as the candor and completeness of the reflection that precedes it. If you are still in damage-control mode or denial, you may be simply making matters worse. That's what Steve Jobs did in failing to acknowledge the iPhone 4's design defect that kept dropping calls.[5] Jeff Bezos did it in belatedly addressing the controversy around Amazon's Orwellian secret deleting of *1984* and *Animal Farm* from its users' Kindles.[6] Sony did it after 77 million of its PlayStation 3 customers' personal data was compromised by a hacker.[7] Those are the Rebound equivalents of air balls.

On the one hand, denial and forgetfulness will only make your problems worse; on the other hand, we don't recommend you dwell on the failure any longer than is necessary to understand its lessons and figure out your most appropriate path forward.

CLEAR THE DECKS FOR AN EFFECTIVE REBOUND

Often an effective Rebound begins with a candid acknowledgment of what just happened. If you made some mistakes early, perhaps by ignoring the situation too long or misstating the scope of the situation, now's the time to make that right. As we've discussed in other stages of the Failure Value Cycle, apology can be an incredibly powerful tool if it is sincere and not overused. Thank your stakeholders for their patience and consideration, and then build on this with your commitments to do right by them going forward.

Make this as personal as you can—visit the site, talk to the employees involved, call some of the customers that were affected. Reestablish your credibility, demonstrate your concern about their reactions to this particular situation, and express your desire to get back on a stronger footing with them. Follow up in a few days and weeks to make sure your Rebound efforts are beginning to pay off. You are building a bank account of trust you may need to draw upon in later circumstances.

YOUR ROLE: FIELD GENERAL

The bleeding has stopped. The lessons have been absorbed and incorporated in your Rebound strategy, which has been converted into your plan and specific tactics. Your executives and teams have their marching orders as you launch your next offensive. As the field general, you might be located just behind the front lines, tracking progress and making battlefield adjustments. This is an execution-intensive stage. Ensure that you have metrics and dashboards in place and drive accountability across the organization. But remember, even with the best of plans and teams, there will often be failures along the way. Employ your failure-savvy leadership and turn those setbacks or experiments into new opportunities for your organization and your people.

Takeaways

Stage Six: Rebound

1. **Get moving:** Rebound is definitely an action stage, where you put into motion the plans you and your team developed during the Reflect stage. Don't blame your customers or other outside parties

for what happened without first examining whether and to what extent your organization is responsible.

2. **Apologize if/as needed:** Acknowledge and, as appropriate, apologize for the failure to your key inside and outside stakeholders. Don't ignore the failure altogether or rationalize it without acknowledging its impact. Worse yet, don't deny it ever existed, hide it, or cover it up.

3. **Rally your own troops:** Broadcast a clear and confident Rebound strategy that reflects what you just learned from the failure in question.

4. **Prove you're serious:** Engage your organization and the affected marketplace with demonstrable evidence of your commitment to your Rebound strategy, whether it is a tenacity strategy for staying the course or a turnabout reversing direction.

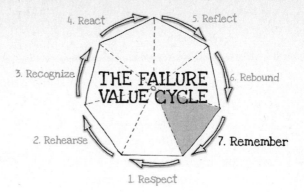

16

Stage Seven: Remember

Embed Failure Savvy in Your Culture

Your Role: Proud Storyteller

WHAT'S WORSE THAN A ROOT CANAL? DOING ONE ON YOURSELF!

In June of 1988, Henry Schein, Inc. was brought to its knees. After 56 years of successful operation—from its original mom-and-pop drugstore to serving dental offices and clinics all over the world—it had just switched over its manual paper-based inventory control process to a new computerized system. With visions of improved efficiency and customer service in their minds, Schein's President, Stan Bergman, and his team looked forward to this new operating platform.

That's when the failure began. No sooner had the new system kicked in then first a trickle, and soon a flood of errors and mistakes started appearing.

173

In the old system, the employees involved knew the customers, their names and addresses, and the products they ordered. They just were not as diligent in keeping that information accurately up-to-date in the records on which the new computer system depended.

As errors began to compound errors, the company knew it had a giant mess on its hands. Its entire business was distribution and that business depended on timely, accurate deliveries to customers who relied on the company's products every day. The real question was whether this would become a company-destroying fiasco or an all-hands-on-deck crisis it would weather.

Bergman knew this was no time for org chart chain-of-command niceties. He needed every able-bodied person to roll up their shirtsleeves and get busy fixing every one of those paper records . . . ASAP! And that's what they did for 24 hours a day for weeks on end as they slowly began the salvage effort. It took almost a year before this self-imposed failure became yesterday's story rather than tomorrow's dreaded reality.[1]

That prolonged failure and the company's recovery became a powerful and lasting story testifying to the resilience, grit, and commitment of the company's leadership and its workforce on Long Island. Today, Henry Schein is a $10 billion, 17,000-employee Fortune 300 global enterprise, boasting a 99+ percent fulfillment accuracy and timeliness performance level. In addition to generating solid financial results, it is one of the few "Triple Crown" companies in business today, meaning it is:

- One of *Fortune*'s "World's Most Admired Companies" (and has been for 13 years in a row)
- Ranked number one in social responsibility among *Fortune*'s list of companies in its industry
- A regular member on Ethisphere's list of the "World's Most Ethical Companies"

* * *

If there's one thing a leader is responsible for besides results, it's the culture of the organization she or he heads. While every leader presumably wants an organization committed to excellence, innovation, integrity, and account-ability, few seem willing to examine the failure culture in their midst. Think about your own enterprise. What was its reaction to the last major failure it encountered? What questions were asked, in what order, and to whom?

What happened to the people involved in that particular failure? Henry Schein's culture continues to apply the core lessons of that 1988 calamity; as recently as 2014, when it mobilized another "let's fix it" squad to solve a temporary operational glitch in its London office.

Culture is what makes you "you" organizationally. It's unique, hard to copy, difficult to sustain, and easy to compromise if you don't pay attention to it. As Tony Hsieh, the founder of Zappos, says: "Your culture is your brand!"[2]

Every organization's culture is rooted in stories, but many leaders miss the opportunity to retell these stories and share the lessons they contain. Some of the most powerful culture stories recount times the organization has successfully navigated the shoals of this failure cycle. So by keeping them in the shadows, leaders miss the chance to make their organization's culture more resilient, competent, and confident going forward. Executives don't use these catalytic experiences nearly enough to create positive, future-directed stories and rituals.

In many ways, the Remember stage is the deepest level of our Failure Value Cycle. This is when truly failure-savvy culture evolves. In this context, failure has the potential to imprint the underlying DNA of an organization by embedding the hard facts and lessons of its prior failures. Done right, this is when you can help your company absorb the other F word's valuable insights and preserve them for future generations.

There are four important ways to do this:

1. **Stories:** This is where the lessons of a failure are informally entered at the most fundamental level in the organization's cultural narrative. Through storytelling, the entire saga becomes part of its memory.
2. **Rituals:** Repeated activities and ceremonies highlight the most important elements, lessons, and actions from the failure episode. These rituals establish how failure is received in an organization.
3. **Relics:** The physical artifacts that remind the organization of its success in learning from those failures. Imagine how refreshing it would be to walk into a corporate headquarters and see a "Things We Learned from Our Failures" showcase next to its trophies.
4. **Reports:** Yes, reports. They can tell the organization's story (even if not in the most gripping format). The other F word deserves its place among the monthly budget, daily production, and quarterly financial reports your organization churns out like clockwork. It's a practical way you can

ensure failure gets taken seriously and productively as a strategic resource in your enterprise.

Out of this process evolves a new organization, better prepared to face its challenges and, having committed its failures to memory, in a superior position to more confidently chart its course forward.

1. Stories: Every Failure Tells One

Silicon Valley gets this. Rather than brushing startup failures under the rug, entrepreneurs often share their failure experiences in highly public blogs, tweets, presentations, and other media. For many entrepreneurs, having at least one failure on your resume is a rite of passage, especially if lessons from that failure help make your next venture-capital-backed startup a success. This approach is so ingrained that (as noted in our discussion of the Respect stage) events such as Fuckup Nights and FailCon have sprung up around this topic. Activities such as these reinforce the importance of telling stories and creating places to discuss failures in a way that the insights and benefits can be remembered and put to work in the future.

These public events might be too open for your tastes or stories, but you and your organization have your own rich trove of failure-and-recovery stories that can drive home the messages of engagement, creativity, resiliency, innovation, and grit that you've probably excluded in your annual reports, formal presentations, and employee handbooks. Stories can resonate more genuinely than those other channels ever can.

Stan Bergman, now CEO of Henry Schein, Inc., has seen and shaped this kind of culture firsthand:

> Highly effective leaders share the same leadership attributes as summer camp leaders: they know how to motivate people to be fully engaged and build a team. Like great summer camp counselors, the leadership at Henry Schein likes to tell stories, and we use the power of those stories to shape and sustain our culture through the years.

As Robert McKee says in his useful guide to storytelling, stories work best because they unite ideas with emotion.[3] They demand truthfulness and authenticity if they are to work with understandably skeptical, if not cynical, audiences.

Your task is to tell stories, not sell PowerPoints. The stories you tell don't need to be perfect, but they have to be real, otherwise they lose their power. Try telling one or two "Other F Word" stories to see what kinds of reactions you get from your fellow workers, and don't forget to ask for—and listen to—their stories as well.

2. Rituals: Ceremonies That Give Failed Experiments Their Due

Other-F-word rituals can contribute to your building a more failure-savvy culture. Like stories, rituals help shape, define, and preserve culture in your organization. They become hallmarks of why yours is different; and hopefully, why your people, customers, and investors prefer working with you.

How you deal with failure is the acid test of your culture. It's just as revealing as how you create and celebrate success. We don't suggest tolerating failure as a norm or setting mediocrity as your benchmark. We presume you seek a culture of excellence, but the gravity of failure doesn't care about your aspirations or rhetoric. It will find you, and you will need to figure out how to best handle and leverage that power to your advantage.

When people die, we hold memorial services to remember them, honor their lives, and help grieving survivors acclimate themselves to a new reality. The same logic can be used to honor the efforts of those still standing after important failures in your organization. Bear in mind there is a fine line here between honoring failure and celebrating it. This is not about holding consolation parades for losers, but neither is it about allowing those involved to slink into oblivion with no acknowledgment of their efforts.

Here's one example of a clever and memorable post-failure ritual: A Norwegian executive we know from a global telecom firm recently shared with us a video of a funny, creative memorial service and "burial" one of his teams held for an intriguing, innovative project that ultimately failed. Rather than quietly disbanding and moving on, the team elected to hold a company ceremony to celebrate its hard work and journey, to recall their successes and teamwork, and to share their failures and insights. The team even con-structed a creative time capsule statue to memorialize the experience.

Our colleague noted that the ritual captured and shared the insights of this project team, including those factors that may have contributed to its failure. It enabled the team's members to gracefully move on to their next project. Simply stated, this ritual showed there was life after failure.

Comic Relief: Make Fun of Yourself (Others Probably Are Anyway)

Poking fun at yourself and your mistakes can be another powerful way to overcome the lingering effects of an important failure (but never poke fun at one involving serious injury, community damage, or loss of life). This is one of those things that may well need permission from you as team or organizational leader, so be willing to go first and let your inner *Saturday Night Live* persona shine through. It'll be a welcome relief to your colleagues, who are probably waiting on pins and needles to see what's safe for them to talk and joke about.

3. Relics: The Hard-Won Trophies of Failures

Every organization has souvenirs from failures. These relics are the products that didn't work, the ad campaigns whose message never took, the acquisition that didn't quite pan out. Most of these end up in the corporate equivalent of the dumpster, destined to be forgotten, but some have talismanic value because they offered some key insight.

Imagine if you went in the lobby of WD-40 and you saw the containers for WD-1 through WD-39, all of which contributed to the final breakthrough that led to this worldwide hit. What if you went on the website of a prominent venture capital firm and you found a humorous mea culpa citing some of the hugely successful investments this crack team had passed up?

That's exactly what you find if you visit Bessemer Venture Partners' website: It's called the "Anti-Portfolio."[4] It includes a dozen companies that went on to become smash successes, even without investment from Bessemer. An early investment in any one would have put a smile on an investor's face, not to mention a sizable bulge in their wallets, but Bessemer missed these opportunities for various reasons. FedEx, Intel, PayPal, eBay, and, of course, Google? Bessemer said, "No, thanks." To give you a flavor for how a failure reliquary can be done with class, here are the most prominent mini-stories from the firm's website:[5]

- **FedEx:** "Incredibly, BVP [Bessemer Venture Partners] passed on Federal Express seven times."
- **Intel:** "BVP's Pete Bancroft never quite settled on terms with Bob Noyce, who instead took venture financing from a guy named Arthur Rock."
- **PayPal:** "David Cowan passed on the Series A round. Rookie team, regulatory nightmare, and, 4 years later, a $1.5 billion acquisition by eBay."
- **eBay:** "Stamps? Coins? Comic books? You've GOT to be kidding,' thought Cowan. 'No-brainer pass.'"
- **Google:** "Cowan's college friend rented her garage to Sergey and Larry for their first year. In 1999 and 2000 she tried to introduce Cowan to 'these two really smart Stanford students writing a search engine.' Students? A new search engine? In the most important moment ever for Bessemer's anti-portfolio, Cowan asked her, 'How can I get out of this house without going anywhere near your garage?'"[6]

What a refreshing acknowledgment of the fallibility of very smart people who occasionally make not-so-smart decisions! Would your organization have the guts and humility to make a comparable admission of its foibles? Amidst all the PR spin to a skeptical public, you might consider how it might actually increase your credibility externally and build more trust internally.

Speaking of Intel, which is included in the Bessemer "Anti-Portfolio," here's another example of a commemorative relic of a very public failure. In 1994, the company initially tried to stonewall and ignore a minor but embarrassing calculation flaw in its new, highly marketed Pentium computer chip. As publicity grew, the company was forced to issue an expensive worldwide recall and suffered damage to its previously sterling reputation. But it also learned an important lesson in rebounding. Andy Grove, Intel's CEO at the time, had the flawed chip made into employee key rings with the inscription: "Bad companies are destroyed by crises; good companies survive them; great companies are improved by them."[7] Mistakes matter, but lessons and memory can matter more.

Chances are your organization has its own counterparts to Bessemer's anti-portfolio, but you may never have thought to talk about them, much less feature them. They may not be as flashy as seeing a bottle of New Coke in the lobby of Coca-Cola or an Edsel at Ford, but imagine how you would react if those failures were acknowledged along with the lessons each company had taken away from those flops.

4. Reports: The Record of Your Efforts, Results, and Progress

If your organization isn't failing or recognizing failures, chances are it isn't learning new things, trying new things, or holding itself sufficiently accountable at all levels. This may be one of the few places where you actually do want to celebrate—or at least commemorate—failure, not for its own sake but for what it taught your organization. One longstanding example is Walmart's "Correction of Errors" practice, a refreshing approach to this issue. As chronicled by former Walmart executive Bill Marquard:

> Correction of Errors isn't aimed at placing blame. It focuses on the problem, not the person. Correction of Errors is all about identifying ways to improve customer experiences, merchandise, processes, cost structure, and the company from within—before competitors beat Wal-Mart [sic] to it.[8]

When's the last time one of your management reports or strategic planning documents illuminated a powerfully unique aspect of your culture? Now imagine if before you had to present your latest strategic plan to senior management or the board, you had to include a "Failure Wisdom Report" to show explicitly how this new strategy incorporates what you learned from prior failures, and what your backup plans are should even this strategy fail, despite your best efforts.[9]

CREATE "WHAT HAVE YOU FAILED FOR US, LATELY?" METRICS

If you're going to tackle the fear of failure in your culture, you're going to have to attack it where it lives, and that's around people's fear that failure will cost them their job, their promotion, or their reputation. You need to take risks to win. Incorporate that into your workplace culture and performance evaluations.

After a recent World Cup upset, the coach of the losing soccer team was asked to explain the result. He said, simply, that his team had been "out-chanced." The winning team had more shots on goal, and converted enough to win. Even though the winning team missed most of their shots, those extra failures *increased* their chances of victory.

You can't win a soccer, basketball, or hockey game if you don't fire shots at the goal. And, chances are, the more shots you take, the greater your odds of winning. Innovation is like that, too. Consultants, academics, and senior executives may not admit it, but nobody knows for sure which particular innovations (in product design, business model, marketing campaign, or manufacturing process) will drive growth for your organization. In fact, some of the biggest innovations have come about not through exhaustive strategy, but through serendipity, good timing, and a dedicated team.

What's all this have to do with failure? It's the flip side. The more shots you take, the more failures you'll likely create, but your real focus is on points scored to win the game. By analogy, think how you can "outchance" your competition in your target markets. You'll still need a solid playbook, and effective training for your players, but your emphasis is getting more shots on goal, and accepting the failures that will accompany them. This is a great way to unlock the natural competitive pride that could be lying fallow in your organization. Just make sure you also connect and reinforce the work and workers off the field with the exploits of those on it—like Cirque du Soleil does with an office setup that visually connects its back-office staff with performers practicing their acts.

But beware: Your organization will sense quickly if you're really serious about incorporating failure and its lessons into that process. Don't become a caricature like the clueless managers in *The Office* or *Dilbert*. They became household names by poking fun at the foibles and pomposity of overly enthusiastic executives who have zero idea about how they come across to the people they supposedly manage.

YOUR ROLE: PROUD STORYTELLER

Think back to those childhood evenings sitting around the campfire telling stories. Stories are one of the oldest ways memories and lessons are handed down from one generation to the next in families, societies, and organizations.

Great stories are a central part of the culture that molds organizations, and they can provide guidance and reminders of values when the way forward may be unclear.

Stories resonate best when they are personal and authentic. Fill them out with those elements that make for a good story: your central characters, motivations, tension and conflict, resolution, and a hero. Finally, as we think back to those days around the campfire, it's not just about the art of telling great stories. It's also about being a great listener to the stories your colleagues like to tell.

Takeaways

Stage Seven: Remember

1. **Culture is job #1!** People come and go, but culture lasts. Yes, you're responsible for results—that goes with your job title—but the real challenge, not to mention legacy, of your leadership is the quality, distinctiveness, and resiliency of the culture you create and leave behind. The phrase attributed to Peter Drucker, "Culture eats strategy for breakfast," gets it right. This is true for your team, your department, and your organization.
2. **Tell stories:** Use the power of personal stories, shared rituals, and memorable relics that demonstrate how your organization approaches, learns from, and leverages failure in its quest for excellence, innovation, and growth. Think of who your organization's other-F-word heroes are, how they contributed to your success, and where they went in their careers inside your company.
3. **Honor the past:** These cultural legends can help you share the lessons your organization has learned from past failures and keep them alive from one generation of employees to the next. Henry Petroski describes this tendency of organizations to repeat errors and failures as "The Historical Future," a 30-year cycle as the cohort of employees who experienced them firsthand retire, leaving their successors to learn them all over again.[10] After all, the worst failure is repeating one you've already made.

17

The Failure Value Report Card

A Practical Tool to Help You Put Failure to Work

"Failure is today's lesson for tomorrow."

—John Danner

We wouldn't be true to our academic roles if we didn't offer you a way to assess your own failure leadership and grade yourself on your progress in making your organization more failure savvy. After all, we don't want you to *flunk* failure. So we've developed a Failure Value Report Card that covers the three different time zones of the Failure Value Cycle: before failure occurs, during a failure event, and afterwards. This tool can help you honestly evaluate how well prepared your organization is to anticipate, deal with, and leverage failure.

Organizations tend to act on what gets measured, so you need a way to keep track of your progress in becoming more failure savvy. Take care that your failure management process doesn't gratuitously celebrate or merely tolerate failure, but elevates and liberates it as an ongoing resource to strengthen performance overall. Keep that goal in mind as you determine what to measure.

Based on the seven stages of the Failure Value Cycle—and the role leaders have at every stage—we have designed this prototype to help you identify where you are strong and where you need to focus your attention. It's a tool that will be most helpful if it reflects the candid assessments of a representative cross-section of your entire workforce and supplier network, and even your external customers and clients. Remember: Your colleagues will not trust this until and unless they see their input reflected in your actions as a more failure-savvy leader.

Feel free to use this information in whatever format works best for your style and organization. You can take a traditional report card approach, or you might use a more visual spider or radar chart format. We have used similar tools effectively with many groups of executives and employees.

We have also purposely left the criteria flexible so you can adapt them to whatever standards fit your particular business situation and leadership expectations. Whichever format you use, make the results as visible and visual as possible, so you can easily collect, capture, and identify patterns and variations. This will facilitate your follow-up conversations about the trends and significant issues behind the grades you receive.

Electronic Report Card

If you'd like to use a digital version of this Report Card, you can go to our website: www.theotherfwordbook.com. Simply enter your e-mail address and the ISBN code from this book. Once we confirm both, you'll have access to it with our compliments. Please let us know how you used it, and send us any suggestions you have for revising it for other readers. We, and they, would appreciate learning from your experience.

These seven stages cover the complete Failure Value Cycle, from before, during, and after a failure event.

Before:	During:	After:
1. Respect	4. React	5. Reflect
2. Rehearse		6. Rebound
3. Recognize		7. Remember

REPORT CARD

Pupil ------------------

Grade

Stage 1. RESPECT

1. Do we encourage smart risk-taking and accept failure as its likely companion in our efforts to become more innovative and grow our organization?	
2. Can people in our organization talk openly and candidly about failure? Do they?	
3. When failure happens, how well do we learn from it and apply its lessons going forward?	
4. Are our people encouraged, and potentially recognized/rewarded, to flag potential difficulties that could turn into failures that matter to our organization?	
5. When failure happens, how fairly and constructively do we treat the individuals and teams involved?	
6. ---	

Grading Guidelines

A = Clearly superior compared with other leading organizations like ours, such as ------------- or -------------

B = Better than most others in our business

C = About average compared to others like our organization

D = Poor, but not at the bottom . . . yet

F = Clearly inadequate relative to most others in our business

Incomplete = Missing or in development

N/A = No basis for evaluation or not relevant

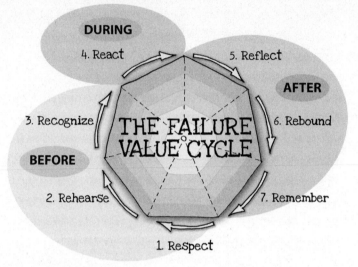

The Failure Value Cycle

Here are sample questions you can use with this Report Card, as you investigate your performance at every stage. We've also included a space to add your own:

BEFORE

The first three stages focus on your organization's failure preparedness.

Stage 1: Respect   *Grade:* _____

1. Do we encourage smart risk-taking and accept failure as its likely companion in our efforts to become more innovative and grow our organization?
2. Can people in our organization talk openly and candidly about failure? Do they?
3. When failure happens, how well do we learn from it and apply its lessons going forward?
4. Are our people encouraged, and potentially recognized/rewarded, to flag potential difficulties that could turn into failures that matter to our organization?

5. When failure happens, how fairly and constructively do we treat the individuals and teams involved?

6. _____

_____

Stage 2: Rehearse   *Grade:* _____

1. Do we have a clear process for identifying and classifying different types of failures that call for different modes of response?
2. How well prepared are we to deal appropriately with failures as they occur?
3. Do we pay sufficient attention to the important and likely failures in our business compared with the time and resources we spend preparing and rehearsing for less likely disasters and emergencies of other types (e.g., fires, storms, etc.)?
4. Are our other-F-word rehearsals realistic, interesting, engaging, and frequent?
5. Have we prepared all relevant parties to handle their appropriate responsibilities in varying failure scenarios, from all-hands-on-deck crises to delegated protocols to handle more isolated situations?

6. _____

_____

Stage 3: Recognize   *Grade:* _____

1. Do we have regularly monitored metrics and processes to adequately anticipate failure in our organization?
2. Are we often surprised by failures we could and should have anticipated?
3. Do we regularly monitor potentially significant events, developments, or trends beyond the perimeters of our existing operations to identify potential opportunities for our "future quo" businesses?
4. Do we routinely probe for potential failure-prone or vulnerable situations (e.g., key competitor initiatives, brand-tarnishing episodes in other companies, etc.) across the portfolio of our activities?

5. Do we use tools like scenario planning and Un–Golden Rule exercises to bring competitively significant trends into sharp focus for our decision making?

6. _____

_____

DURING

The next stage focuses on how well your company performs in the moment. It can have both defensive as well as offensive dimensions.

Stage 4: React   *Grade:* _____

1. When unanticipated failures happen, how well and appropriately does our organization typically respond?
2. How clear, confident, and calm are we in communicating to affected stakeholders while addressing failure scenarios?
3. How well do we strike a balance between improvised, spur-of-the-moment responses and execution of rehearsed protocols?
4. Do we tend to treat failure as an isolated event as opposed to part of a process, as we might in other areas of our operations?
5. How well do our values influence our decisions and actions in the middle of a failure situation?
6. _____

_____

AFTER

The final three stages look at how well your organization deals with the aftermath of failure.

Stage 5: Reflect   *Grade:* _____

1. Do we have and follow useful procedures to carefully review important failure situations to understand clearly *what* happened, *where* and *how*

events unfolded—including the impacts that were felt where and by whom—and *why* this particular situation developed? And do we do all this *before* we focus on *who* was responsible?

2. How well do we take care of the team members involved in and impacted by the failure?

3. How open, honest, and thorough are our after-the-fact evaluations of failure events, and how well trained are our people in that process?

4. How well do we employ an experimental mindset when analyzing the positive and negative outcomes from our failures, whether they are unintentional or the result of our own discovery efforts?

5. How well do we incorporate lessons learned into our recovery and rebound plans?

6. _____

_____

Stage 6: Rebound   *Grade:* _____

1. Once we've defined our new post-failure strategy, how well do we mobilize to put it in action?

2. Do we include members of the team involved with the failure in our Rebound effort?

3. Do we apologize appropriately and genuinely to those affected by our failures?

4. How well do we communicate, both internally and externally, our new direction and its rationale?

5. Are we sufficiently decisive and aggressive in getting back in the game?

6. _____

_____

Stage 7: Remember   *Grade:* _____

1. Do we share stories and lessons learned from how we've dealt with prior failures?

2. Do we have any traditions, relics, and rituals that honor noble failures from our past?

3. Can we point to individuals and/or teams whose careers were not compromised by their involvement with acknowledged failure situations?

4. Do we have accurate, up-to-date, and well-reasoned reports about prior failures and how they can improve our future strategies and decisions?
5. Do we tend to repeat our mistakes as opposed to learning from them and improving our activities?
6. _____

_____

These are just suggestions of the kinds of questions you might ask about each stage of the Failure Value Cycle. We have included 35 questions here, in our prototype version; you may wish to modify them or replace some with your own. The important thing is to remember the real purpose of this exercise: to increase your organization's openness around the other F word and ability to put it to work for you. In other words, the precise metrics are less important at this point than the quality and honesty of the conversations you can trigger and, most importantly, the performance improvement you can realize from the insights you learn.

GRADING GUIDELINES

Feel free to substitute your own standards here, but we'd recommend you start with something like this, just to make it interesting:

A = Clearly superior compared with other leading organizations like ours, such as _____ or _____
B = Better than most others in our business
C = About average compared to others like our organization
D = Poor, but not at the bottom . . . yet
F = Clearly inadequate relative to most others in our business
Incomplete = Missing or in development
N/A = No basis for evaluation or not relevant

We understand there is ambiguity in this exercise and the criteria you will use to grade yourselves. It'll probably drive your engineers and accountants nuts, but remember: This is an exercise about your *culture*, not your balance sheet or purchase orders. It's designed to invite a level of candor not often found in many organizations to help you start a more productive relationship with the other F word and what it can offer you. In fact, you may want to ask your graders what specific exemplars they think are most relevant for comparison.

Takeaways

Here's your drill from now on:

1. **Decide how specific you want the grading criteria to be.** For instance, you might let each grader use his or her own method, or you might prefer to prescribe guidelines for what should constitute each grade in each stage. There's merit to both approaches, as you can imagine.
2. **You can print out a master copy of our prototype Report Card from our website, www.theotherfwordbook.com.** Determine what format you want to use for this Report Card (e.g., hard copy or online). There are benefits and disadvantages to each concerning security, privacy, and convenience. Think about how you can keep the results inside your organization, until and unless you're comfortable with sharing them more widely.
3. **Identify who your graders will be.** You might want to start with yourself, but keep your results to yourself initially. From there, you can branch out to other members of your core leadership team, and later invite a broader mix of individuals both inside and outside the organization to contribute their own perspectives *anonymously* and with whatever degree of confidentiality you can reasonably assure.
4. **Ask participants to offer specific examples that support or explain their particular grades in each stage.** This may offer you a fertile set of situations with which to anchor your efforts to take the other F word out of the realm of taboo and bring it into your organization's daily conversation.
5. **Without indicating whose grades are whose, make the results big and visible in one of your conference rooms so your team can immerse themselves in the information.** If you decide to use the radar or spider diagram version from our website, we suggest you print hard copies so you can lay them out side-by-side on the wall. Step back and invite your team to look at the patterns or diversity they see. Consider the examples behind people's grades.
6. **Imagine yourself as the teacher in a proverbial parent–teacher conference when you discuss these grades.** The only difference is, in this case, the parents are your colleagues, and you are there to help

(continued)

(*continued*)

them understand your grading and map out a game plan to reinforce the positives and improve the negatives between now and the next grading period.

7. **Try it out.** If you have never invited this kind of feedback around an issue as sensitive and potentially off-limits as failure, be prepared to be surprised at what you discover. Remember: People will be looking closely at how you respond to the grades, examples, and implications from this exercise. Your job as a leader is not to bemoan but to understand, not to blame but to listen, and not to defend but to invite. This Report Card process could prove to be pivotal in moving your organization to a more trusting pro-innovation culture, open to experimentation and discovery of new opportunities. That prize is worth a little pain.

PART IV

Now

Put the Other F Word to Work

We promised when we started this tour that this book could make you a better leader, entrepreneur, and team member. We've suggested that you're sitting on top of a rich, largely untapped, strategic resource you've already paid for: failure. Managed thoughtfully and creatively, it has the power to unleash more honest engagement and trust from your employees and colleagues. If you can reduce fear of failure in your organization, you can free their innate creativity and ingenuity to help drive innovation and growth.

It's up to you to figure out how you'd like to use the ideas, tools, and frameworks we've provided to become a more failure-savvy leader. These two concluding chapters will get you started.

18

Creating the Failure–Savvy Organization

OUR JOURNEY SO FAR

Everybody wants to talk about success, but we began this book by discussing and defining failure. We suggested that failure's like gravity: It's a pervasive fact and force of life. We investigated the insidious power of the fear and memory of failure to paralyze teams, limit experimentation and risk-taking, and reduce innovation. We explored how the other F word manifests itself across different organizational phases—from nascent Start-Ups to small and medium-sized Keep-Ups to global Grown-Ups. We also introduced our seven-stage Failure Value Cycle to help you avoid failure in the first place, better prepare for it and, in particular, leverage it more effectively when it happens.

Throughout this journey we have provided exercises, to-do's, and takeaways, along with our Failure Value Report Card to help you assess the failure-savvy of your organization. We also provided examples and illustrations of how once-proud organizations such as Kodak stumbled and never recovered, while others such as Netflix were sufficiently failure savvy to respond effectively to failure, recover, innovate, and thrive.

Now, we turn to you. Think back on the various exercises we've suggested and the results you've seen from yourself and your colleagues. As a refresher, here are the key exercises we introduced:

- Assess Your Failure Leadership Profile (Chapter 2)
- Your Definition of Failure (Chapter 4)
- Fear of Failure (Chapter 5)
- Exercises and recommendations in the "Takeaways" section for each of the different organizational phases of Start-Ups, Keep-Ups, and Grown-Ups (Chapters 6, 7, and 8); and also in "Takeaways" for each of the seven stages of the Failure Value Cycle (Chapters 10–16)
- The Failure Value Report Card (Chapter 17)

Together, the insights from these exercises will help clarify where you are now, where you need to take your organization, and how to best get from here to there.

The other F word poses different types of challenges for entrepreneurs, executives, and team members alike. Nobody, including us, has a foolproof formula guaranteed to work when managing this complicated essential issue. We've offered specific recommendations throughout the book, and we encourage you to refine and interpret them to suit your own organizational context and personal leadership style.

We invite you to share your experiences and ideas with us through our website: www.theotherfwordbook.com.

Before we finish, we'd like to suggest six specific actions your organization can take as it steps up its ability to leverage the power of failure and become more innovative, faster growing, and more resilient.

1. DECIDE WHERE YOUR ORGANIZATION NEEDS TO GO

We presume that, like most organizations, yours strives for stronger innovation and growth. You seek greater involvement and more commitment from your employees. Leveraging the other F word as a strategic resource can help. Not as an end in itself, but as a means to help you achieve the success you want.

This requires a high-performance, failure-savvy culture—and that takes balance and judgment. It doesn't mean tolerating careless failures or encouraging failures in areas of your business where failure is not acceptable. Nor is it about celebrating failures that don't contribute to your organization's intelligence or capability. It is about acknowledging and respecting the potential of failure to reveal new knowledge and possibilities. In simple terms, you have to balance Six Sigma with Zero Stigma, simultaneously expecting excellence in performance while depersonalizing the failures you will inevitably encounter in pursuing ambitious objectives. Failure-savvy leaders know how to put failure to work in just these ways.

2. TAKE STOCK OF WHERE YOU ARE, BUT BEWARE

Nobody has a perfect organization. But wherever yours is with regard to its relationship with failure, better to acknowledge it before you embark on this journey.

Decide the True Risks Your Organization Faces

Fear of failure keeps most of us from trying new things. We don't want to fumble, stumble, or fall. We don't want to look foolish or be embarrassed, laughed at, or ridiculed. Nor do we want to sacrifice our credit rating, professional reputation, or job. But in our avoidance of the new or unknown, we amplify the risks of sticking with the old.

Let's say your organization is facing a potentially existential threat. It could be from a competitor who's developed a better product or business model, like Apple did to BlackBerry, Amazon did to bookstores, and Uber is doing to taxis. Maybe there's a new technology that fundamentally changes how people do things in your market, like craigslist and classified ads, cable and television, and Airbnb and hotels. Perhaps a new law or regulation threatens the foundation of your business, like deregulation did to Pan Am, TWA, and others. Fundamental shifts in demography or customer tastes can also have a severe impact on your business, as seen with JCPenney and The Sharper Image. Threats come in many forms, from many directions, and often in disguise.

Now ask yourself where the real risk lies. Is it in staying the course like Blockbuster and Polaroid did, or aggressively exploring new frontiers for your organization before it's too late? In other words, if fear of failure is causing you to cling too tightly to today's way of doing things, you may ultimately pay a far bigger price than the failures you will likely encounter in your search for tomorrow's business.

Frank Blake, the former CEO at Home Depot, captured this perfectly:

> There are parallel tracks carrying the fear of failure and the fear of being wrong. My experience is that leaders are very focused on being right. And as a colleague said to me a few years ago: If you want to be right 98% of the time, say "no." But what you miss in the 2% is what matters.[1]

Understand the Grip of the Status Quo: Foundation of Strength or Tar Pit?

The gravitational force of failure can guide you as well as ground you; that is, if you're willing to openly address it and incorporate it into your key decisions. You can use its power to unlock new possibilities for your organization. It has the ability to show you how to improve your thinking, create better options in your strategy, fix glitches in your product, and mend relations with your customers. We've said: *Failure is today's lesson for tomorrow.* But that lesson will be lost if you deny, defy, or trivialize failure in the first place.

Failure and the fear of failure have a very strong ally: the status quo. The status quo is powerful. After all, it's extremely important you do the best you can in running today's operations. It's familiar, but it has the unique ability to create a false sense of security for those inside it. In fact, if you are an executive trying to change your organization, you'd be better off to think of the status quo as the *static* quo, because that's the effect it has. It keeps your organization locked in the grip of today, at the expense of moving forcefully and confidently into tomorrow.

Stan the Dinosaur

Google is a modern poster child for innovation. Its Googleplex headquarters is loaded with examples of spontaneous, creative, and informal artifacts—from yurts and pink flamingos to thought-provoking articles routinely posted in the restrooms. When you visit, you'll also see Stan the dinosaur, a life-size replica of a T-Rex whose bones were found nearby. On the one hand, Stan makes for great eye candy. On the other hand, and more symbolically, he is a perfect reminder of how easy it can be for a once-mighty king of the world to become extinct. Google's campus, after all, is built on the former headquarters of a former Silicon Valley heavyweight, Silicon Graphics. If you want to know more, Google "Stan the dinosaur at Google."

Doubt this? Talk, as we have many times, to any executive who had the misfortune to preside over the demise of a once-strong company, and ask what should have been done differently. Chances are you'll hear regret that the organization hadn't acted sooner and more boldly to shake things up and overcome its fear of failure in embracing a different strategy or moving to a new position in its market. In fact, a 2014 study of hundreds of turnaround experts identified the two most frequent, serious causes of business crises: (1) continuing strategies that were no longer working, or (2) losing touch with markets and customers and thus not effectively adapting to changes.[2] No surprise there.

How can you avoid a similar fate? First of all, don't get overwhelmed by it. You are up against daunting forces, but leadership is an act of assertion in the face of those forces. Like a skilled practitioner of jujitsu, you can integrate those powerful forces into your own strategy and actions, ultimately emerging more nimble, stronger, and victorious.

3. FOCUS ON A FOUNDATION OF TRUST

When we spoke with Great Place to Work CEO China Gorman, she stressed that the most important ingredient of a great workplace is *trust*.

Imagine that! What employees really look for in a place they spend most of their adult lives is the feeling that they can be trusted and, in turn, can trust their leaders and colleagues. Easy enough to say, but apparently incredibly difficult for the vast majority of organizations to live up to.

Why does trust matter?

Trust matters because it has an immense impact on performance. Great Place to Work has shown that its award-winning companies routinely outperform their competition across measures that range from employee loyalty and voluntary turnover to financial performance and stock market returns.[3] From 1997 to 2013, publicly traded companies on the "Best Companies to Work For" list outperformed the overall stock market almost two to one.[4]

Trust matters to employee engagement. This goes well beyond typical measures of employee satisfaction. Committed employees are more likely to go the extra mile, recruit their best contacts as prospective hires, and talk up their companies in their other interactions. They personify the brands they work for and enhance their organization's visibility and reputation. Gallup has found similar results in its studies linking employee engagement and company performance.[5,6]

Trust and the Other F Word: Escaping, Embarking, and Employee Engagement

Trust doesn't excuse or make up for bad judgment, or even bad luck, but it can help cushion the blows every organization will absorb when failure happens. It can stiffen the resolve to rebound when things don't go as planned, and can help you to better harness the innate capabilities of the human talent available inside your organization.

Trust is at the core of the values you instill and exemplify across your organization, whether it's a Start-Up, Keep-Up, or Grown-Up enterprise in the business, public, or nonprofit sector. We're not talking about values you periodically post on the wall, your website, or your annual report, but the ones your people know in their gut. Those values are most often tested and defined by how you and your company deal with the other F word. Failure is the crucible in which those values are forged.

Consider for a moment when trust *really* matters. Here are two times when it is particularly important.

First is when you need help after you find yourself in a vulnerable situation, whether it's on a high-stakes sales call or trying to fix a problem on the manufacturing floor. You want to know you can count on your organization and fellow workers to help you *escape* from a mess.

Second is when you're *embarking* on a new and uncertain effort. You want to know that you'll be supported to improve the chances for success and backed up when you make key decisions en route to that objective. At these high-stress times, you want to know you will be treated honorably and fairly should things go sideways.

Both those situations—escaping and embarking—are directly tied to failure and how you handle it in your organization. If your workers feel alone and abandoned when they meet with failure, they are less likely to acknowledge those failures when they do occur, or willingly take on risky assignments. If they've seen your company scapegoat the individuals and teams involved in prior failures, they know what lesson to draw: Stay away from the other F word!

If colleagues about to start a high-risk initiative (e.g., a new product launch, a major strategic endeavor, installing a big new IT system, etc.) feel that they may not have your support if things get tough, they're likely to spend as much time looking over their shoulders as looking ahead. By simply not giving your people the confidence that you're behind them, you increase the riskiness of that project.

Too many organizations, perhaps yours included, embrace a *fail once and you're out* mindset; or so it seems to many employees. It's easy to celebrate the wins; what differentiates great places to work is how they demonstrate trust when the news is less rosy.

Escaping and embarking represent the outer edges of your day-to-day reality. But what about the in-between times—the everyday work that is more routine and predictable? What's the connection between trust and the other F word there?

This is the prime territory of everyday employee engagement. It determines how genuinely involved employees are with their jobs, careers, and organizational agendas. Unfortunately, the verdict here is nothing short of a condemnation of so many American workplaces and the cultural practices their leaders have created. You can avoid repeating their mistakes by focusing on the primary unit most employees deal with every day: the team.

Think of it like math. Without trust, at best you have individuals using addition, along with subtraction and division. In other words, the whole can be less than the sum of its parts. With trust, you can deploy multiplication and maybe even exponential math in your organization. That's what sets apart those "Great Places to Work" organizations from their counterparts in every industry. That's a key reason why they tend to outperform their peers in other ways as well, in the market and with customers.

4. TEAMS—YOUR CULTURE'S PROVING GROUND

Most leadership books focus on the vertical dimension of leadership, i.e., between leaders and followers. We suggest you look at leadership through the lens of where most work really gets done—in and by teams.

This is the horizontal axis of leadership: how your employees lead and support one another when you're not around. In other words, it's not about us and them, or leaders and followers, but how we lead, support, and inspire one another in our day-to-day activities. It's that elusive but transcendent team dimension that makes for distinctive organizational cultures and contributes to the results they produce.

Often the real culture that counts is not that of the umbrella organization but the day-to-day teams in which individuals interact with one another. We've all seen examples of how team culture may or may not reflect umbrella culture. Teams can corrode, complement, or reinforce organizational culture. In any case, they are important components of a failure-savvy leader's agenda.

There are probably as many clichés written about teams as about failure, so we're in dicey territory here. Even so, it's worth exploring because, although failure is a very personal experience, it often happens in team settings. This is a complicated dynamic, as it operates on so many different levels and plays out in so many different configurations.

We've all been on winning and losing teams. We know how one team member can let down, or even take down, the whole team. Conversely, we know what it's like when each member pulls her or his own weight and someone turns in a truly heroic or almost superhuman performance on the way to success.

The essentials are easy enough to recite: shared purpose, camaraderie, reciprocity, commitment, training, and skilled execution. But that's like listing the ingredients of a soufflé and assuming it will turn out just like the pictures in the magazine. So, let's cut to the chase. Just as we suggested that the major problem Grown-Up organizations have with the other F word is the appalling absence of genuine employee engagement, we note that a primary failing of many teams is the absence of real trust.

The Boston Consulting Group (BCG, another of *Fortune* magazine's "100 Great Places to Work") has thought a lot about this dimension of corporate performance. We talked to Rich Lesser, BCG's CEO, and Roselinde Torres, its partner in charge of global leadership practice. They talked about it this way:

> It's not just about top-down recognition, but whether you get peer-to-peer reinforcement when things get tough. People want to know their teammates will be there for [them]. We did a study called "Agile Adaptive Leadership Teams" to examine the link between team dynamics and business performance. The key factor? Whether people "felt like [their] team members have [their] back[s]." That contributed to greater willingness to express diverse opinions and take risks to advance the organization's agenda.[7]

Torres continued with the example of a large retail client who initiated a new leadership operating model to focus on this aspect of peer-to-peer support. Among the ten questions asked of its leadership team about each other were the following two, which we paraphrased here:

- Did Person X support me in a risk we were trying to take?
- Did Person X help me when we asked for funds to support this initiative?[8]

During the first year of this new model, the results were shared simply to drive awareness. The second year's results were used as a key input for individual performance assessments and compensation reviews, reinforcing the collegial support dimension of the company's cultural commitment.

Both Lesser and Torres emphasized the importance of stories, often more than formal metrics, as a powerful force to shape a more failure-savvy culture where innovation and experimentation are genuinely encouraged. Stories say it all. Who do companies make heroes of? Only individuals and teams with great successes? Or also those who participated in failures that proved significant steppingstones to future improvement?

5. METRICS THAT PROVE YOU'RE SERIOUS

"If you want to succeed, double your failure rate."[9]
—Tom Watson, former CEO of IBM

Most organizations, to use a common phrase, *measure what they treasure*. If you're serious about addressing the other F word in your company, you need to figure out appropriate metrics to demonstrate that failure savvy is a competency that matters to you. If you're going to tackle the fear of failure in your culture, you're going to have to attack it where it lives, and that's around people's fear that failure will cost them their livelihood. That means you need to incorporate failure, in a constructive way, into how you evaluate performance, individually and in teams, and make promotion and compensation decisions.

If your organization is not failing or recognizing failures as they occur, chances are it isn't learning new things, trying new solutions for the benefit of your customers and sponsors, or holding itself sufficiently accountable at all levels. This may be one of the few places where you actually do want to occasionally celebrate failure, not for its own sake but for what it taught your organization.

We are not suggesting you encourage failure per se, or that you tolerate it if it results from carelessness or incompetence. But establishing explicit metrics at the organizational and business-unit levels can help you liberate the power of the other F word as an ongoing resource to strengthen performance overall. Fundamentally, these metrics need to balance your organization's focus on execution of its current portfolio against its need for experimentation to improve and innovate for tomorrow.

We look at these as prototype *today-to-tomorrow* (T2T) metrics. They help you focus on the resources you're dedicating to executing *today's* business relative to those devoted to experimenting and exploring for *tomorrow's* (you might recall we introduced this concept in the questions we posed in Chapter 2). Jennifer Granholm, the former governor of Michigan, captured this T2T tension nicely. She suggested leaders think about the "trajectory" of their leadership tenure. "How do you strike the right balance between the quick wins and short-term things you can do with the longer-term legacy issues you should try to do? It's like that ancient proverb: Leaders have to be willing to plant trees under whose shade they know they will never sit."[10]

We know you probably have many different measures of how well your company is doing in various departments and areas, from sales and marketing to finance and human resources. You may well have performance dashboards and management systems to track those indicators; we've helped design those ourselves.

But when it comes to failure metrics, we're talking about a more fundamental set of data. This goes to the core of our premise. How well you manage the other F word is a significant strategic lever that affects the most important aspects of your business. We encourage you to test and develop measures around just three core questions, each of which reinforces the other:

1. **Trust: Do your people, on a basic level, actually trust one another and you?** This is the single most important indicator of whether yours is a "Great Place to Work." While it might be nice to have that kind of public recognition, that's not the real reason to focus on trust. It's because trust, like failure, is an essential accelerator to get to your real organizational objectives: higher levels of performance, increased competitive success, and longer-term viability. It can unlock the inherent potential of the people you already have working for you, and help you attract the talent you need to complement them going forward.

   If you're not getting the desired intensity of real employee engagement, look and listen here. If you don't feel the teams in your organization are genuinely delivering what they could, focus on trust and what you can do to help build it across your company. Trust doesn't come from the applause and high-fives you use to celebrate success. It's the hard currency you mint by how your company and colleagues handle failure.

   For examples, take a look at the Great Place to Work process, Gallup's employee engagement approach, or the instrument used in the

American Psychological Association's Center for Organizational Excellence reports for possible examples of trust-related metrics.

2. **Fear of failure: How afraid are your people to voice their real opinions, share their best ideas, and try out their notions to improve or transform your business?** If your company isn't getting the kind of improvements or innovations you want, look here. If your business is stagnating or stuck in neutral while your competitors are forging ahead, look here. Your problem may not be your people; it may be the culture of caution and compliance that is stifling their innate creativity and spirit of experimentation.

   You might use the "Failure-Savvy Leadership Profile" exercise in Chapter 2 and the "Aretha Challenge" questions in Chapter 9 to get you started.

3. **Customer enthusiasm: How willing are your customers to enthusiastically recommend your company to others?** You've all seen pictures of the lines of customers waiting outside Apple stores to get their hands on the newest "iThing." Even Apple's competitors use those images to try to differentiate their own offerings. What's keeping your company from generating comparable levels of intense loyalty?

   Chances are it's some combination of complacency, lack of imagination, or frustrated sense of experimentation that is compromising your own capability to design and deliver a comparably avid set of customers. You may need to strike a better balance between your desire for steady incremental improvement in your core business with your tolerance for the risk and failure required to leapfrog to a higher, preemptive level in your market.

   Take a look at the Net Promoter Score[11] methodology and its variants for ideas to focus on this critical dimension of your business.

This is not as easy as looking at the percentage of your budget devoted to research and development (R&D), since that is only one arena in which your organization may need experimentation. In many sectors, R&D investments may take too long to pay off, given your company's need for more rapid innovation.

Another complicating factor with failure metrics is they may represent different measurements and criteria across your various business units. For example, your manufacturing unit may want to have a very high T2T (today-to-tomorrow) ratio, reflecting its concentration on traditional operational improvement regimens like Six Sigma. But if your industry is characterized by rapid change in technology, regulation, or other strategic platforms, then your product development, sales, and marketing (not to mention your strategic planning and possible merger and acquisition units) might need to have a much lower T2T ratio.

In developing your own metrics, think of your organization—as we've suggested—not just in terms of its formal organizational chart but rather as a portfolio of "failure zones." For example, if your business involves activities with life-or-death consequences, then every zone should be focused on a zero-failure benchmark. In other circumstances, however, you may want to create a no-fault failure zone to encourage bold experimentation and unfettered creativity focused around the issues that may redefine and revitalize your future. Since failure itself usually ignores organizational boundaries, your metrics need to do the same.

This still requires an open environment where failure can be talked about freely, regardless of the particular T2T ratio or failure zone involved. As a leader, you simply want to make sure your approach to failure is as nuanced as the phenomenon you are trying to leverage.

SOME SIMPLE WAYS TO GET STARTED

So how do you get started? Here are a few very specific ideas that might jump-start your thinking:

- Consider requiring your strategy and product planning teams to include a "Failure Wisdom Report" to illustrate what previous failures taught you on the path to developing this plan, and outlining your fallbacks should it falter as well.
- Why not create a "Workaround Reward" for the team that develops an effective, practical improvement to some process that, despite how much you spent on its design and installation, actually got in the way of efficient work?
- Borrow a page from Sheri McCoy's team at Avon. They started a "Copy with Pride" award for employees who borrowed and deployed a successful idea originated in another department. Both the borrowing and originating departments get credit. As Sheri says, "I want to emphasize that we all work for Avon, not just one person or one department."[12]
- Or how about a "Failure Bounty" to encourage your employees and suppliers to flag product, process, or other failures *before* your customers

and users have to? After all, they are your front line and your allies. Why not enlist—and reward—their active involvement in anticipating and fixing failure-prone areas of your business? General Motors probably wishes they'd had a better system like this in advance of their latest ignition recall headaches.

The Great Catch Award

Every month Barnes-Jewish Hospital in Cleveland recognizes hospital team members who go above and beyond their usual responsibilities to prevent harm to patients. The recipients of these awards don't let go of a problematic situation until it is resolved, even if it affects care for just one patient, like the catering associate who noticed an unresponsive patient, and called for care just in time. By investigating where something might have gone wrong and collaborating with other team members, they save patients' lives. In addition to these monthly honors, annual Great Catch Award–winners are formally recognized in the hospital's annual report. In this way Barnes has made it a part of its culture to acknowledge that failure happens, and to recognize and support those employees who are extra diligent in helping address failure to save lives.[13]

What's all this have to do with innovation and success? It's the other side of the same coin. The more initiatives you launch, the more failures you'll likely create; but your real focus is on the innovation and performance agenda you need to advance. The more your employees get engaged in improvement and innovation, the better they understand your business, and the better your chances of noteworthy results.

These are practical ways you can engage the natural ingenuity in people across your organization. Together with the ideas, frameworks, and resources laid out earlier in our book, the actions we suggest in this chapter will accelerate your effectiveness as a failure-savvy leader, whether you are a corporate executive, entrepreneur, manager, or team member.

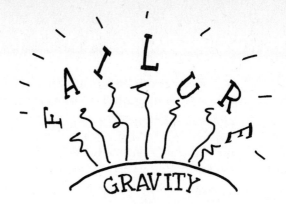

19 | Escape the Gravity of Failure: Leading the Fallible Organization

We named this book *The Other "F" Word* for a very simple reason: We want our readers to move the topic of failure from taboo to a regular focus of their leadership agenda. Our suggestions can help you turn your failures from unfortunate regrets into valuable resources.

The good news is, there are five additional powerful capabilities inside your organization—just on the other side of the other-F-word taboo—waiting to be liberated. As you become more failure-savvy, these five—honesty, curiosity, pride, humility, and engagement—can themselves become force multipliers for your leadership:

1. **Honesty:** Think how much wiser your decisions would be if you had the benefit of real candor from your colleagues. Rather than presiding

over meetings in which people are afraid to share their ideas, much less talk about the proverbial elephant in the room, develop a culture where productive conversations take place about projects and initiatives that failed. The meetings we profiled at Google, ONTRAPORT, and Twitter serve as helpful examples.

2. **Curiosity:** Imagine how invigorating it would be to hear new product, strategy, or business model ideas and questions bubbling up from your organization, rather than awaiting signals from on high. Face it, no single person in your organization —including you—is as smart or brings as much perspective as many people collaborating. Tap into that innate pool of insight and ideas, including your customers and partners, to create an atmosphere that invites learning from all sources. Recall how Instagram's founders leveraged their customer feedback to transform an overly complicated mobile app into a phenomenon.

3. **Pride:** Consider the hard-earned pride your team might derive not just from their successes, which are easy to celebrate, but from rebounding from an honest, best-efforts failure. That, one could argue, is an even greater accomplishment than succeeding with a low-risk pursuit. Henry Schein's employees know they can count on the same kind of all-hands-on-deck support their colleagues in London received should they ever need it in a pinch, just as Johnson & Johnson's employees still point with pride at how their company handled the Tylenol tampering crisis decades ago. But you don't need failures that dramatic to anchor your own culture's positive memory about how it has managed adversity.

4. **Humility:** Accept the irony that your fallibility is the foundation of the very kind of trust you and your colleagues are looking for. We understand this doesn't come naturally to some of you, and we appreciate that leaders have to demonstrate self-confidence, especially in times of crisis. But admitting and even poking fun at some of your own failures can send a strong signal throughout your organization that it can be okay to fail, as long as you learn something constructive in the process and don't use failure as an excuse for otherwise poor performance or lower expectations. Indiegogo's Danae Ringelmann shared how she processes failures and includes her team in the debriefing process, as did Chris Michel with his various venture teams.

5. **Engagement:** Envision your employees as willing to dedicate greater effort to your mission once they feel more connected to it, inspired by it, and freer to contribute to it without fear of recrimination or ridicule if they fail occasionally despite their best efforts. That depends on mutual trust. Take a look at some of the key characteristics of those small, medium, and big "Great Places to Work"—firms like the Mayo Clinic,

REI, USAA, Genentech, and American Express—and you will see time and again the value employees place on being trusted, respected, and acknowledged.

Each of these resources is often stifled in organizations whose cultures have not yet unlocked the positive potential of failure. Their impact goes far beyond the actual learning from a specific failure. In a sense, they are the real bonuses you can capture by moving your organization to a more mature and savvy level of failure management.

To do that, you need to understand your own attitudes about the other F word. You need to be candid with your colleagues about the failures you've encountered, if you want to earn their trust and support. In that sense, acknowledging failure can be an act of confident humility. Far from being a sign of weakness, it simply recognizes the reality that you and the organization you lead are fallible. You don't have all the answers and, often, you are making decisions in the face of the unknown. That doesn't make you ignorant; it just makes you human.

Open a genuine conversation about failure in your organization. Be willing to separate the failure from the person, since the most valuable failures are not those caused by incompetence or inattention, but those that result from the best efforts of smart, talented people testing the limits of your organization's thinking, knowledge, and resources. The fact that they may not have succeeded in the ways you and they had hoped is unfortunate, but it also can help you make better decisions the next time around.

Failure is one strategic resource you and your team create every day. It has the power to teach you what to do and not to do next. After all, you've already paid the tuition. You might as well get the education that goes with it.

Afterword

By China Gorman
CEO, Great Place to Work Institute

Our mission at Great Place to Work is in our name: helping leaders turn their organizations into places where their employees are proud to work. We've studied this issue for more than 25 years, and survey millions of employees in thousands of workplaces around the world every year.

If we had to distill our insights into a single word, that word without doubt would be "trust." It's the single most important ingredient that characterizes a great place to work—trust between colleagues across the organization, and trust between employees and their leaders.

Yet trust, while easy to talk about, is often elusive. It can be hard to build and easy to lose. That's where failure and how organizations deal with it become so important. In most settings, it's failure that tests the bonds and boundaries of real trust. Do my team members have my back when things go bad? Do my managers accept honest mistakes as a part of doing business without blaming or scapegoating those involved? Can my organization accommodate the risks involved in becoming more innovative?

Trust is as interconnected as innovation is with failure. Both require risk and a willingness to constantly challenge and strengthen the prevailing culture of the organization.

That's why my colleagues and I were happy to connect with John Danner and Mark Coopersmith during their research on this book, and I'm honored to write this afterword. As you've read, these authors have shown how we can create a more open and productive relationship with failure—not as an end unto itself, but as a key lever to improve performance. Their pioneering, seven-stage Failure Value Cycle is just one of the many practical tools here that can help teams and leaders at all phases of an organization's life. They show how to turn "the other F word" to your advantage—encouraging real innovation, tapping employee creativity, and strengthening genuine commitment. These performance drivers complement trust in delivering competitive superiority.

With the publication of *The Other "F" Word*, smart leaders now have an essential resource to help anchor trust throughout their organizations when it can matter most: during the tough times, when dealing with a failed project, product, or strategy. I look forward to learning more from Danner and Coopersmith's ongoing work in this frontier, and how it can benefit companies striving to create the next generation of Great Places to Work.

—China Gorman

Appendix
Our Classrooms:
Putting Failure
to Work in
Creating Value

As you know, both of us teach several courses at UC Berkeley's Haas School of Business, while also anchoring various leadership education programs for U.S. and international executives. Berkeley-Haas has a significant but simple mission: developing leaders who redefine how we do business. Our campus cherishes its tradition of independent thinking, discovery, and dynamism on many levels, both in and out of the classroom and research labs. Against that background, Dean Rich Lyons has centered the school's approach around four defining principles:

1. **Question the status quo:** It doesn't get more Berkeley than that
2. **Confidence without attitude:** We want our students to be effective collaborators as well as leaders
3. **Students always:** Our invitation to continued curiosity and humility
4. **Beyond yourself:** We hope our graduates produce not just shareholder but societal value

Our classes deal with innovation, leadership, entre- and intrapreneurship, and strategy. But regardless of their focus, failure and fear of it play significant roles in all these arenas. We thought some of you might be interested in how we teach about that interplay. Here's a profile of two of our classes, our "Workshop for Startups" and our "Other F Word" course, which gave this book its title.

"WORKSHOP FOR STARTUPS": PRESSURE-TESTING NEW VENTURE CONCEPTS

Before they open on Broadway, many shows do trial openings elsewhere. Not to pick on our friends at Yale, but many productions, for some reason, choose New Haven as their proving ground. This is where they rewrite scripts, modify staging details, and even change cast members. Soft openings are also frequent with new restaurants, which invite informal groups of friends and contacts to try things out—providing the restaurant time to work out menus, procedures, and ambience before its official debut. Similarly, movie producers run audience tests to finalize storylines and even endings for their films. And, generals and admirals conduct elaborate war games to pressure-test military strategy and readiness.

So the idea of "off-off Broadway" testing before launching big-time is not new. We use a similar philosophy in the "Workshop for Startups" course we launched a dozen years ago. We want potential entrepreneurs to have lots of opportunities to test, fail, and refine their ideas while they're in graduate school classrooms *before* they decide whether to make the personal, financial, and career commitment to actually launch a new venture.

Launching a venture is never easy. Nor does it lend itself to simple formulas or frameworks. Despite the use of quasi-scientific language like *hypothesis-testing* or *evidence-based entrepreneurship*, it's much more art than science, with a lot of hard work and luck required. There are just too many variables at play to create anything like the controlled environment of a real laboratory. The truth is, nobody really knows how to evaluate whether a particular idea in the hands of a particular team will become a huge, or even modest, success in the marketplace. Despite all the planning, detailed analysis, hard work, and tenacity devoted by startup teams, most will fail. That's true even for ventures hand-picked by seasoned and sophisticated venture-capital firms.

That's why we approach our workshop class with humility, fully aware of the daunting and unpredictable path that lies ahead for our would-be entrepreneurs. We don't require students to prepare elaborate business plans with complicated spreadsheets showing hockey-stick growth curves. While well-thought-out business plans can help crystallize a team's go-to-market strategy and business model—and also align members around that game plan—they remain largely works of fiction that rarely survive contact with real customers.

We'd rather have our students create basic prototypes or demos of the products or services they intend to offer a skeptical market. By taking their concepts out of the classroom and talking to potential users and customers early, they get firsthand intelligence about the market and likely competitors.

Therefore, our workshop centers on a series of weekly informal test-show-critique-refine cycles, in which student teams regularly present in-progress reports on the important elements of their venture strategy, each one grounded in focused analysis and/or real-world explorations. For example, one cycle might require students to storyboard their customer's user experience or develop a simple prototype of the product they have in mind. This forces them to identify key features and potential challenges associated with converting their idea into a physical or technological form. Other times, students might be challenged to create a video demonstrating how the proposed product solves a problem or meets a need. Another cycle might focus on refining their pitch based on close observation and listening to potential customers instead of relying on Internet research.

Each cycle involves "stand-and-deliver" presentations, which are candidly but constructively critiqued by the students' colleagues in class, each of whom understands that the collaborative goal is to maximize everyone's chances of success. This is a variant of the grand rounds that medical residents go through, complete with intensive reviews by peers and instructors.

We start each class with lightning-round summaries of key developments from the previous week. Periodically we hand out "Aha!" and "Oh, shit!" cards that describe actual moments of serendipity and disasters that their predecessors have experienced, asking students to reflect on how their teams would respond in similar situations.

In addition to developing their own venture ideas, each student acts as a consultant to another venture in class. In that role, they are expected to offer more detailed advice to help another team's efforts during the semester, exposing them in more depth to at least one other venture.

Many of our students actually launch their businesses, and some beat the odds in the process. The co-founders of Timbre Technologies met in this class, when one was a PhD candidate in computer sciences and the other an experienced venture capitalist. They went on to launch and then sell a venture that improved the efficiency of computer chip design. Two other classmates developed the idea for Indiegogo, which has become one of the largest crowdfunding platforms in the world. TubeMogul went from an idea about monitoring the exploding world of online video to a successful IPO as a digital media and marketing firm. Others have launched enterprises to change how we buy houses online, negotiate for used cars, design clothing for gay consumers, create super-thin batteries, develop a new approach to cancer research and treatment, and design a better breast pump for nursing mothers. And they are not alone.

Patrick Awuah used this class to refine his idea for Ashesi University in Ghana, which has now become one of Africa's most respected institutions for higher education. Priya Haji, Siddharth Sanghvi, and their colleagues crafted the early plans for World of Good, a global marketplace for products native to developing countries, before launching what is now part of eBay. Carlos Orellana, working with his partner who was moonlighting from his investment banking job, hatched the idea for SalaUno, which now offers affordable cataract surgery to eye patients in Mexico City.

It's a hard class in the middle of an intense MBA curriculum, definitely not for window shoppers. For admission, we require that students commit to at least trying their ideas for new ventures and candidly sharing their ideas and experiences.

Our philosophy with this course is very simple: Don't postpone early opportunities to fail. Every startup fails at something; some failures are fatal, but most are valuable and survivable. We want our workshop students to squeeze as much risk out of their ideas as possible before they have to make the really big commitments to actually launch a venture. Our class is certainly no guarantee of success, but it provides aspiring entrepreneurs with a real-life laboratory in which to test core assumptions, develop understandable prototypes, and refine pitches to both investors and customers.

We don't care how rough their performances are when they start our class. We just want to make sure they are more ready for showtime when they leave it.

OUR "OTHER F WORD" COURSE

If you're serious about innovation or entrepreneurship, you need to be ready to tango with the other F word. That's what we help our MBA students do in our Berkeley course officially titled "Failure and Its Importance to Innovation and Entrepreneurship," better known by its nickname, "The Other F Word."

John has the rare privilege of teaching at two of the world's finest universities. Every fall, he and his wife migrate eastward for his semester at Princeton, where he teaches courses on entrepreneurship and innovation. It was there that the idea for a course about failure originated, with a pilot session before an overflow audience of high-achieving students eager to talk about failure.

When he returned to Berkeley, he broached the idea for an experimental MBA course on the other F word with Dean Rich Lyons. In light of those four defining principles we mentioned initially, Rich was an easy sell. He gave us the green light to launch the course during the next academic year, and we were off and running.

Most of you know that the tried and true curriculum at many business schools is case-based. This approach centers on in-depth, after-the-fact examination of specific organizations and leaders dealing with specific thorny issues in various circumstances. Cases give students a vicarious opportunity to consider how they might react in those settings, and to challenge one another in the search for the most effective decision or strategy. It makes for intense discussions as they step into the drama of the case, frequently adopting the protagonists' roles, much like taking on roles in a play.

As useful as these simulations can be, most of us learn best through direct personal experience. We need to make our own mistakes—even when we know better. Most of the colossal mistakes made by respected, established organizations—sometimes on the advice of comparably respected, established consulting firms—are made by highly trained professionals who graduated from the best schools, including ours.

Vicarious education has its limits, if we faculty are honest enough to admit it. That is particularly true around a topic as personal as the other F word. That's why we decided to take a different approach to our experimental course on failure. We thought you might be interested in understanding how we did this and what we learned in the process.

The first class had several dozen MBA students, from all kinds of backgrounds and countries. When they arrived for the first session, we began by sharing with them our "un-resumes." Those included some of the setbacks, mistakes, disappointments, and failures that accompany most careers. We felt it was only right, if we wanted to have an honest and collaborative classroom, to begin by acknowledging our own experiences with the other F word. It's an unusual start for a class at a prestigious business school, used to what we call "résumé drag racing"—but it set the right tone.

In each session, we look at iconic business failure examples through the lens of the Failure Value Cycle. We complement those retrospectives with examination of late-breaking current failure scenarios across the business landscape.

Next we asked them to *draw* their views of failure. We saw pictures of dark pits, mountain-climbing paths, fiery explosions, mazes, logic trees, and engineering flow charts—a visual kaleidoscope of failure. Many students talked about the loneliness that often accompanies failure, not to mention ostracism by colleagues. That, in turn, reinforced a sense of personal and professional embarrassment that made it difficult to talk about failure and the circumstances surrounding it. We explored the difficulties those issues pose for managers and leaders to create an environment in which employees feel comfortable enough to talk about failure, and then establish a culture of inquiry that facilitates pragmatic learning from it.

Other students viewed failure in a more positive light. The images they drew were of bridges (from ignorance to insight), rites of passage to new understanding, and even badges of honor attesting to their fortitude in weathering past challenges. Those images, in turn, opened up conversations about the difficulty leaders have in presenting failure as the necessary companion to serious innovation.

It's almost as if failure had both magnetic poles. On the one side, students recognized intellectually the positive pull of failure as necessary to discovery and learning. On the other side, the psychological, emotional, and professional impacts of failure had an opposite effect, pushing us away from a desire to re-encounter the experience, think carefully about it, and openly discuss it.

An Intellectual Scout for Everyone

We also asked each student to act as an intellectual scout on behalf of the whole class. This assignment involved outside research across different disciplines such as engineering, architecture, and science, in addition to personal interviews with senior executives about their leadership experiences dealing with the other F word. Their choice of interviewees ran the gamut, including corporate executives, government officials, athletes, academics, investors, and nonprofit leaders. The diversity of choices sparked interesting and wide-ranging discussion. In our final class, one student who had read about innovation in the context of science and the scientific method, shared how language plays a really important part in shaping our attitudes about failure and its relationship to innovation and learning.

She noted that most businesses talk in terms of strategies, projects, products, markets, and transactions. When these fail, those involved distance themselves as quickly as possible. But if we used the term "experiment" for those activities, we probably would expect a certain number of negative outcomes to go along with them. The class nodded their heads in agreement, struck by the different expectations triggered by just that word "experiment." It was an *Aha!* insight. The language of experimentation anticipates both negative and positive outcomes. Experiments beget failure on the way to discovery.

After all, what are all strategies, projects, and other organizational initiatives if not experiments? They are all assertions founded on supposition and usually imperfect analysis, regardless of how confidently they are communicated. They are full of untested assumptions, but the language leaders tend to surround them with, not to mention the metrics used to measure them, connote failure as unlikely, off-limits, or hardly worth noticing.

Failure Journals: Making It Personal

The students' third assignment was to keep a handwritten journal to capture their thoughts about failure during the semester. This was not intended to be an intimate diary, but rather an old-fashioned way for them to keep track of how their thinking about and awareness of failure evolved. To give you a feel for the kinds of postings, here are a few anonymous examples (paraphrased for brevity):

- "Funny how failure sometimes makes people make things worse for themselves . . . I guess the stress of failure is so all-encompassing that it acts to momentarily blind people from looking at the long term . . . I came to see how failure can become a self-fulfilling cycle."
- "Failure might be defined as 'losing' but in reality, it's never that black or white."
- "Is a failure more heart-breaking if you know you won't have a chance to redeem yourself?"

A fairly common conclusion was the increased awareness of both the ubiquity and complexity of this failure issue, and the intensity with which it is felt and avoided. Students discovered failures in unexpected places and found themselves trying to develop their own consistent framework for coping with it.

Go Fail

On the theory that each of us is an expert in failure, but none of us probably knows as much as we should about it, we asked students to pick an activity at which they would be highly likely to fail. Nothing life-threatening or too dangerous, but nonetheless challenging, at least, to one's ego and comfort level. Between classes, they were to embark on this challenge and then summarize lessons learned for later discussion.

Again, creativity ruled. Students changed their diets, pursued athletic endeavors like rock climbing or skiing, or tried a completely alien skill like an unusual language or computer programming. The results? There was a lot of failure to be sure; but even more insights from the experience of consciously embarking on a high-failure initiative. There were also more than a few surprises when students actually succeeded in their endeavors. As one student put it: "The satisfaction [of doing better than expected] as I walked out . . . was not quite as extreme as the fear I felt walking in, but it was close."

So what have we (and more importantly our students) gained from these classes? To be sure, a deepened appreciation for the subtlety, ubiquity, and importance of the other F word in both professional and personal settings. As much as we might like to think of ourselves as intrepid adventurers or creative thinkers, the default for most of us is much less exciting and noble. We like our comfort zones, thank you very much.

That may be the most important insight of all for a leader. Because innovation, competition, ambition, and aspiration all require discomfort—in how we think, what we do, and how we do it. Shaking loose from our organizational and personal comfort zone is no easy task. That's why we say failure's biggest ally is the status quo.

Acknowledgments

We wrote this book as much to satisfy our own curiosity as the requests of our audiences, clients, and students. Throughout our careers, both of us have been struck by how often organizations staffed with intelligent professionals, supported by adequate funding, and led by capable men and women simply fail to achieve their fundamental mission, or worse, fail outright.

Having worked in very large and very small organizations, we understand the dynamics that can compromise a company's focus and dedication to that mission. But we sense that there is something far more basic going on. Organizations, their leaders and people, have difficulty dealing with failure and overcoming the fear of failure—and that, in turn, stifles initiative, creativity, and engagement.

At times, finishing this book began to feel like trying to escape the very metaphor we've used to explain the other F word: gravity. On the one hand, the gravitational pull of our topic kept moving us forward, from issue to issue, example to example. But on the other, as our evenings and weekends with our families and friends evaporated amidst the book's rough drafts and research, it felt at times as if we were in our own version of a black hole, unsure we would escape.

But escape we did, with a book we hope will repay both you and us for the time we've each spent with it. Getting here has been the result of help we received from many quarters. We offer profound thanks to our family, friends, colleagues, and complete strangers. There are too many to list them all by name, but let us thank a few on behalf of those many: First, we thank our wives, Peach and Lori, whose love, support, and patience remained steadfast despite our countless hours collaborating and upending our homes and routines.

Second, we thank our kids—Eliot, Chris, Will, Ali, and Matt—who were curious and amused enough about what their dads were doing to accommodate us and, more importantly, share their ideas and enthusiasm. As did other members of our families, including Alice Coopersmith Furst; and Bry, Bill, and Katharine Danner.

Third, we thank our friends like Guy Kawasaki, Eli Noyes, Georgia Nelson, Tom Higgins, Jim Mitchell, Jennifer Granholm, Jim and Gigi Goldman, Laura Melendy, Jeff Rosenthal, and many others, who were all generous with their ideas, time, and connections to help us at critical points. Two special, posthumous thank-yous to Michael Cronan, muse on many matters; and Warren Bennis, who was so encouraging when John first mentioned this book idea more than a decade ago.

Colleagues from both UC Berkeley and Princeton, as well as elsewhere, contributed critical thinking and suggestions, not to mention patient flexibility in juggling teaching duties, that helped shape the book you've read. At Berkeley, they include Whitney Hischier, Dan Mulhern, Clark Kellogg, Greg Le Blanc, Andre Marquis and our colleagues at the Lester Center for Entrepreneurship, and others. Also thanks to Dean Rich Lyons and the Berkeley-Haas staff for supporting our "Other F Word" pilot course when it was just a gleam in our eyes. At Princeton, Ed Zschau, Derek Lidow, and Chris Kuenne were steadfast supporters, as were John's colleagues at The Keller Center. People like Jodi Hendry, Dana Baker-Williams, and Elizabeth Saunders gave us crucial help at various stages.

Our students on both campuses sharpened our thinking in ways only upstart students can, and many of them will see the results of their independent perspectives in these pages. It's why we love teaching as part of our professional portfolios.

At John Wiley & Sons, Shannon Vargo and Elizabeth Gildea have been our partners from start to finish, with Deborah Schindlar as our expert production editor. We tapped John Kador's pre-publication experience early on, as well as that of our agent, John Willig. Carolyn Monaco, Alicia Simons, and Jill Totenberg have helped orient us to the after-publication world, which we are delighted to now enter as published authors rather than aspiring writers.

Finally, each of us owes an incalculable debt to our fathers, who introduced us to the world of important ideas, questioning, and experimentation. We think they'd be as proud of this book as we are.

About the Authors

John Danner is a thought leader, trusted advisor, and respected teacher at the intersection of leadership, innovation, strategy, and entrepreneurship. For more than four decades, he has helped senior business, nonprofit, and government executives navigate rapidly changing environments like high-tech, healthcare, energy, financial services, and consumer products.

John is a sought-after advisor to Fortune 500 enterprises, mid-market businesses, and emerging ventures worldwide. He co-founded a widely read national business newspaper in healthcare. He has held senior-level state and federal positions, working for then-Governor Bill Clinton and the first U.S. Secretary of Education. At Morrison & Foerster, he represented major legal clients in telecommunications, real estate, energy, and investment banking.

He teaches at two of the nation's finest universities: the University of California Berkeley and Princeton University, in addition to anchoring executive education programs on five continents, including Aspen Institute leadership seminars.

John's media coverage includes the *New York Times, The Economist,* and the *Los Angeles Times.* He created the idea for TED U[niversity], and is a popular keynote speaker for executive and industry audiences globally.

He earned JD, MPH, and MAEd degrees at UC Berkeley, and his BA from Harvard. For more information, visit JohnDanner.com.

* * *

Mark Coopersmith is a seasoned corporate executive, successful entrepreneur, and sought-after advisor and teacher. He has spent more than 25 years leading businesses at the convergence of technology, media, and brands.

As a Senior Fellow at the Haas School of Business at UC Berkeley, he is an award-winning teacher of innovation and entrepreneurship. Mark also leads executive education and distance learning programs for executives around the world.

Mark advises companies ranging from global enterprises to early stage ventures, and is an active board member. He founded and built a significant new business unit for Sony, was founding CEO of online payments pioneer WebOrder (now part of Google), and led the $350M Global Technology Brands group at Newell Rubbermaid. Previously he was a strategy and M&A consultant for Ernst & Young.

Mark is an in-demand speaker and advisor who focuses on leadership, innovation, entrepreneurship, and growth. He has been featured in the *New York Times, The Economist,* CNN, Fox News, *NPR, Huffington Post,* and *USA Today.*

Mark earned his MBA and BA degrees at UC Berkeley. For more, visit MarkCoopersmith.com.

Notes

CHAPTER 1: What's in It for Me? Your Personal Guided Book Tour

1. For those of you unfamiliar with *Dilbert*, it's a satirical cartoon strip by Scott Adams that pokes fun at the foibles of everyday office life—with officious managers, clueless workers, and meaningless agendas.
2. Jim Collins, *Good to Great* (New York: HarperCollins, 2001).
3. Clayton Christensen, *The Innovator's Dilemma* (New York: Harper-Collins, 2003).
4. Clayton M. Christensen and Michael E. Raynor, *The Innovator's Solution: Creating and Sustaining Successful Growth* (Boston: Harvard Business School Press, 2003).

CHAPTER 2: The Other F Word: "Failure" Is Such a Loaded Word

1. Drawn in part from: *failure*. http://www.thesaurus.com/browse/failure?s=t (accessed November 1, 2014).

CHAPTER 3: The Gravity of Failure and Failure's Gravity

1. Pamela Engel, "Small Business Owners Don't Fear the Devastatingly High Failure Rate," *Business Insider*, June 5, 2013, http://www.businessinsider.com/small-business-owners-are-optimistic-2013-6.
2. Deborah Gage, "The Venture Capital Secret: 3 out of 4 Start-Ups Fail," *Wall Street Journal*, September 20, 2012, http://online.wsj.com/news/articles/SB10000872396390443720204578004980476429190?mg=ren

064-wsj&url=http%3A%2F%2Fonline.wsj.com%2Farticle%2FSB10000
8723963904437202045780049804 76429190.html.

3. John Hagel, III, John Seely Brown, Tamara Samoylova, and Matt Frost, "The Burdens of the Past," *Deloitte University Press*, November 11, 2013, http://dupress.com/articles/the-burdens-of-the-past/.

4. Ray B. Williams, "Why Every CEO Needs a Coach," *Psychology Today*, August 13, 2012, http://www.psychologytoday.com/blog/wired-success/201208/why-every-ceo-needs-coach.

5. Laurie Burkitt, "Brand Flops: Ford, GE, Coca-Cola Know Hype Can Hurt New Products," *Forbes*, March 31, 2010, http://www.forbes.com/2010/03/31/brand-flops-apple-ford-pepsi-coors-cmo-network-brand-fail.html.

6. Timothy J. Galpin and Mark Herndon, *The Complete Guide to Mergers & Acquisitions* (San Francisco: Jossey-Bass, 2007).

7. Andrew Greenberg, "Hiring for Attitude: Why 81% of New Hires Will Fail," Recruiting Division, April 23, 2014, http://www.recruitingdivision.com/why-new-hires-fail/.

8. Gallup, Inc., *The State of the American Workplace* (Washington, DC: Gallup, Inc., 2013).

9. Dave Chaffey, "Display Advertising Clickthrough Rates," Smart Insights, November 13, 2013, http://www.smartinsights.com/internet-advertising/internet-advertising-analytics/display-advertising-clickthrough-rates/.

10. "Avoiding the Inventor's Lament," *BloombergBusinessweek*, November 9, 2005, http://www.businessweek.com/stories/2005-11-09/avoiding-the-inventors-lament.

11. Michael Krigsman, "Study: 68 Percent of IT Projects Fail," ZDNet, December 11, 2008, http://www.zdnet.com/blog/projectfailures/study-68-percent-of-it-projects-fail/1175.

12. The Standish Group, *CHAOS Summary*, 2009, http://www.portal.state.pa.us/portal/server.pt/document/standish_group_chaos_summary_2009_pdf (accessed November 6, 2014).

13. Dan Hurley, Divorce Rate: It's Not as High as You Think, *New York Times*, April 19, 2005, http://www.nytimes.com/2005/04/19/health/19divo.html?_r=0.

14. National Basketball Association, "Michael Jordan," *NBA Encyclopedia, Playoff Edition*. http://www.nba.com/history/players/jordan_stats.html (accessed November 24, 2014).

15. Major League Baseball, "Ty Cobb Career Stats," MLB.com, http://mlb.mlb.com/team/player.jsp?player_id=112431#gameType=%27R%27 (accessed November 24, 2014).

16. National Hockey League, "Wayne Gretzky," NHL.com, http://www
.nhl.com/ice/player.htm?id=8447400 (accessed November 24, 2014).

17. Richard Wiseman, "The New Year's Resolution Experiment,"
Quirkology, 2007, http://www.quirkology.com/UK/Experiment_resolution
.shtml.

18. Barnard Schutz, *Gravity from the Ground Up: An Introductory Guide to Gravity
and General Relativity* (Cambridge, UK: Cambridge University Press, 2003).

CHAPTER 4: Defining Failure: Mistakes and Unwelcome Outcomes That Matter

1. Oxford Dictionaries, "Failure," Oxford Dictionaries online, http://www
.oxforddictionaries.com/us/definition/american_english/failure (accessed
October 28, 2014).

2. BrainyQuote, "Jean Giraudoux Quotes," http://www.brainyquote
.com/quotes/authors/j/jean_giraudoux.html (accessed November 25,
2014).

3. Author conversation with Guy Kawasaki.

4. Author's note (John): I first mentioned the idea for this book to Warren
during a seminar at the Aspen Institute. His enthusiasm for it was a key
reason I kept working on this topic in the years since.

5. Joel Kurtzman, "An Interview with Warren Bennis," *Strategy+Business*,
no. 8 (July 1997).

6. Warren Bennis, "The 4 Competencies of Leadership," *Training and
Development Journal* 38, no. 8 (August 1984): 14–19.

7. Author conversation with Bryan Roberts.

8. Author conversation with Kef Kasdin.

9. Author conversation with Bob King.

10. Author conversation with Michael Hinshaw.

11. Author conversation with Jennifer Granholm.

12. Author conversation with Michael Sippey.

13. For more on Henry Chesbrough's Open Innovation, we recommend
several of his books: *Open Business Models: How to Thrive in the New
Innovation Landscape* (Boston: Harvard Business School Press, 2006); *Open
Innovation: Researching a New Paradigm* (New York: Oxford University
Press, 2008); *Open Innovation: The New Imperative for Creating and Profiting
from Technology* (Boston: Harvard Business School Press, 2006); and *Open
Services Innovation: Rethinking Your Business to Grow and Compete in a New
Era* (San Francisco: Jossey-Bass, 2011).

14. Author conversation with Henry Chesbrough.

15. George Hurdalek, Howard Lindsay, Russel Crouse, and Ernest Lehman. *The Sound of Music*. Directed by Robert Wise. Performed by Julie Andrews. 1965.
16. WD-40 Company, "WD-40 FAQs," http://wd40.com/faqs (accessed October 27, 2014).
17. Tom Cheshire, "In Depth: How Rovio Made Angry Birds a Winner (and what's next)," *Wired*, March 7, 2011, http://www.wired.co.uk/magazine/archive/2011/04/features/how-rovio-made-angry-birds-a-winner.
18. *Merriam-Webster Dictionary*, "Snafu," http://www.merriam-webster.com/dictionary/snafu (accessed November 24, 2014).
19. Nassim Nicholas Taleb, *Fooled by Randomness* (New York: Random House, 2004).
20. "Value-killer losses" are those losses of company value that are 20 percent or greater relative to changes in the MSCI All Country World Index within the same one-month period. This study updated Deloitte's 2005 report, "Disarming the Value Killers," which documented the devastation of value caused by the earlier array of black-swan events (e.g., savings-and-loan crisis of the 1980s, Asian financial crisis, dot-com bubble burst, post-9/11 economic downturn, accounting frauds, etc.).
21. "The Value Killers Revisited: A Risk Management Study," Deloitte LLP, 2014.

CHAPTER 5: Fear and Memory: Failure's Force Multipliers

1. John Gardner, an influential American leader, author, and thinker, nailed this point.
2. Stanley Coopersmith, "Implications on Studies of Self-Esteem for Educational Research and Practice," paper presented at American Educational Research Association, Los Angeles, February 6, 1969.
3. Angie LeVan, "The F Word (and the C Word)," *Psychology Today*, January 13, 2011, http://www.psychologytoday.com/blog/flourish/201101/the-f-word-and-the-c-word (accessed November 26, 2014).
4. Mark Twain, *The Tragedy of Pudd'nhead Wilson*, http://www.gutenberg.org/files/102/102-h/102-h.htm#link2HCH0012 (accessed October 29, 2012).
5. Author conversation with Rich Lyons.
6. Andy Grove, *Only the Paranoid Survive: How to Exploit the Crisis Points That Challenge Every Company* (New York: Crown Business, 1999).

7. Author conversation with Randy Komisar. Komisar further investigated this sentiment of learning from failure in his book *Getting to Plan B, Breaking Through to a Better Business Model* (Boston: Harvard Business Press, 2009).

8. Author conversation with Joe Kraus.

9. Paul Rozin and Edward B. Royzman, "Negativity Bias, Negativity Dominance, and Contagion," *Personality and Social Psychology Review* 5 (November, 2001): 296–320.

10. Daniel Kahneman, "The Riddle of Experience vs. Memory," TED Talk, February 2010. http://www.ted.com/talks/daniel_kahneman_the_riddle_of_experience_vs_memory.

11. John Kremer, Aidan Moran, Graham Walker, and Cathy Craig. *Key Concepts in Sport Psychology* (London: SAGE Publications Ltd., 2012).

12. D. E. Conroy, "Fear of Failure: An Exemplar for Social Development Research in Sport," *Quest*, no. 53 (2001): 165-183.

CHAPTER 6: Start-Ups: Launching Your Venture in the Land of Failure

1. Lim Yung-Hui, "Inspiring Insights by Instagram CEO Kevin Systrom, the Man Who Built a $1 Billion Startup," *Forbes*, April 9, 2012, http://www.forbes.com/sites/limyunghui/2012/04/09/inspiring-insights-by-instagram-ceo-kevin-systrom-the-man-who-built-a-1-billion-startup/.

2. U.S. Small Business Administration, "Frequently Asked Questions," SBA.gov, September 2012, http://www.sba.gov/sites/default/files/FAQ_Sept_2012.pdf.

3. Fundable, "Startup Funding Infographic," Fundable.com, https://www.fundable.com/learn/resources/infographics/startup-funding-infographic (accessed November 10, 2014).

4. Ibid.

5. U.S. Census Bureau, Table 764, 2012, https://www.census.gov/compendia/statab/2012/tables/12s0764.pdf (accessed November 1, 2014).

6. Fundable, "Startup Funding Infographic."

7. Ibid.

8. Dane Stangler, *Infographic: Kauffman Index of Entrepreneurial Activity, 1996-2013*, April 9, 2014, http://www.kauffman.org/multimedia/infographics/2014/infographic-kauffman-index-of-entrepreneurial-activity-1996-2013.

9. Rip Empson, "Silicon Valley, London, NYC: Startup Genome Data Reveals How the World's Top Tech Hubs Stack Up," TechCrunch.com, April 10, 2012, http://techcrunch.com/2012/04/10/startup-genome-compares-top-startup-hubs/.

10. Moya K. Mason, "Worldwide Business Startups," Moya K. website, 2014, http://www.moyak.com/papers/business-startups-entrepreneurs.html.
11. Ibid.
12. José Ernesto Amorós and Niels Bosma, "2013 Global Report," *Global Entrepreneurship Monitor*, 2014, http://www.gemconsortium.org/docs/download/3106 (accessed November 1, 2014).
13. Ibid.
14. Melissa Tsang, "When Startups Fail: 12 Founders, and Advice Moving Forward," *Referral Candy* (blog), July 8, 2014, http://blog.referralcandy.com/2014/07/08/when-startups-fail-12-founders-and-advice-moving-forward/.
15. Louis Rheaume, "Why Startups Fail," TechVibes infographic, June 18, 2012, http://www.techvibes.com/blog/why-92-of-startups-fail-infographic-2012-06-18.

    The exact percentage is open to interpretation, depending on your definition of startup failure and whose data you use. Some sources define it as the inability of the new venture to at least repay its investors the amount invested, preferably with some return on investment. Other definitions include shutting down with no return to investors, or even consuming additional capital as the venture winds down. But no matter how you look at it, the mortality rate of startups is extremely high.
16. Statistic Brain, "Startup Business Failure Rate by Industry," http://www.statisticbrain.com/startup-failure-by-industry/ (accessed November 10, 2014).
17. Ibid.
18. CB Insights, *The R.I.P. Report—Startup Death Trends*, January 18, 2014, http://www.cbinsights.com/blog/startup-death-data/.
19. Author conversation with Duncan Logan.
20. Author conversation with Justin Kan.
21. Author conversation with Randy Komisar. See also John Mullins and Randy Komisar, *Getting to Plan B* (Boston: Harvard Business Press, 2009).
22. Author conversation with Chris Michel.
23. See, for example: M. Caliendo, F. M. Fossen, and A. S. Kritikos, "Risk Attitudes of Nascent Entrepreneurs: New Evidence from an Experimentally Validated Survey," *Small Business Economics* 32 (2009): 153-167.

    The Global Entrepreneurship & Development Index, *GEDI Index*, http://www.thegedi.org/research/gedi-index/ (accessed November 9, 2014).

    Amorós and Bosma, "2013 Global Report."
24. Ewing Marion Kauffman Foundation, "Kauffman Index of Entrepreneurial Activity," online interactive version, April 9, 2014, http://www.kauffman.org/multimedia/infographics/2013/kiea-interactive.

25. Amar V. Bhide, *The Origin and Evolution of New Businesses* (New York: Oxford University Press, 1999).

26. Guy Kawasaki, *The Art of the Start* (London: Penguin Books, 2004). In this book, Kawasaki, recognizing that most entrepreneurs are better creators than operators, recommends that early-stage ventures need three kinds of players on their teams: kamikazes willing to work 80 hours a week to launch; implementers who come in after the kamikazes and create infrastructure and scalability; and operators who are most at home running the infrastructure and building the business.

27. Geoffrey Moore, *Crossing the Chasm* (New York: HarperCollins, 2002).

28. Max Marmer, Bjoern Lasse Herrmann, and Ertan Dogrultan, *Startup Genome Report Extra on Premature Scaling*, Startup Genome, 2011.

29. Webvan was an online grocery store and delivery service. The company was founded in the mid 1990s, went public in 1999, raised a total of $1.2 billion, and went bankrupt in 2001. In 2008, CNET named Webvan as the "#1 dot-com flop" in history. As of this writing what remains of Webvan is owned by Amazon.

30. Carmen Nobel, "Why Companies Fail—and How Their Founders Can Bounce Back," Harvard Business School Working Knowledge blog, March 7, 2011, http://hbswk.hbs.edu/item/6591.html.

31. Scott Adams, *How to Fail at Almost Everything and Still Win Big: Kind of the Story of My Life* (New York: Penguin Group, 2013).

32. Author conversation with Scott Adams.

33. Eric Ries, *The Lean Startup* (New York: Crown Business, 2011).

34. An A:B test is a real-time experiment to determine how two different configurations of a similar product, service, advertisement, or other offering perform vis-à-vis one another, with metrics that help measure and define success.

35. Patrick Vlaskovits, "Henry Ford, Innovation, and That 'Faster Horse,' *Harvard Business Review* blog, August 29, 2011, https://hbr.org/2011/08/henry-ford-never-said-the-fast/.

36. Andy Reinhardt, "Steve Jobs on Apple's Resurgence: 'Not a One-Man Show,'" *BusinessWeek online*, May 12, 1998, http://www.businessweek.com/bwdaily/dnflash/may1998/nf80512d.htm.

37. Author conversation with Julie Wainwright.

38. Author conversation with Michael Berolzheimer.

39. CNET News, "Steve Jobs and His 'Reality Distortion Field,'" CNET.com, October 23, 2011. http://www.cnet.com/news/steve-jobs-and-his-reality-distortion-field/.

CHAPTER 7: Keep-Ups: Surviving and Thriving After You Meet Payroll

1. Erik Hurst and Benjamin Wild Pugsley. "What Do Small Businesses Do?" *Brookings Papers on Economic Activity, Economic Studies Program, The Brookings Institution* 43, no. 2 (Fall 2011): 73-142.

2. U.S. Small Business Administration, "Frequently Asked Questions," *SBA.gov*, September 2012, http://www.sba.gov/sites/default/files/ FAQ_Sept_2012.pdf. Note: There is a fair amount of fuzziness in defining this sector, but the SBA considers businesses with fewer than 500 employees to be small businesses.

3. U.S. Census, "2012 Nonemployer Statistics," Censtats website, http://censtats.census.gov/cgi-bin/nonemployer/nonsect.pl (accessed November 11, 2010).

4. Business Insurance, "Who Employs America? Scale Model by Company Size," *Business Insurance*, August 30, 2012, http://www.businessinsurance .org/wp-content/uploads/2012/08/sizes-of-small-businesses-2.jpg. By comparison, firms with 500 to 5,000 workers employ roughly 61 million men and women. Even larger firms (those with 5,000 to 10,000 employees) employ 40 million, and those with 10,000+ employees provide jobs for 33 million.

5. Association of Chartered Certified Accountants, *Small Business: A Global Agenda*, September 2010, http://www.accaglobal.com/content/dam/ acca/global/PDF-technical/small-business/pol-afb-sbaga.pdf.

6. Cihan Aktaş, "The SMEs in the Global World: Issues and Prospects," Association of National Development Finances Institutions in Member Countries of the Islamic Development Bank, October 5, 2010, http:// adfimi.org/dosyalar/seminerler/128/pdf/4.pdf.

7. Ibid.

8. Note that home-based does not necessarily mean working at or in the home. (See: U.S. Small Business Administration, "Frequently Asked Questions.")

9. Joseph H. Astrachan and Melissa Carey Shanker, "Family Businesses' Contribution to the U.S. Economy: A Closer Look," *Family Business Review* 16, no. 3 (September 2003): 211-219.

10. The University of Vermont, *Family Business Facts*, http://www .uvm.edu/business/vfbi/?Page=facts.html (accessed November 5, 2014).

11. Morten Bennedsen, Francisco Pérez-González, and Daniel Wolfenzon, "The Governance of Family Firms." In *Corporate Governance*, edited by

H. Kent Baker and Ronald Anderson (Hoboken, NJ: John Wiley & Sons, 2010), 371–389.

12. Karlee Weinmann and Aimee Groth, "The 10 Largest Family Businesses in the U.S.," *Business Insider*, November 17, 2011, http://www .businessinsider.com/the-10-largest-family-businesses-in-america-2011- 11?op=1.

13. Ibid.

14. ADP, "U.S. Added 16,930 Franchise Jobs in September, According to ADP National Franchise Report," press release, October 1, 2014, http:// www.adp.com/media/press-releases/2014-press-releases/us-added-16930- franchise-jobs-in-september-according-to-adp-national-franchise-report .aspx.

15. Sarah E. Needleman and Coulter Jones, "Franchise Brands with Higher- Than-Average Default Rates," *Wall Street Journal*, September 10, 2014, http://online.wsj.com/articles/some-franchise-brands-have-higher- than-average-default-rates-1410392545.

16. Ibid. To put this into another context, in FY 2012, the SBA repurchased 3.4 percent of defaulted franchisee loans, compared to a 2.8 percent repurchase rate for non-franchise small businesses in default.

17. Cihan Aktaş, "The SMEs in the Global World: Issues and Prospects."

18. U.S. Small Business Administration, "Frequently Asked Questions."

19. Katherine Duncan, "Despite Challenges, Franchising Continues to Rebound in 2014," *Entrepreneur*, December 19, 2013, http://www .entrepreneur.com/article/230288.

20. Author conversation with Lena Requist.

21. Jason Nazar, "The State of US Small Businesses," Infographic, *Business Insider*, September 10, 2013, http://www.businessinsider.com/info graphic-the-state-of-us-small-businesses-2013-9.

22. Nicholas Kachaner, George Stalk, and Alain Bloch, "What You Can Learn from Family Business," *Harvard Business Review*, November 2012, http:// hbr.org/2012/11/what-you-can-learn-from-family-business/ar/1.

23. Author conversation with Fred Stuart, owner of ELMS Puzzles.

24. Christian Caspar, Ana Karina Dias, and and Heinz-Peter Elstrodt, "The Five Attributes of Enduring Family Businesses," McKinsey & Company, January 2010, http://www.mckinsey.com/insights/organization/ the_five_attributes_of_enduring_family_businesses.

25. The Ohio State University and General Electric Capital Corporation, *The Market That Moves America*, 2011, http://www.middlemarketcenter.org/

Media/Documents/the-market-that-moves-america-insights-perspectives-and-opportunities-from-middle-market-companies_the_market_that_moves_america_white_paper.pdf (accessed October 29, 2014).

CHAPTER 8: Grown-Ups: Dodging the Oxymoron of "Big Company Agility"

1. SimpsonsWiki.com, "The PTA Disbands Quotes," http://simpsonswiki .com/wiki/The_PTA_Disbands/Quotes (accessed November 2, 2014).

2. For six years in a row, beginning in 1995, Sony was named the number-one global brand in Harris Interactive's Annual Best Brands Survey.

3. Author conversation with Carl Yankowski.

4. Author conversation with Rich Lesser.

5. Alan Murray, ed. "Fortune 500," *Fortune Magazine*, June 16, 2014.

6. The World Bank, "Data: GDP (current US$)," WorldBank.org, http://data.worldbank.org/indicator/NY.GDP.MKTP.CD (accessed November 10, 2014).

7. U.S. Small Business Administration, "How Important are Small Businesses to the U.S. Economy?" Small Business FAQs on the SBA.gov website, http://www.sba.gov/sites/default/files/sbfaq.pdf (accessed November 10, 2014).

8. Matthew J. Slaughter, "How U.S. Multinational Companies Strengthen the U.S. Economy," The United States Council for International Business, 2009, http://www.uscib.org/docs/foundation_multinationals.pdf.

9. U.S. Census Bureau, *Statistics about Business Size; Table 2a*, http://www .census.gov/econ/smallbus.html (accessed November 2, 2014).

10. Nancy Folbre, "Small vs. Big, Local vs. Global," *New York Times*, May 6, 2013, http://economix.blogs.nytimes.com/2013/05/06/small-vs-big-local-vs-global/?_r=0.

11. Pew Research Center, *Beyond Red vs. Blue: The Political Typology*, June 26, 2014, http://www.people-press.org/files/2014/06/6-26-14-Political-Typology-release1.pdf.

12. Richard Dobbs, Jaana Remes, Sven Smit, and James Manyi, "Urban World: The Shifting Global Business Landscape," McKinsey & Company, October 2013, http://www.mckinsey.com/insights/urbanization/urban_world_the_shifting_global_business_landscape.

13. The Economist Online, "Defending Jobs," September 12, 2011, http://www.economist.com/blogs/dailychart/2011/09/employment?fsrc=scn/tw/te/dc/defending.

14. Ibid.

15. David S. Pottruck, *Stacking the Deck* (San Francisco: Jossey-Bass, 2014).

16. Author conversation with David Pottruck.

17. Timothy J. Galpin and Mark Herndon, *The Complete Guide to Mergers & Acquisitions* (San Francisco: Jossey-Bass, 2007).

18. Laurie Burkitt, "Brand Flops: Ford, GE, Coca-Cola Know Hype Can Hurt New Products," *Forbes*, March 31, 2010, http://www.forbes.com/2010/03/31/brand-flops-apple-ford-pepsi-coors-cmo-network-brand-fail.html.

19. Author conversation with Justin Kan.

20. Author conversation with Stanley Bergman, CEO of Henry Schein, Inc.

21. Gallup, Inc., *The State of the American Workplace* (Washington, DC: Gallup, 2013).

22. Ibid.

23. Ibid.

24. Author conversation with Scott Adams.

25. Vivian Giang and Melissa Stanger, "The 50 Best Companies to Work for in 2013," *Business Insider*, December 12, 2012, http://www.businessinsider.com/the-50-best-companies-to-work-for-in-glassdoor-2013-2012-12?op=1.

26. *Fortune*, "100 Best Companies to Work For, 2013," http://archive.fortune.com/magazines/fortune/best-companies/2013/snapshots/5.html (accessed November 9, 2014).

27. Great Place to Work Institute, *Great Places to Work,* http://www.greatplacetowork.com/ (accessed November 10, 2014).

28. For those of you interested in a resource to help you better understand this trust issue and what you can do about it, Chris Michel, one of our interviewees, suggests this as one that has helped him in his career as an entrepreneur and board member: Charles Feltman, *The Thin Book of Trust; An Essential Primer for Building Trust at Work*, edited by Sue Annis Hammond (Bend, OR: Thin Book Publishing, 2009).

29. China Gorman, "China Gorman: How to Become a Great CEO," *Business Review Europe*, November 6, 2014, http://www.businessrevieweurope.eu/leadership/272/China-Gorman:-How-to-Become-a-Great-CEO.

30. American Psychological Association, *2014 Work and Well-Being Survey*, April 2014, http://www.apaexcellence.org/assets/general/2014-work-and-wellbeing-survey-results.pdf.

31. Author conversation with Scott Delman.

32. Vince Marsh, Deloitte, "Employee Engagement is Key," http://www .deloitte.com/view/en_by/by/0dc63bfd53b93210VgnVCM100000ba 42f00aRCRD.htm.
33. Author conversation with Johan Aurik.
34. Since 1943, Lockheed Martin's Skunk Works group has developed new flight technologies. http://www.lockheedmartin.com/us/aeronautics/ skunkworks.html.
35. An excellent example is: Charles A. O'Reilly III, and Michael L. Tushman, "The Ambidextrous Organization," *Harvard Business Review* 82, no. 4 (April 2004): 74-81.
36. Author conversation with Mark Hoplamazian.

CHAPTER 9: The Failure Value Cycle: Seven Stages Where You Can Leverage or Flunk Failure

1. Gregory Ferenstein, "Zuckerberg's Advice for Entrepreneurs: 'What Ends Up Mattering Is the Stuff You Get Right,'" *VentureBeat*, December 12, 2014, http://venturebeat.com/category/business.
2. Specifically, a so-called regular heptagon (with equal sides and angles) is one of the hardest geometric figures to draw with a compass and straightedge ruler. So don't feel too bad—even mathematicians have difficulty handling seven-sided challenges.

CHAPTER 10: Stage One—Respect: Acknowledge the Gravity of Failure

1. Shelley DuBois, "7 Most Admired Companies That Fell Off the Map," *Fortune*, February 28, 2013, http://fortune.com/2013/02/28/7-most-admired-companies-that-fell-off-the-map/.
2. When we were growing up, the expression "that's a Kodak moment" was commonly used to describe when something memorable or funny happened that would have made for a good picture.
3. Oxford Dictionaries, "taboo," http://www.oxforddictionaries.com/us/ definition/american_english/taboo (accessed August 31, 2014).
4. Walmart, *Annual Report*, 2013, http://stock.walmart.com/annual-reports.
5. GE, *GE 2013 Annual Report*, 2013, http://www.ge.com/ar2013/.
6. Toyota, "True Competitiveness for Sustainable Growth," *Annual Report*, 2013, http://www.toyota-global.com/investors/ir_library/annual/pdf/ 2013/ (accessed November 30, 2014).

7. Daimler, *Annual Report 2013*. 2013, http://www.daimler.com/Projects/c2c/channel/documents/2432177_Daimler_2013_Annual_Report.pdf.

8. Enron Corp., *Annual Report*, 2000, http://picker.uchicago.edu/Enron/EnronAnnualReport2000.pdf (accessed November 10, 2014).

9. Giovanni Gavetti, Rebecca Henderson, and Simona Giorgi, *Kodak and the Digital Revolution (A)*, Case Study, Harvard Business School (Boston: Harvard Business School Press, 2005).

10. BlackBerry Limited, *Form 40-F Annual Report*, 2013, http://us.blackberry.com/content/dam/bbCompany/Desktop/Global/PDF/Investors/Documents/2014/Q4_FY14_Filing.pdf.

11. Helene Cooper, "Air Force Fires 9 Officers in Scandal over Cheating on Proficiency Tests," *New York Times*, March 27, 2014. http://www.nytimes.com/2014/03/28/us/air-force-fires-9-officers-accused-in-cheating-scandal.html.

12. Bill Murphy, Jr., *The Intelligent Entrepreneur* (New York: Henry Holt and Company, 2010).

13. Author conversation with Chris Michel.

14. Author conversation with Danae Ringelmann.

15. Kathy Caprino, "10 Lessons I Learned from Sara Blakely That You Won't Hear in Business School," *Forbes*, May 23, 2012, http://www.forbes.com/sites/kathycaprino/2012/05/23/10-lessons-i-learned-from-sara-blakely-that-you-wont-hear-in-business-school/.

16. Author conversation with Sheri McCoy.

17. For more information on these events visit http://fuckupnights.com/.

18. This is a shortened version of the Pecha Kucha presentation style, developed in Japan: http://www.pechakucha.org.

19. We attended one of their inaugural U.S. events, and can attest to the mix of humor and candor that permeates the audience, as well as a strong sense of relief in being able to share those stories openly with one another.

20. FailCon, "About FailCon," http://thefailcon.com/about.html (accessed November 10, 2014).

21. Ibid.

22. Author conversation with Bob King.

23. Ibid. 16.

24. Author conversation with Henry Chesbrough.

25. Quoted in Goodreads.com, "Thomas A. Edison," Quotable Quotes. http://www.goodreads.com/quotes/9788-negative-results-are-just-what-i-want-they-re-just-as (accessed November 9, 2014).

26. "Muckers" was the name that Thomas Edison gave to his assistants.

27. 99.999 percent performance.

28. Author conversation with Johan Aurik.
29. Savings attributed to the period 1986-2004. For more see the web archive of: Motorola University, "About Motorola University: The Impact of Six Sigma," Motorola.com, https://web.archive.org/web/20051106025758/http://www.motorola.com/content/0,,3081,00.html (accessed November 11, 2014).
30. Author conversation with Peter L. West.
31. Author conversation with Mark Hoplamazian.
32. Author conversation with David Pottruck.
33. The concept of "noble failure" is further described by David Pottruck in his book *Stacking the Deck* (San Francisco: Jossey-Bass, 2014).
34. WikiQuote, "Thomas J. Watson," http://en.wikiquote.org/wiki/Thomas_J._Watson (accessed November 2, 2014).
35. Caroline Copley and Ben Hirschler. "For Roche CEO, Celebrating Faiure Is Key to Success," Reuters, September 17, 2014, http://www.reuters.com/article/2014/09/17/us-roche-ceo-failure-idUSKBN0HC16N20140917.
36. For a more in-depth discussion of "grit," see: Angela Lee Duckworth, "The Key to Success? Grit," TED Talks, April 2013, http://www.ted.com/talks/angela_lee_duckworth_the_key_to_success_grit?language=en. Also refer to https://sites.sas.upenn.edu/duckworth/pages/research for research on grit being done at the Duckworth Lab, University of Pennsylvania.

CHAPTER 11: Stage Two—Rehearse: It's Not Just About Fire Drills

1. Author conversation with Mark Laret.
2. Author conversation with Kurt Beyer.
3. Author conversation with Michael Sippey.
4. Author conversation with Joe Kraus.

CHAPTER 12: Stage Three—Recognize: Pick Up the Signals of Failure Earlier

1. Author conversation with Dave Williams.
2. Chamath Palihapitiya, who ran Facebook's growth team, shared this fact in a talk at the 2012 GrowHack conference, "Discovering Your Aha! Moment," December 4, 2012, http://www.growhack.com/2012/12/04/discovering-your-aha-moment/.

3. Obi-Wan Kenobi was a lead character in the *Star Wars* movies. He was a Jedi warrior who was able to feel a "disturbance in the force" when something grave happened, such as a disaster on a different planet.

4. W. Michael Cox and Richard Alm, "Creative Destruction," *The Concise Encyclopedia of Economics*, Library of Economics and Liberty, http://www.econlib.org/library/Enc/CreativeDestruction.html (accessed November 2, 2014).

5. Riley Woodford, "Running Water Is Sound of Spring for Beavers," *Juneau Empire*, May 4, 2008, http://juneauempire.com/stories/050408/out_275269543.shtml.

6. Del Harvey, "Transcript: Protecting Twitter Users (sometimes from themselves)," TED Talk, March 2014, http://www.ted.com/talks/del_harvey_the_strangeness_of_scale_at_twitter/transcript?language=en#t-246593.

7. Tony Hsieh, *Delivering Happiness* (New York: Hachette Book Group, 2010).

8. Description of Navy SEALs Hell Week, http://navyseals.com/nsw/hell-week-0/ (accessed December 15, 2014).

9. Gregory C. Elliott, "Self-Esteem and Self-Consistency: A Theoretical and Empirical Link Between Two Primary Motivations," *Social Psychology Quarterly* 49, no. 3 (1986): 207-218.

10. Author conversation with Jed Katz.

11. Bruce Schneier, "Airport Security Failure," blog post, March 14, 2006, https://www.schneier.com/blog/archives/2006/03/airport_securit_2.html.

CHAPTER 13: Stage Four—React: Deal with It!

1. Chip Wilson interview by Trish Regan, "Some Women Just Can't Wear Lululemon Pants: Founder," *Street Smart*, Bloomberg Television, November 5, 2013.

2. Melissa Lustrin and Felicia Patinkin, "Lululemon Founder Chip Wilson Blames Women's Bodies for Yoga Pants Problem," ABC News. November 7, 2013. http://abcnews.go.com/US/lululemon-founder-chip-wilson-blames-womens-bodies-yoga/story?id=20815278.

3. In 1982, seven people died after taking Tylenol capsules laced with potassium cyanide. All of the deaths occurred in Chicago, but nonetheless Johnson and Johnson, the maker of Tylenol, acted quickly and instituted a nationwide recall of an estimated 31 million bottles of Tylenol representing a retail value of $100 million. This incident accelerated the development of tamper-resistant packaging for drugs, which Johnson and Johnson

introduced when Tylenol capsules were once again shipped, months later. No killer was ever found. Source: Dan Fletcher, "A Brief History of the Tylenol Poisonings," *TIME*, February 9, 2009.

4. John W. Schoen, "As Gulf Spill Spreads, Blame Game Begins," *Today*, May 3, 2010, http://www.today.com/id/36917929/ns/today-today_news/t/gulf-spill-spreads-blame-game-begins/#.VGFCBoe4mRs.

5. Robert Wood Johnson Foundation, "Higher Hospital Costs Linked to Triage Decisions," September 10, 2013, http://www.rwjf.org/en/about-rwjf/newsroom/newsroom-content/2013/09/higher-hospital-costs-linked-to-triage-decisions.html (accessed Dec 15, 2014).

6. James B. Stewart, "The Real Heroes Are Dead," *New Yorker*, February 11, 2002, http://www.newyorker.com/magazine/2002/02/11/the-real-heroes-are-dead.

7. John Kador, *Effective Apology* (San Francisco: Berrett-Koehler, 2009).

8. Perhaps less well-known, but equally deserving of attention, was Susan B. Anthony's quote to close her final public speech on women's rights in 1905: "Failure is impossible!"

9. Gene Kranz, *Failure Is Not an Option* (New York: Simon & Schuster Paperbacks, 2009).

10. Quoted in Kranz, ibid.

CHAPTER 14: Stage Five—Reflect: Turn Failure from a Regret to a Resource

1. Author conversation with Joe Kraus.

2. Author conversation with Lena Requist.

3. Author conversation with Johan Aurik.

4. Dean A. Shepherd, Holger Patzelt, and Marcus Wolfe, "Moving Forward from Project Failure: Negative Emotions, Affective Commitment, and Learning from the Experience," *Academy of Management Journal* 54, no. 6 (December 2011): 1229-1259.

5. Ibid.

6. Caroline Copley and Ben Hirschler, "For Roche CEO, Celebrating Failure Is Key to Success," Reuters, September 17, 2014, http://www.reuters.com/article/2014/09/17/us-roche-ceo-failure-idUSKBN0HC16N20140917.

7. Leo Esaki, Ivar Giaever, and Brian D. Josephson, "Electron Tunneling and Superconductivity," Nobel Lecture, December 12, 1973, http://www.nobelprize.org/nobel_prizes/physics/laureates/1973/giaever-lecture.html.

8. Elisabeth Kübler-Ross, *On Death and Dying* (New York: Scribner, 2014).
9. Charles Francis, ed., *Wisdom Well Said* (El Prado: Levine Mesa Press, 2009). See also: Robert Palestini, *From Leadership Theory to Practice: A Game Plan for Success as a Leader* (Lanham, MD: Rowman & Littlefield Education, 2009).
10. Ingelheim Boehringer, "Boehringer Ingelheim Awards Predictive Data Prize," press release, June 22, 2012, http://us.boehringer-ingelheim. com/news_events/press_releases/press_release_archive/2012/june_22_ 2012.html.
11. Here, consider using a tool like the "5 Whys." Originally developed by Sakichi Toyoda, it was used within the Toyota Motor Corporation during the evolution of its manufacturing methodologies, as the company grew to a global market and quality leader through consistent innovation and evolution. Toyota executive Taiichi Ohno described the 5 Whys method as "the basis of Toyota's scientific approach . . . by repeating why five times, the nature of the problem as well as its solution becomes clear."

CHAPTER 15: Stage Six—Rebound: Retake the Initiative

1. Julianne Pepitone, "Netflix Loses 800,000 Subscribers," CNN Money, October 24, 2011, http://money.cnn.com/2011/10/24/technology/ netflix_earnings/.
2. Jim Cramer, "Cramer: Netflix Nails It," *TheStreet*, April 23, 2013, http://www.thestreet.com/story/11903257/1/netflix-nails-it.html.
3. Nancy Hass, "And the Award for the Next HBO Goes To . . . ," *GQ*, February 2013, http://www.gq.com/entertainment/movies-and- tv/201302/netflix-founder-reed-hastings-house-of-cards-arrested- development.
4. For a more successful example, see how Home Depot's CEO, Frank Blake, handled the early stages of its Rebound after it suffered a serious cyberattack in late summer 2014. "How Home Depot CEO Frank Blake kept his legacy from being hacked," *Fortune*, Jennifer Reingold, October 29, 2014, http://fortune.com/2014/10/29/home-depot-cybersecurity- reputation-frank-blake/.
5. Joshua Topolsky, "Apple Responds to iPhone 4 Reception Issues: You're Holding the Phone the Wrong Way," Engadget.com, June 24, 2010, http://www.engadget.com/2010/06/24/apple-responds- over-iphone-4-reception-issues-youre-holding-th/.
6. Bobbie Johnson, "Amazon Boss Bezos: Kindle Move Was 'Stupid,'" *The Guardian*, July 23, 2009, http://www.theguardian.com/technology/ blog/2009/jul/24/amazon-drm.

7. Keith Stuart and Charles Arthur, "PlayStation Network Hack: Why It Took Sony Seven Days to Tell the World," *The Guardian*, April 27, 2011, http://www.theguardian.com/technology/gamesblog/2011/apr/27/playstation-network-hack-sony.

CHAPTER 16: Stage Seven—Remember: Embed Failure Savvy in Your Culture

1. Author conversation with Stanley Bergman.
2. Tony Hsieh, "Your Culture Is Your Brand," *Huffington Post*, November 15, 2010, http://www.huffingtonpost.com/tony-hsieh/zappos-founder-tony-hsieh_1_b_783333.html.
3. Robert McKee, *Story: Style, Structure, Substance, and the Principles of Screenwriting* (New York: HarperCollins, 1997). As a director, producer, and writer, McKee has created a storied string of successes, including *Toy Story, Gandhi, Sleepless in Seattle, Erin Brockovich, Nixon*, and *Forrest Gump*. See also McKee's interview in: Bronwyn Fryer, "Storytelling That Moves People," *Harvard Business Review*, June 2003, http://hbr.org/2003/06/storytelling-that-moves-people/ar.
4. Bessemer Venture Partners, "Anti-portfolio," http://www.bvp.com/portfolio/antiportfolio (accessed November 1, 2014).
5. Ibid.
6. By the way, lest you think Dave Cowan was singled out here, he was just one of the BVP partners mentioned in this self-deprecatory gesture. Henry Chesbrough likes the anti-portfolio as well, as a visible reminder of how Bessemer Venture Partners balances its commitment to innovation with a recognition and acceptance of failures in pursuit of that goal.
7. Chips Etc, "Intel Keychains," http://www.chipsetc.com/intel-keychains-page-3.html (accessed November 1, 2014).
8. William Marquard, *Wal-Smart: What It Really Takes to Profit in a Wal-Mart World* (New York: McGraw-Hill, 2006).
9. This idea originally came out of a conversation John had about this book with Jim Goldman, recent CEO of Godiva Chocolatier, and his wife, Gigi, a former brand manager at General Mills. We liked it almost as much as we like those chocolates.
10. Henry Petroski, *Success through Failure: The Paradox of Design* (Princeton, NJ: Princeton University Press, 2008).

CHAPTER 18: Creating the Failure-Savvy Organization

1. Author e-mail exchange with Frank Blake, CEO of Home Depot.
2. Christoph Lymbersky, *Why Do Companies Fail? 2014 Survey Results*, Turnaround Society, February 10, 2014, http://turnaround-society .com/companies-fail-2014-survey-results/.
3. Great Place to Work, "What Are the Benefits?," http://www .greatplacetowork.com/our-approach/what-are-the-benefits-great-workplaces (accessed November 4, 2014).
4. China Gorman, "2014 World's Best Multinational Workplaces: Trends for Thought," ChinaGorman.com, October 21, 2014, http://china gorman.com/tag/employee-satisfaction/.
5. Gallup, Inc., *Engagement Predicts Earnings per Share* (Washington, DC: Gallup, 2006). Note: In 2006, Gallup looked at more than 23,000 business units and compared top quartile and bottom quartile financial performance with its own engagement scores. Bottom quartile units averaged 31–51 percent more employee turnover, 51 percent more inventory shrinkage, and 62 percent more accidents. Top quartile engagers averaged 12 percent higher customer advocacy, 18 percent higher productivity, and 12 percent higher profitability. Another 2006 Gallup study of 89 organizations top quartile engagement companies experienced earnings per share growth 2.6 times that of below-average engagers.
6. James K. Harter, Frank L. Schmidt, Emily A. Killham, and James W. Asplund, "Q12 Meta-Analysis," Gallup, Inc., http://strengths.gallup .com/private/resources/q12meta-analysis_flyer_gen_08%2008_bp.pdf (accessed November 1, 2014).
7. Author conversation with Rich Lesser.
8. Author conversation with Roselinde Torres.
9. *Thomas J. Watson*, http://en.wikiquote.org/wiki/Thomas_J._Watson (accessed November 2, 2014).
10. Author conversation with Jennifer Granholm.
11. For more on the Net Promoter Score, visit the company's website at www.netpromoter.com.
12. Author conversation with Sheri McCoy.
13. Barnes-Jewish Hospital, *2011 Patient Safety & Quality Report to Board of Directors*, 2011, http://www.barnesjewish.org/upload/docs/AboutUs/ Annual%20Reports/BJH_PSQ_Board_Report_11.pdf.

Index

Celebrating success is easy. But leveraging failure—defining it, de-stigmatizing it, measuring its full value, and putting it to work in your organization—is hard. It can also be invaluable.

Authors **John Danner** and **Mark Coopersmith** have spent their careers helping leaders and organizations expand their repertoire of strategies to be more successful in high-stakes times. They understand that failure is a powerful catalyst and accelerator for innovation—if you know how to use it.

Get more of these insights by bringing John or Mark to your organization. Thanks to fresh case studies, a pragmatic approach, and their new Failure Value Cycle, every audience can walk away with a greater understanding of:

- **Failure's full value:** its facts, facets, and power
- **Where failure shows up:** surviving and thriving at every stage and in every type of organization
- **Limiting failure's damage and leveraging its opportunities:** how to put the seven stages of the Failure Value Cycle to work
- **Creating the failure-savvy organization:** the five powers that smart leaders unleash for greater resilience and employee engagement

Start leveraging *The Other "F" Word*, and gain the cutting-edge advantages you need to drive innovation and accelerate growth.

Contact John@JohnDanner.com or Mark@MarkCoopersmith.com today.